A Picture of
DEVON

Contemporary Artists and the Inspirational Landscape

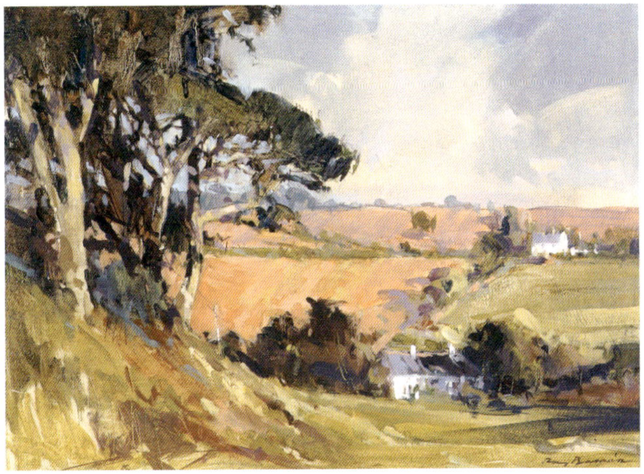

Ray Balkwill

HALSGROVE

First published in Great Britain in 2008

Ray Balkwill. *Summer Fields, Ashcombe*
Oil 10x14in (25x36cm)

British Library Cataloguing-in-Publication Data
A CIP record for this title is available from the British Library

ISBN 978 1 84114 734 5

HALSGROVE
Halsgrove House
Ryelands Industrial Estate
Bagley Road, Wellington,
Somerset TA21 9PZ
Tel: 01823 653777
Fax: 01823 216796
email: sales@halsgrove.com
website: www.halsgrove.com

Printed and bound by D'Auria Industrie Grafiche, Italy

Contents

Acknowledgements

The preparation and production of this book have involved many people, and I am grateful to them all for their cooperation. In particular I would like to thank all the contributing artists:

Lionel Aggett, Stephen Brown, Colin Allbrook, Andrew Coates, Alan Cotton, Alwyn Crawshaw, Stewart Edmondson, John Hammond, Judy Hempstead, Michael Hill, John Hoar, Robert Jennison, Paul Lewin, Michael Morgan, Tina Morgan, Robert Mountjoy, Martin Procter, Keith Stott, Richard Thorn, Barry Watkin and Tony Williams. Without their valued help this book would not have been possible. However, in thanking these artists, one is also conscious of the many, for reason of space, who could not be included. Also my thanks to Nigel Cheffers-Heard and John Melville for photographing my paintings, and also special thanks to Nigel for the back cover portrait photograph. Warren Collum, Curator of the Burton Art Gallery and Museum, Bideford for use of the Hubert Coop photograph and Rosemary Jones of Elford Fine Art, Tavistock for use of the F.J. Widgery photograph. John Butler, Tom Brown, Thelma Reddington and Priscilla Hull for their assistance with my research. Alwyn Crawshaw images are courtesy Harper Collins Publishers.

My sincere thanks to Directors and Staff at Halsgove, in particular Simon Butler, Karen Binaccioni, Sharon O'Inn and Denise Lyons. It has been a real pleasure working with the publishers on this book.

Finally, not forgetting my wife Jane for her continued help, encouragement and patience.

DEDICATION

To my dear mother, Phyllis

Preface

Devon means many things to many people. It might be her picturesque thatched cottages of colour-washed cob, the deep-cut lanes, rolling green hills and embosomed farms that epitomise Devon. Or perhaps it is her rugged wave-lashed cliffs, sandy coves or sweeping moorland that first spring to mind. Whatever it may be, one thing is agreed, her scenery is unsurpassed and of a variety that is unequalled in all England. Devon is the third largest county in England, covering about 2,500 square miles, but it also has the unique distinction of two separate, totally contrasting coastlines. Its landscape is often regarded as quintessentially English and has provided artists with a rich source of inspiration for over 200 years.

A Picture of Devon is a celebration of the Devonshire landscape viewed through the eyes of those who aim to capture its essential qualities in paint. Artists bring their own vision to a place, often revealing to us things that we may have encountered, but have not really *seen*. It draws together for the first time, twenty-two of its most celebrated contemporary artists; some published for the first time, alongside others who have received much international acclaim. Between them they encompass a wide variety of subjects, styles, media as well as working methods. Images reveal a lot about what artists think and feel about themselves, but the commentary also provides a fascinating insight into the artist's own personal and physical relationship with the landscape.

This haven for the creative spirit has inspired poets and writers too, and the power wielded with the pen has at times been as mighty as that of the brush. Some of these literary connections to the landscape are also referred to within the pages of this book.

Devon has always reached out, welcomed and embraced all who rejoice in her natural beauty. Being a Devonian as well as an artist, I have a deep-rooted empathy with my native county and my passion for it runs as deep as the red earth itself. I hope that within the confines of a few thousand words and a hundred or so paintings, this book is able to voice a deeper understanding of what this landscape means to those who love it. I sincerely hope that this book will enhance your appreciation further and if that is the case, then I will have succeeded. Or as they say down here, 'that'll be 'ansome!'

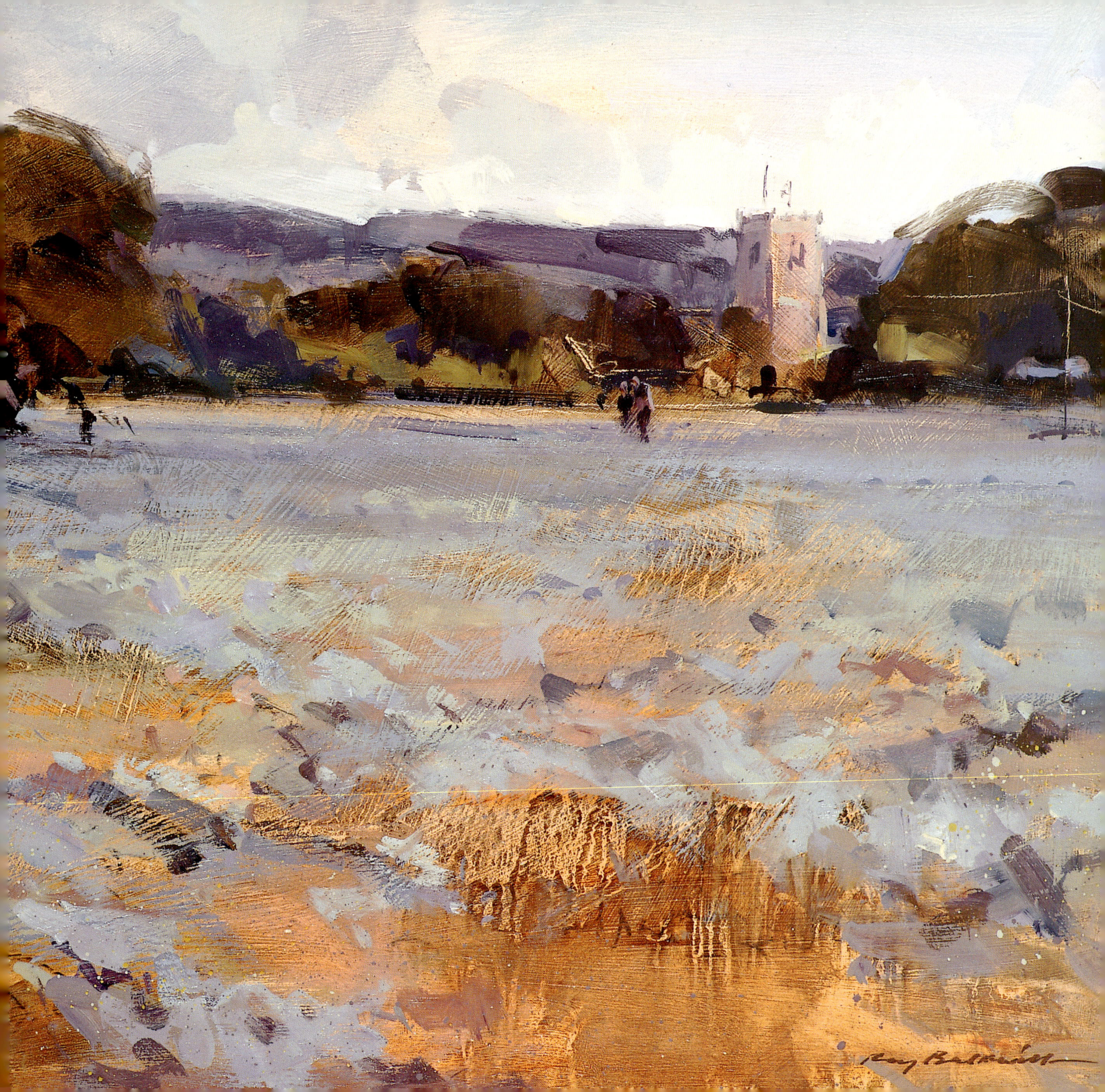

INTRODUCTION

An English Eden

The year was 1813 and it was a beautiful English summer's day. A warm breeze shepherded tangled cloud across the sky, whilst sunlight and shadows played over the landscape. High overhead rose great shapely billows of gleaming cumuli, their edges sharply outlined against a brilliantly blue sky. Swallows twisted and turned in graceful aerobics across the lawns, and the hum of insects filled the air. In the idyllic setting of Mount Edgcumbe, beside the banks of the River Tamar, a picnic party was taking place. The party sat and talked and enjoyed the spectacular views across the waters of Plymouth Sound and to the Devon countryside beyond. After they had eaten their picnic of cold meats and shellfish, accompanied by fine wines, the host, who was a painter, produced and showed the ladies his most recent oil sketches of the Devon landscape, which he had brought with him. Nothing unusual in that, except the artist was J.M.W. Turner, Britain's greatest landscape artist.

One of the guests in the party was Cyrus Redding, a local journalist who had accompanied Turner on parts of a Westcountry tour undertaken in that same year. He later wrote of the experience: 'In that delightful spot we spent the best part of a summer's day. Never was there more social pleasure partaken by any party in that English Eden.' Visiting Devon and Cornwall in 1811 and returning to Devon in 1813 and 1814, the work Turner produced here was at an important stage in the artist's development. His omnivorous gaze prompted some early experiments in his oil sketches shown on that beautiful summer's day in 1813. Redding also recalled Turner's admiration and idealistic reactions to the hinterland of Plymouth: 'Turner said that he had never seen so many natural beauties in so limited an extent of country as he saw in the vicinity of Plymouth'. Adding that 'Some of the scenes hardly appeared to belong to this island.'

Ray Balkwill. *Across the Fields to Powderham*
Oil 10x14in (25x36cm)

Turner was not alone in his appreciation of the magnificence of the Devon scenery. Plymouth painter Benjamin Robert Haydon gives us a particularly fervent entry in his diary in 1829, when he recalls:

> *Never more impressed in my life with the beauty of Devon. I walked to a favourite haunt when a child... and found it as woody and sequestered and beautiful as ever – never was such a spot! I can now account for all my early aspirations; no wonder Devonshire is so prolific in painters. Devonshire is a gem. I remember when a child I used to loiter behind my nurse to look and muse on the scenery of this enchanting place, and could not tell what was there to make my heart beat so. The fact is, the Scenery is so poetic it was impossible not to affect a Poetick mind. The deep shadows of umbrageous trees, the green emerald masses of Foliage, the crystal ripple of the limpid springs, were fit to excite emotions deep and passionate...*

The eminent landscape painter Samuel Palmer was also inspired by it, so much so that he described himself 'quite haunted' by the scenery of the county in attempting to 'capture its quintessence.'

Devon has proved an attractive source of subject matter for landscape artists for over 200 years. Some of these were native Devonians, others settled here for various lengths of time, whilst many came on shorter visits, often with commissions for specific subjects. Most of the noted nineteenth century watercolourists were to visit Devon in their travels around the British Isles, including such eminent artists as Thomas Girtin, Peter de Wint and of course J.M.W. Turner. However, the artistic scene in Exeter and Plymouth never really developed a distinctive identity as seen in Norwich, Birmingham and Liverpool for example. Neither did its coastline attract the schools of artists to the area as Cornwall did to Newlyn and St Ives. Painters tended to concentrate more on its natural features, developing a more picturesque approach rather than the social scenes generally associated with its Cornish neighbour. Despite this though, apart from Middlesex, Devon has produced more notable painters than any other county in England. It is arguable, but even Turner once claimed that he was of Devon birth. His family certainly originated from North Devon, with his father being born and bred in South Molton. It was perhaps these connections that may possibly have inspired his son to claim the same tie.

Paul Lewin. *Low Tide to Hartland*
Mixed Media 17.5x20.5in (45x52cm)

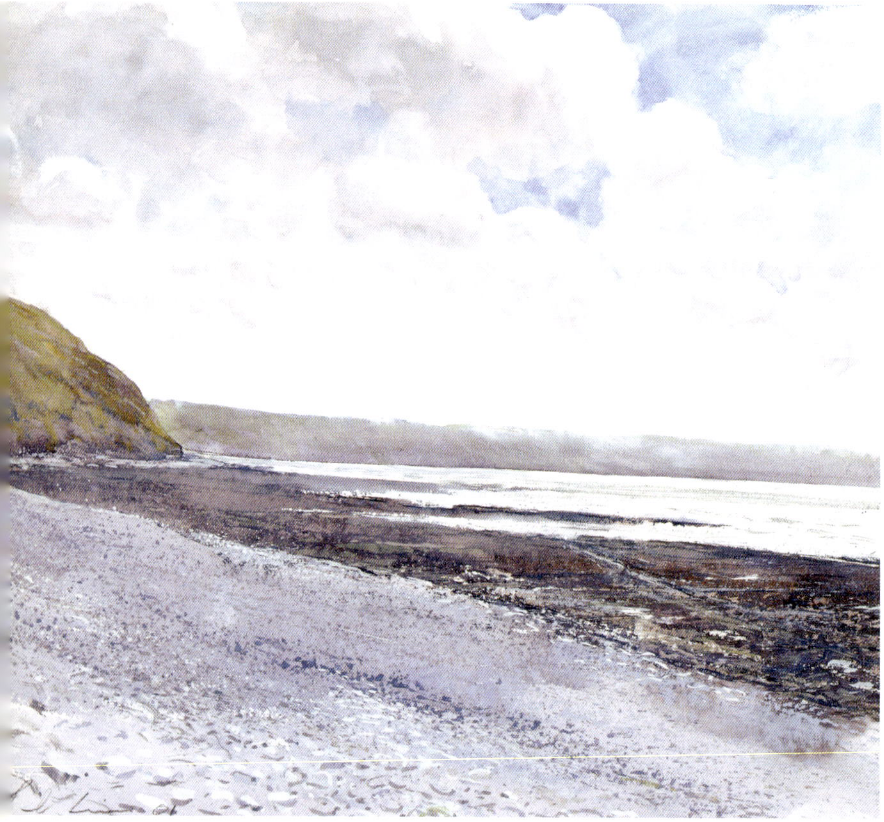

Like their eighteenth and nineteenth century counterparts, today's painters continue to be beguiled by the beauty of its scenery and for the artists drawn together here it has more than matched their internal creative needs. A painter responds to the landscape differently to most and is blessed with a special pair of eyes. These eyes not only look at the subtleties in nature, but also see beauty in the mundane. Alan Cotton described it thus: 'I love this old fashioned word 'inspiration' because I don't really start painting unless I am inspired to do it. It's some trick of light, or shapes in the landscape, it's the intangible thing, I can't describe exactly what it is. When you see it, you know it, it's a gut reaction to something very strong.'

Some painters, Robert Mountjoy and Colin Allbrook for instance, have found that the ordinary things around them are equally as exciting as the bigger picture. Corners of old barns and farmyards, where man's neglect and indolence are evident, have fascinated Robert. Whereas for Colin it is capturing the daily life of the farmer in the barns and livestock markets around his home.

In contrast, for artists such as Alan Cotton and Lionel Aggett, it is from the essence of the pictorial drama of land, sea and the skies above it, that their inspiration has been drawn. For Alan it is often the rugged terrain of the north coast at Hartland, lashed by its Atlantic waves, whilst for Lionel it may be the heartland, with its vast sweeps of rolling hills and undulating moorland. Paul Lewin's connection with the landscape has even extended to his use of a pigment known as 'Bideford Black', made from the Devon soil itself, in his drawings and paintings.

Painting Methods and Materials

When one thinks of the traditional English landscape, then it is usually the medium of watercolour that will first spring to mind. In Britain the practice of working in the open air spread rapidly during the late eighteenth century in conjunction with the growing popularity of the medium of watercolour. By comparison with oil painting, materials for watercolour were more practical, being compact, portable, ready to use, and quick drying. It still remains the most popular medium today, despite it being the most difficult to master. Its popularity stems from not only being an extremely portable medium, but also for its properties of translucency, expressiveness and unpredictability. This makes an exciting medium for artists to use, especially for capturing the subtle nuances of light and colour in nature. Gouache, or body colour as it is sometimes called, is also water-based, but is more opaque than watercolour. In addition to being used as a medium in its own right, gouache can be combined with watercolour to give highlights, solidity and contrast.

By the middle of the nineteenth century a revolution was taking place in the techniques and appearance of oil painting, as commercial colourmen took over manufacture of artists' materials. Workshop traditions of tempering paints broke down as they became readily available in collapsible lead tubes. From then on it became practical for oil painters to work on location directly from nature and to develop new visions. Oils are immediately attractive due to their smooth, rich, buttery consistency, and their popularity with patrons and galleries spans hundreds of years. Soft pastels also have a long history and are a dry medium made from finely ground pigments. They bridge the gap between drawing and painting, but tend to be regarded commonly as a painting medium. Being light and portable, they provide an immediate effect, without the problems found in paints, primarily drying speed and colour mixing on the palette. This also makes it the ideal medium for working on location. Acrylic paints are a modern medium derived from materials produced by the plastics industry. It is now the second most popular medium, primarily because it is so extraordinarily versatile. These paints can be applied straight from the tube, or diluted with water, as well as being mixed with a number of gels. Mixed media paintings give a really broad range of possibilities to the artist. With watercolour being a transparent medium and pastel being opaque, for instance, I like to explore the contrasts between the two when they are combined in the same painting.

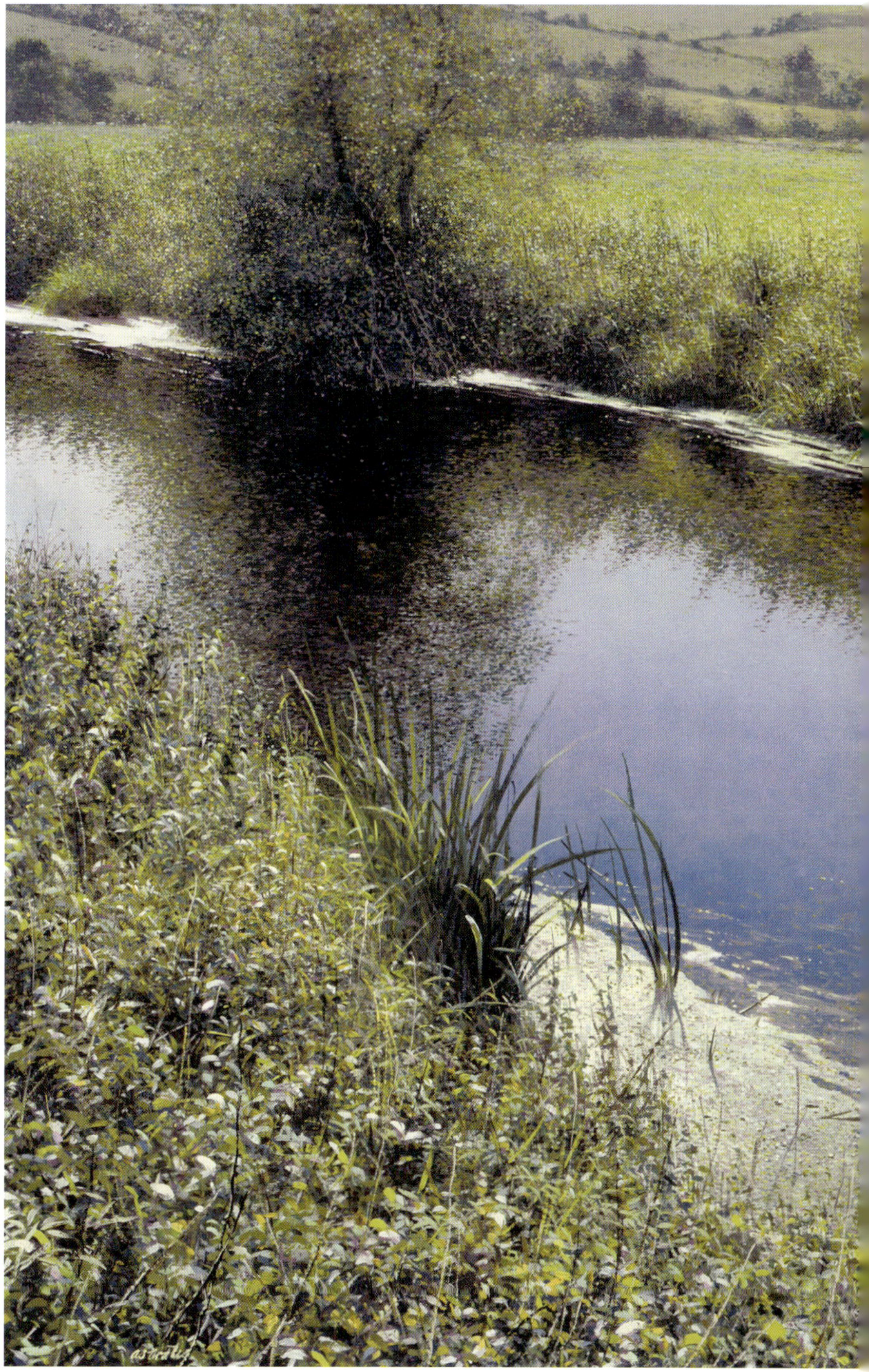

Andrew Coates. *Peaceful Water, River Axe*
24x18in (61x46cm)

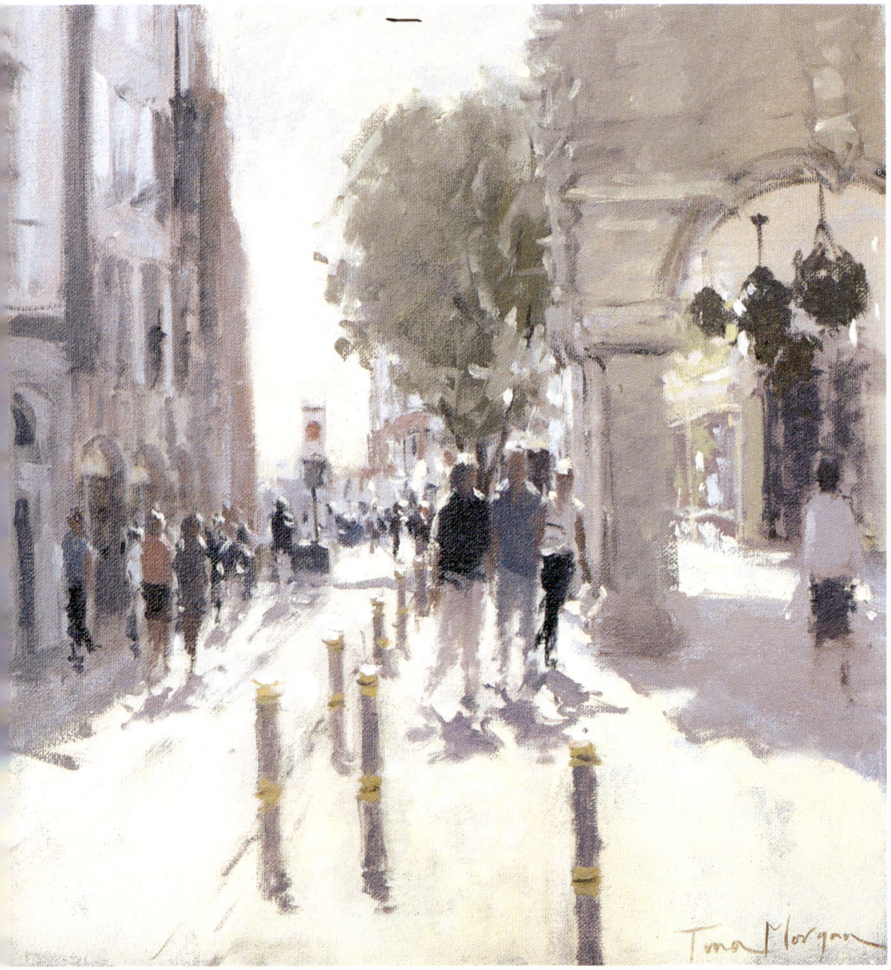

Tina Morgan. *A View of Exeter*
Oil 12x12in (30x30cm)

Many artists enjoy the challenge of combining other media in the same painting, such as oil pastels, inks and pen work. Collage can also be an integral part of the painting with some using such materials as gesso, tissue paper and PVA glue to achieve various effects.

All painters of course, gather information and ideas in their sketchbooks, but although many choose to work in their studios, for some it is the challenge of actually painting in the landscape itself that is important. Although I divide my time between painting in the studio as well as on location, it is the latter that I advocate. Stewart Edmondson is another painter who relishes this, working on Dartmoor in all weathers, sometimes from a portable shelter when the rain pours.

Painting in the great outdoors is never easy, the sun beating down one minute and rain the next. Battling in high winds to keep the easel upright, or waiting for what seems like an eternity for watercolour washes to dry. I am sure that there are times though when onlookers must look on in utter amazement and question whether artists are indeed even quite sane! After all it does appear a rather eccentric occupation in this day and age to suffer for our art as we do. However, connecting with the great outdoors touches all the senses and I find there is nothing more exhilarating. It not only seems to add a 'living presence' to my work, but it has also provided me with some of nature's truly memorable moments. Every experience in front of the motif is important to a painter, no matter how brief it may be. One of my favourite quotes is from Monet who once said: 'Three brushstrokes before nature are worth three days' work in the studio'. However, there are no rules, and painting is, of course open to individual interpretation and every artist has his or her own thoughts on the subject. To paint any subject well means immersing oneself in it and actually 'getting under the skin' of it, as it were. This involves not only seeing, but also understanding the history and ecology of the place.

Whatever working practice is chosen, whether painting *en plein air* or in the studio, one thing is certain, each of the artists featured in this book carries the same conviction in their work. After many years of working in locations throughout the British Isles, I still maintain that you will see nothing more beautiful, or varied than the landscape of Devon. I also firmly believe that an artist can paint his own land better than anywhere else - after all, artists who have chosen to paint the land because they love and understand it are bound to paint the best landscapes.

A perfect example of this was John Constable, one of Britain's greatest landscape painters. Perhaps more than any other artist his work was a response to and love of his native landscape of the Stour, born out of a lifelong acquaintance and a profound sense of belonging. He urged young painters 'to become the patient pupil of nature,' and we are indebted to Constable for opening our eyes to the unexpected beauty that is all around us. The depth of his concentration is illustrated in a lovely story that describes how he was sitting so still at his easel in the landscape, that a field mouse crept into his pocket without him noticing it. He once said, 'The art of seeing nature is a thing almost as much to be acquired as the art of reading the Egyptian hieroglyphics.'

Painters like Turner expressed a concept of the World quite different from our own today and as we enter a new century, we see our planet in a new way, unique to our time. Concern for its conservation makes landscape painting important again. Out of the rich traditions of the past, I believe today's landscape painters can still make a difference, however modest. Progress has meant that we have become more removed from the natural world than is safe, or healthy to be. Painters both past and present play their part in weaving the rich tapestry that is the heritage of Devon today.

Through their art, landscape painters can help change perceptions and offer real aesthetic richness and diversity. The pressures on this fragile landscape have never been greater, but it is reassuring to know that painters stand against the flow of time to define our being. As the renowned Exeter-born historian W.G. Hoskins once wrote: 'Devon, for all its faults and deficiencies, is the best of all places in which to live. Some of us think that Paradise may be no better.'

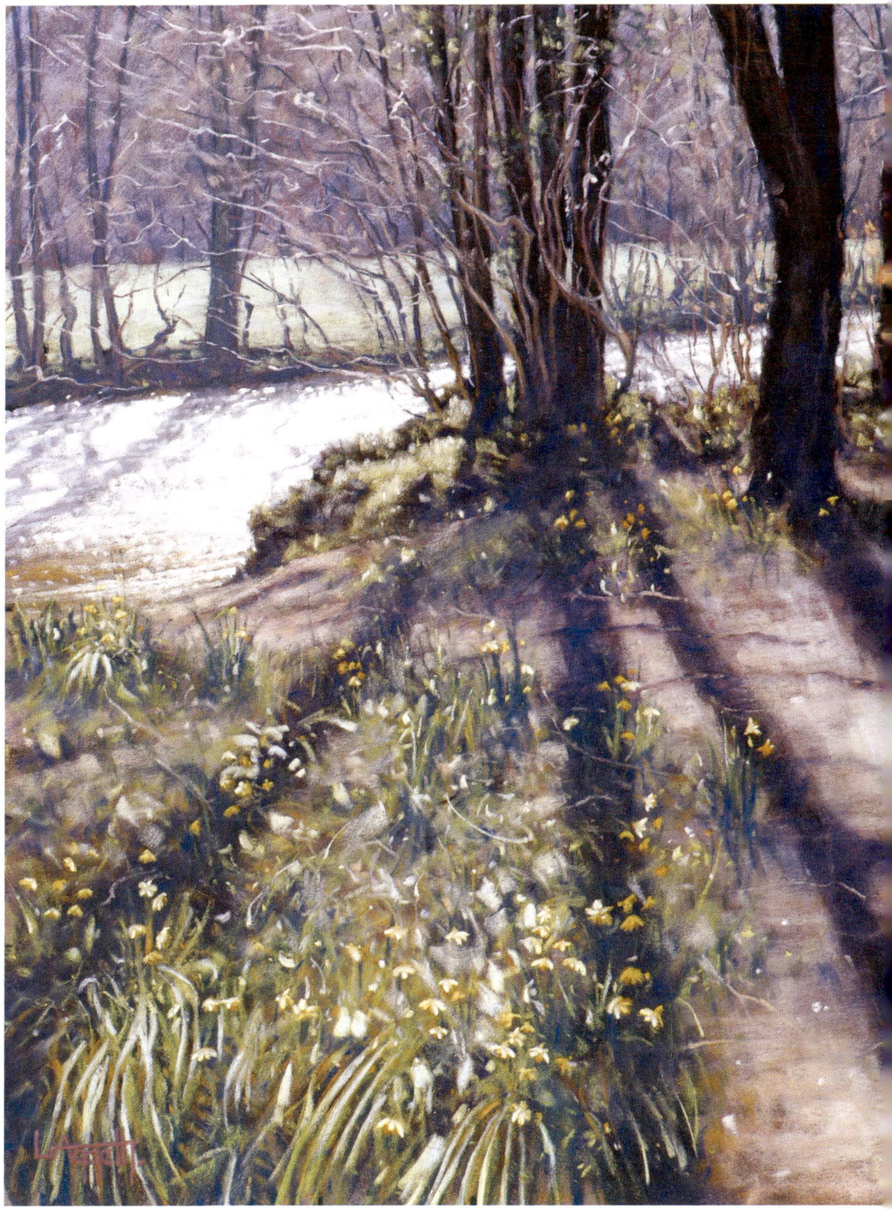

Lionel Aggett. *Spring, Teign Valley*
Pastel 20x16in (500x400cm)

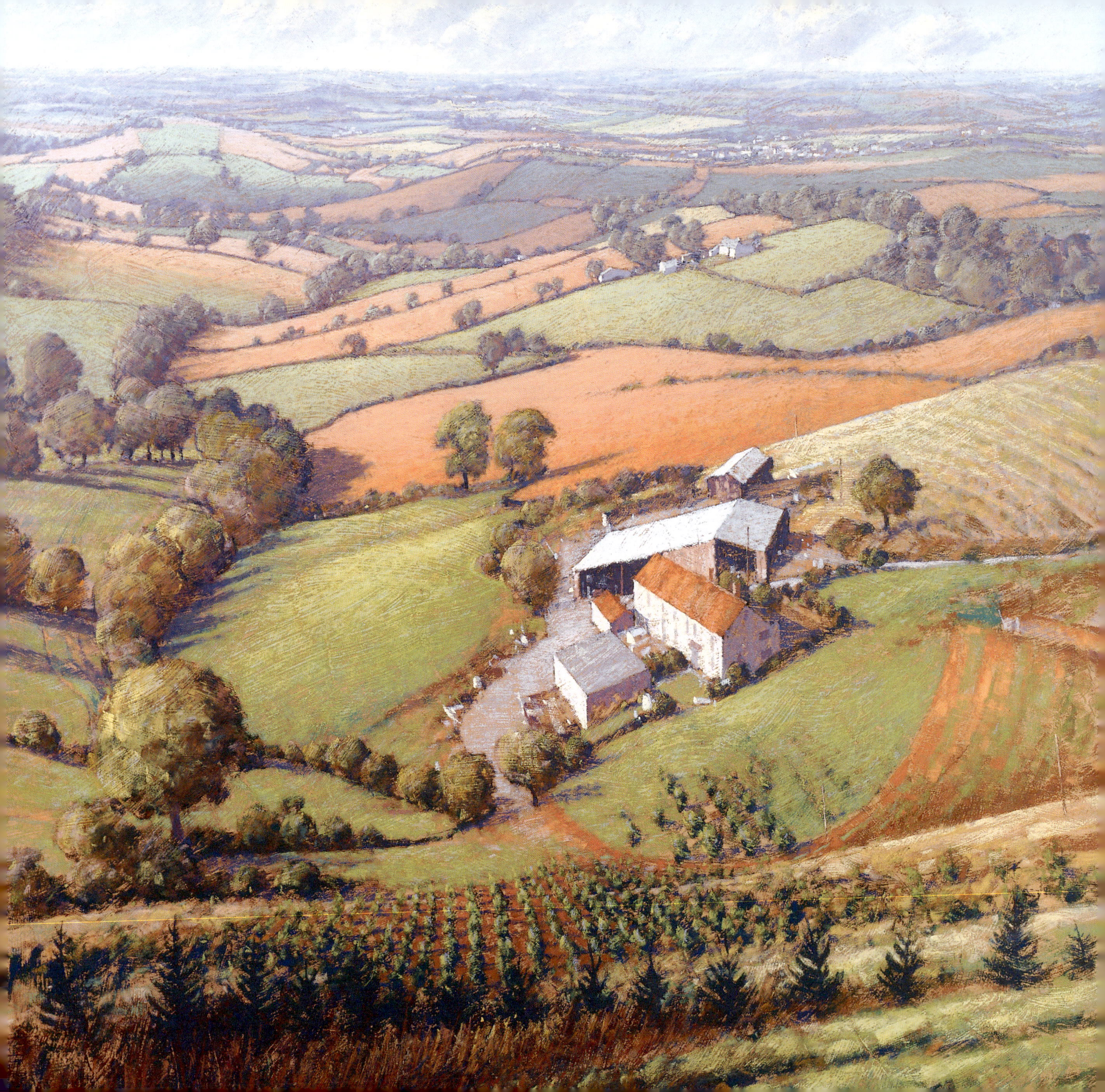

CHAPTER ONE

From deep-cut lanes to rolling green hills...

There can be fewer heart-swelling sensations than to look down from the top of any Devon hill and see the rich pattern of the countryside stretched out before you. A mosaic of hundreds of little hedged fields of rich red soil, contrasting with golden corn and fresh green growth. Its rivers and streams winding like blue threads, adding their own individual personality to the lie of the land. Stitched into this very fabric are the splashes of colour of its red sandstone churches, whitewashed cottages and farms. One such view, and in my opinion one of the finest in the county, is from Balle's Obelisk at Mamhead Point, on the lofty wooded summit of the Haldon Hills. On a clear day, one cannot only take in the pastoral beauty that gently unrolls itself down to meet the banks of the Exe, but also much of East Devon's fine coastline beyond. It is a highly cultivated landscape that we see before us today, created by more than fifty generations of farmers. For centuries they have been faithful stewards of the countryside and have created not only a cornerstone of English identity, but also a fertile subject for its many artists and writers.

My deep passion for the countryside, as well as for art, goes back to my childhood spent on the northern edge of Dartmoor. It was here that I first became entranced by nature's wonders, and before long I was caught under its magic spell. I consider it to have been a privileged childhood, one of building dens in the woods and playing in the morland streams. It was here that I first experienced the freedom, mystery and unpredictability that nature offers, something that has stayed with me ever since. When I left Art College in Exeter in 1969, I became a commercial artist, working in a number of advertising agencies in London, Bristol and Bath. Then in the late seventies I returned to my native land to work in Exeter. Our first home was at Starcross and I still have fond memories of walking our collie-cross 'Mij' from the front door, straight out into the luxuriant countryside around the village. Its close proximities to the estuary, as well as the coast, soon prompted me to pick up my paintbrushes again. Then after a number of years of painting alongside my job, demand for my watercolours led me to resign as Art Director in 1990 to become a professional artist.

The special quality of this stretch of countryside nestled in the shadows of the Haldon Hills is hard to define. It is a man-made landscape, but an ancient one, perfectly defined by its high-banked lanes, ancient woods, water meadows, orchards and enclosed farms. It is typified by undulating countryside so typical of Devon, which supports mixed farming on its deep red soils. Tucked away within its folded valleys, down its deep winding lanes lies a secret and almost timeless scene of ancient farms, hamlets and villages. Standing proudly at the heart of these are its noble sandstone churches, against a backdrop of fields crowned, in summer, with golden coronets of ripened corn. Kenn, Ashcombe, Powderham, these are all magical places to paint. Yet despite its close proximity to Exeter, no matter what time of the year I visit, there is always a feeling of remoteness in its sunken lanes. The embracing stillness is almost palpable at times, broken only by the occasional sound of the startled 'clatter' of pheasants as they scurry across the fields and the soft 'mewing' of buzzards as they soar majestically overhead. I believe we all have a need to belong, and in particular to have a place we feel an emotional affinity to, and I think this is mine.

Lionel Aggett. *Devon Red*
Pastel 40.5x40.5in (103x103cm)

No matter which part of the county one visits each area is unique. It has been said that the difference between the North and South Devon landscape is reflected in the appearance of its cows. Those in the south being happy and content, cream producers, grown fat on the 'milk and honey' sward of the South Hams; while those of the North are angular and tough, self-sufficient, chewing cud, a bit on the wild side. Then there are Devon's famous 'Ruby Red' cattle. There cannot be many places in England, where even its cattle complement the landscape quite so beautifully. Ideal for thriving on heavy clay soil, they have been an historic part of the scene for generations, and were, it is said, taken to America with the Pilgrim Fathers.

A painter, who has truly responded to the colours to be found in the landscape here, is **Lionel Aggett, RIBA, PS, SWAc**. A Devonian and proud of it, he was born in an old cob and thatched farmhouse beneath the backcloth of Dartmoor, in the very heart of the county at Whiddon Down. Since 1980 he and his wife Ann, who is also a painter, have worked from their home in Mid Devon. It affords tremendous views of distant Dartmoor and the red-enriched landscape that inspires him. He has also travelled extensively in Europe to explore a wider range of subject matter with his mobile studio – a VW camper van. His vibrant paintings of Italy, France and Spain have won him much international acclaim. However, it is his studies of the rolling Mid-Devon landscape and the city of Exeter, which have been part of the artist's wide popularity and success.

Lionel is a painter who enjoys working equally on location, as well as in the studio. He is rarely without a pencil and sketchbook in his hand and to view his sketches is a real pleasure. These sometimes take the form of diaries, with his masterly watercolour views accompanied by beautiful handwritten notes. His pastel paintings, often on a large scale, have been developed upon a firm foundation of skilful drawing and sound draughtsmanship, which comes from his architectural background. He says, 'Paintings should speak for themselves, but regarding my approach to landscape painting, well we all see things differently. In this respect my ability to read detail far into the distance certainly influences the way I paint. Most importantly, I firmly believe that the essence of good topographical painting is the capturing of the moment in every respect, and all that this entails.'

Another painter, who evokes this same 'spirit' in his work, is **Stephen Brown, RBA** He draws his inspiration from the rich history of man's relationship with the landscape, particularly around his East Devon home. He is a master at depicting its warm summer days, as cows graze in the fields, or as combines cut the corn and wheat. One can almost feel the very heat of the sun being emitted from his canvases. Painting almost exclusively in oils, he considers himself a true Westcountryman. As he says: 'I was born in Chard in Somerset, very close to a point where you could stand in Somerset, lean forward and put one hand in Dorset and the other hand in Devon.' At school it was the art classes he enjoyed most, but it was not until he was in his early twenties that he took up painting seriously. This came about after seeing the impressionistic watercolours of A.H. Knighton-Hammond in a small art shop in Chard.

Stephen Brown. *Landscape near Salcombe*
Oil 24x30in (60x76cm)

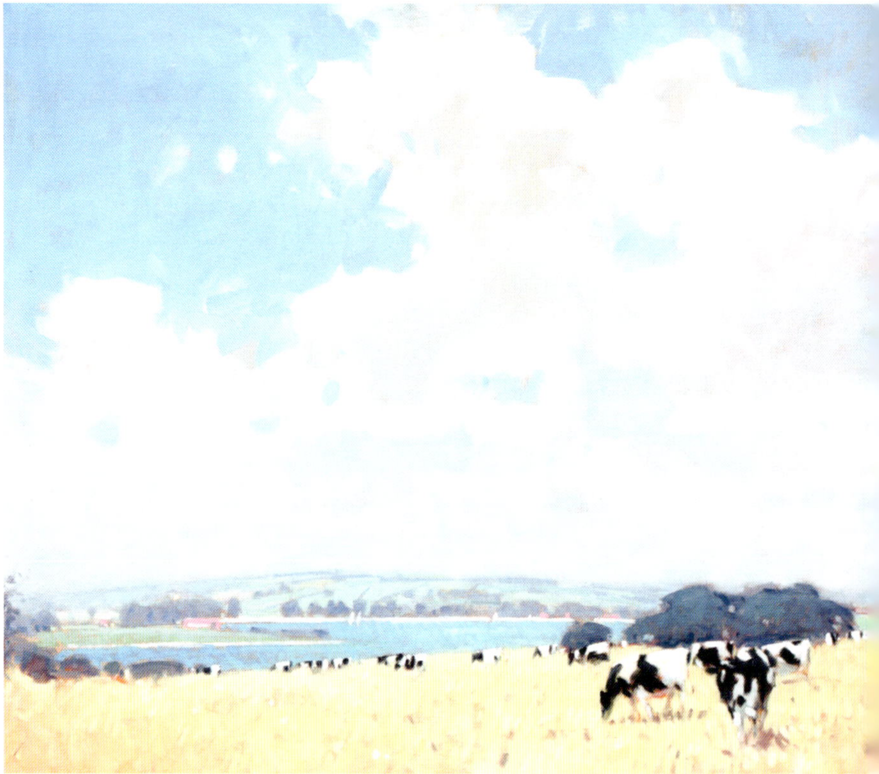

It was the owner who introduced Stephen to the artist Patrick Larking RP, ROI who was then living in Colyton after a long career in London. They became good friends and painted the landscape around Colyton together for a little over ten years. Painting trips rarely include a canvas and easel though, as he prefers to work in the studio from pencil sketches and notes and photographs. 'Pat Larking once told me that he was not at his best as a painter with a cow licking the back of his neck!' He added: 'In today's world, it may seem old-fashioned and out of date, but Ruskin's comment: "Paint what you love and love what you paint," firmly applies to my philosophy. It sums up my preferred subject matter – people, often family, enjoying the Devon coast and landscape; the day-to-day working of farms near our home in Sidmouth; and possibly the most painted border collie in England, Ben.'

Another painter associated with the East Devon landscape is **Alwyn Crawshaw, SEA, BWS, UA(Hons), FRSA, P.NAPA**. Alwyn is an internationally known artist, author and television presenter, and for nearly four decades, with support from his wife June, has championed the cause of practical art to millions of amateur painters worldwide. Born in Mirfield, Yorkshire, he trained at Hastings School of Art and then started his own commercial art studio in Russell Square, London before deciding to paint fulltime; something that he had wanted to do from the age of seven. Alwyn moved to Devon from Woking and, until recently, resided in the county for 18 years, which he loved. Firstly living at Metcombe, deep in the Otter Valley and then on the coast at Dawlish, where he and June also ran their own gallery. 'The Otter Valley was fantastic painting country, but it took eighteen months to come to terms with the hills, which seemed to close in the landscape and take away a lot of visible sky.'

Alwyn's painting skills are built on a sound foundation of drawing and observation, honed from years of working in the landscape. 'It is the influence of Constable's work that played such a great part in my love of landscape and in the choice of it as my painting subject.' This is evident in whichever medium he happens to be using, whether it is watercolour, acrylics or oils. He says that he is often asked which medium he prefers, to which he offers the reply: 'The one that I am working with at the moment. If it wasn't my favourite I couldn't give it my hundred per cent. Therefore whatever medium I am working with, that is my favourite.'

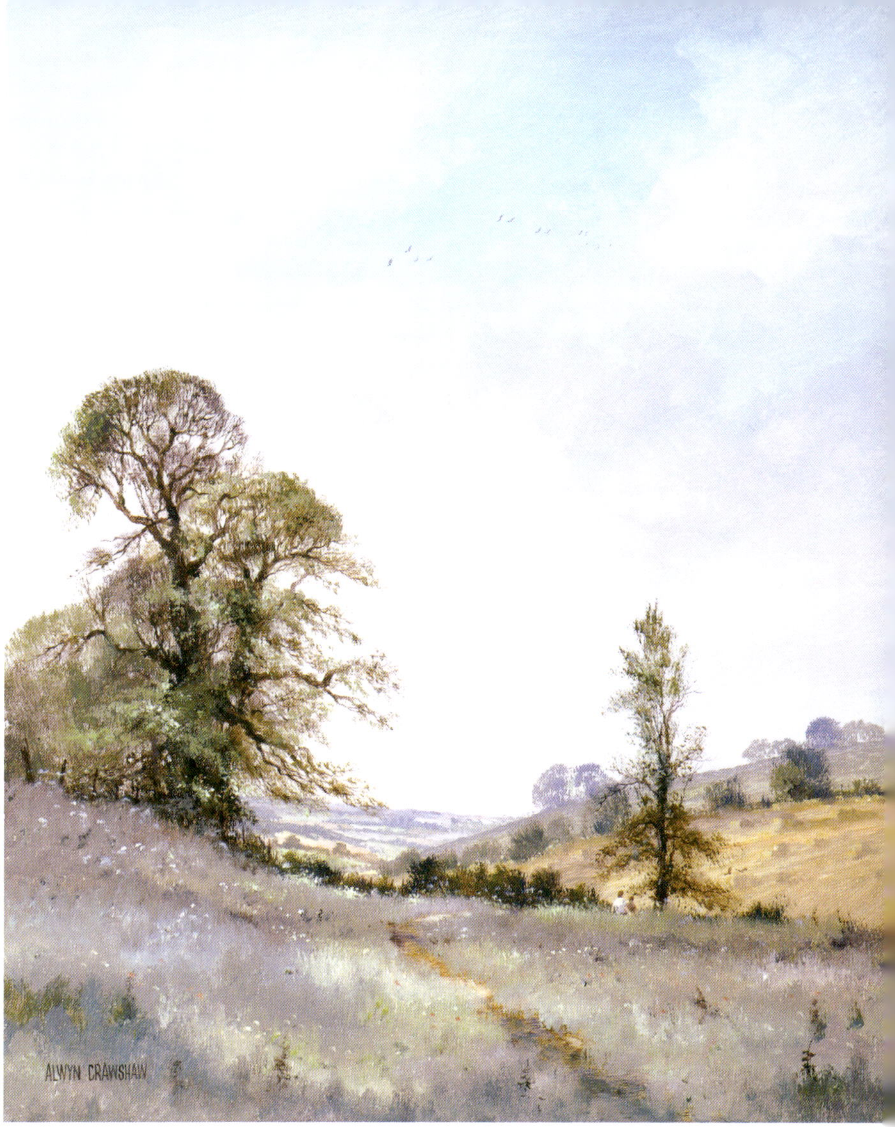

Alwyn Crawshaw. *Summertime, Otter Valley*
Acrylic 20x16in (51x41cm)

It was in the Otter Valley that he also ran many of his popular painting courses. Alwyn told me one amusing story when on one occasion his group of painters were surrounded in a field by a herd of inquisitive cows and whilst most fled one defiant lady continued to paint unconcerned. Her easel was promptly knocked over by one curious cow and then to her astonishment, it preceded to lick the painting! The student then remarked 'I don't know if it was better before or after the cows licking!' There are shades of Patrick Larking here and from that day Alwyn never took students into fields where cows were grazing.

For some painters, it is not the sweeping landscapes or big skies that inspire, but the more intimate subjects found at the very heart of the countryside. This is the case for **Colin Allbrook, RI, ARSMA, SEA, SWAc** who has found a wealth of material in the farmsteads around his home in the Taw valley. Born in Hertfordshire, he studied at St Martins School of Art and then joined a commercial studio in London before moving to North Devon in 1979. From discovering the work of American painter Andrew Wyeth, he soon realised that the ordinary things around you were equally as important as the bigger picture. Colin began by painting many interiors in and around the house, often featuring his wife and children. Fascinated by the light and colour in these spaces led him to look at bigger interior spaces which he found in the barns and livestock markets in the area. He finds the barns have a lovely quality of light in them and there is nearly always activity like milking or feeding going on. He says: 'I love working in these places with their clutter of machinery, sacks, boxes and livestock. The light, often coming from high up through roof lights or perhaps half-doors lower down, is filtered through dust and cobwebs and the straw reflects it back in ochre greens illuminating the dark corners or perhaps someone working. Sometimes the buildings are viewed from outside, maybe standing in the yard on a winter evening during milking or lambing. Then the electric light glows warmly from the shed and contrasts with the cool colours outside.' In them he lovingly celebrates the quintessential nature of the region's gentle, yet ever threatened pace of life, thus providing a unique record of a fast changing scene. However, capturing the daily life of the Devon farmer in his soft atmospheric watercolours and oils has its drawbacks as he added: 'Standing in a cold yard gradually freezing from the feet up, drawing an animal that is constantly moving is certainly an encouragement to take up still life.'

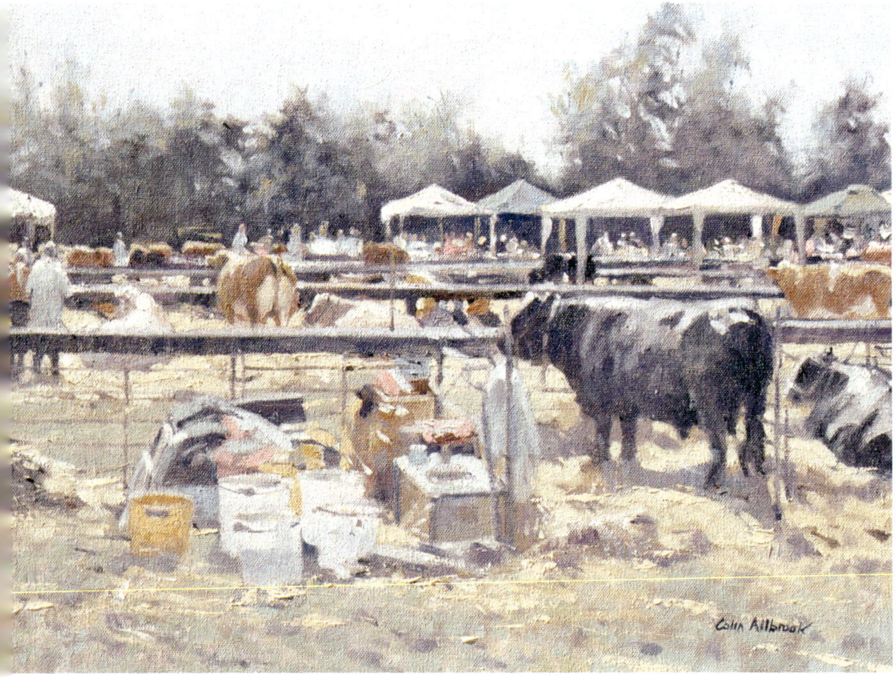

Colin Allbrook. *At the County Show*
Oil 14x18in (36x46cm)

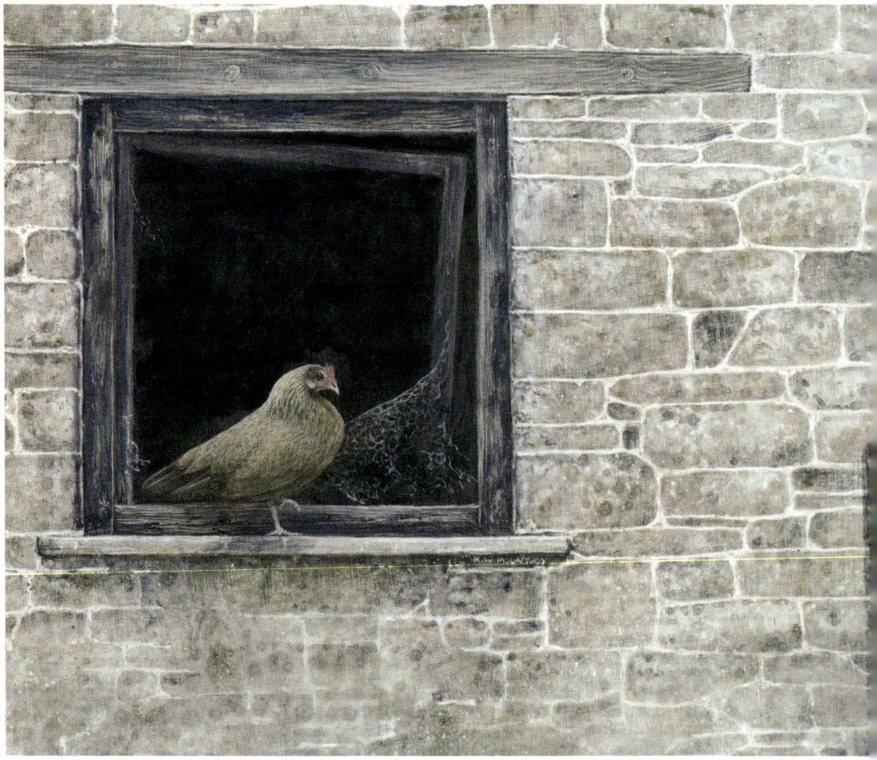

Robert Mountjoy. *Mike's Bantam Hen*
Watercolour 10x12.5in (25x32cm)

Plymouth watercolorist **Robert Mountjoy, SWAc** is equally passionate about old barns and farmyards, but it is the corners where man's neglect and indolence has allowed nature to claw back some space that appeals to him more. He has a rare talent for capturing the commonplace and revealing it as a significant moment in time. Robert was born and grew up in Appledore and at an early age was encouraged to carry an unlined school exercise book and a few stubs of pencils by his grandfather, who was captain of a small steam ship. It was these ships and sailing vessels on the busy Torridge estuary that first inspired him to draw. But he also admits that it was the frequent visits he made to the Burton Art Gallery which were also invaluable in his development as a painter. The turning point came later when he was roving the Taw and Torridge valleys in a futile search for the home of one of his ancestors. He says: 'The dwelling, like so many vernacular buildings in Devon, had shrunk back into the earth and I could find little evidence of habitation in the given location. The protective thatch had decayed and the rain had penetrated, rotting the timbers and washing out the cob walls. The stone footings had gone and all that remained was a rectangular mound of rough grass and bramble. The way that these man-made structures were melting into the landscape fascinated me and I sought out other structures which had fallen into disuse and disrepair. Across North and West Devon there were many. I wanted to document the slow but inevitable repossession. Old lichen covered walls that had lost their mortar and had been invaded by ivy and wild flowers. Unused barns and abandoned sheds that had been patched and repaired with ill-fitting planks or sheets of rusting iron drew me and I drew them. Once discovered I rushed to record them before they were spoilt by renovation or destroyed by an impulse to tidy up.'

Robert works on a relatively small scale, holistically, through a series of watercolour washes and underpainting, gradually getting more detailed as the composition develops. Paintings may be started in situ but will be then finished in the studio, often being worked and reworked over months and even years. His search to fully get inside the subject has resulted in more than just photo-realism; his paintings evoke the layering of time itself and are a meditative experience for both the painter as well as the viewer.

Another fine watercolourist in the true tradition of the word is **John Hoar**. He too has a deep-rooted empathy with the landscape he inhabits and his

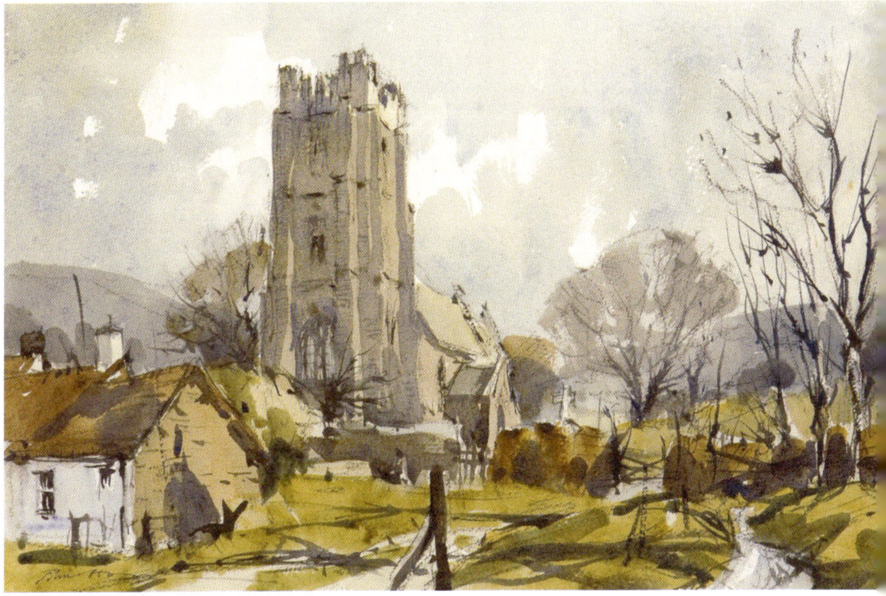

John Hoar. *Kentisbury*
Watercolour 12x18in (30x46cm)

painting philosophy is as direct and honest as his paintings. 'If you feel like painting, be straightforward and simple and enjoy yourself.'

The son of an architect who was also a distinguished watercolorist, John studied architecture at Cambridge until he realised that he had no aptitude for its modern form and switched to painting. He became a student of Ruskin Spear RA, and spent a lot of time studying the work of the great water-colorists, concentrating on those who had perfected an economy of drawing and wash in particular more recently Wilson Steer and Edward Wesson. Since 1987 he has lived in South Molton, in the heart of North Devon. He has a family of seven sons of whom Tom and Jack have also taken up the mantle. Although John also travels further a field to paint, he agrees that there really is no need. Some of his favourite subjects are all around him in the towns and villages, many with their whitewashed cottages and fine church towers. To watch John paint in watercolour is an exhilarating experience as he handles the medium in the way that it should be used, with fluidity, clarity and unpredictability. He tends to draw outside and paint inside, but on occasion will paint on the spot. I remember asking John once whether he stretched his watercolour paper on to a board prior to painting on it. 'Heavens no!' he replied in a flash, 'Life's far too short.'

Tony Williams' career as a painter came very much out of adversity. He did not start painting until 2001, when the foot and mouth outbreak threatened their Bed & Breakfast business in rural North Devon. He says: 'I had to teach myself to paint in isolation, drawing on a lifetime of looking at the Devon landscape as a series of paintings and drawings.' Perhaps partly due to this, he has evolved a distinctive style and since then has not looked back. Tony was born in London into a family of artists and after studying at Art College he worked as a Creative Director in advertising. He spent all his childhood holidays in Devon and has lived in the county since 1966. His home is in the heart of small family-run farms and it is often these subjects of cattle, or local farm workings that provides his main inspiration. He is a great admirer of the Suffolk artist Harry Becker, with his powerful and intuitive studies of farm labourers and their stock of the 1900s. Tony says he works best in his studio from colour notes and drawings, 'My style of painting has come from a love of drawing and seeing subjects graphically and design is also an important element in the painting.'

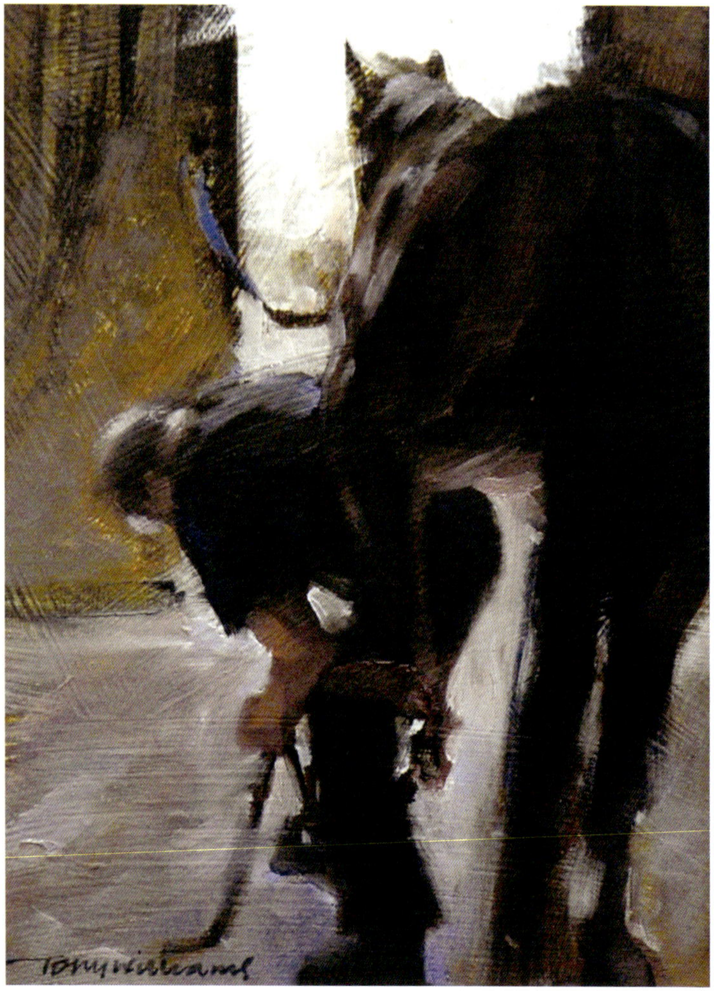

Tony Williams. *Colin Trimming Paddy*
Oil 8x6in (20x15cm)

For **Robert Jennison, RWA** there is also a sensitive awareness of the various effects of man's involvement with the landscape. The graphic geometry and linear rhythms of buildings, boundaries and tracks, the textures and pattern of hedges and fences, and the wonderful muscular forms of fields and woods echoed in the sky and clouds. He has lived and worked in East Devon for over forty years and the landscape around his home has had a profound effect on his work. Robert's paintings are built on a sound foundation of drawing skills and he has always regarded drawing as a valid picture-making medium in its own right. As he explained: 'Drawing has always been an essential part of my work, exploring the subject itself and the change from being "of" the subject to being "about" it.' As Degas once said: 'Drawing is not what one sees but what one can make others see.' He prefers to paint in the studio rather than on the spot, working from drawings and photographs. His paintings are mainly concerned with the dual action of climate and man on the land. Weather and changing light are constantly modifying his experience of it. His approach to painting aims to go beyond the descriptive 'capture' of nature on canvas towards a dialogue between the painter and subject, a process that frees him from rigid topographical representation. The resulting work is an exploration of meaning defined through form, pattern and colour that have evolved through the process of painting itself.

Robert Jennison. *Pines, Woodbury Common*
Oil 36x36in (92x92cm)

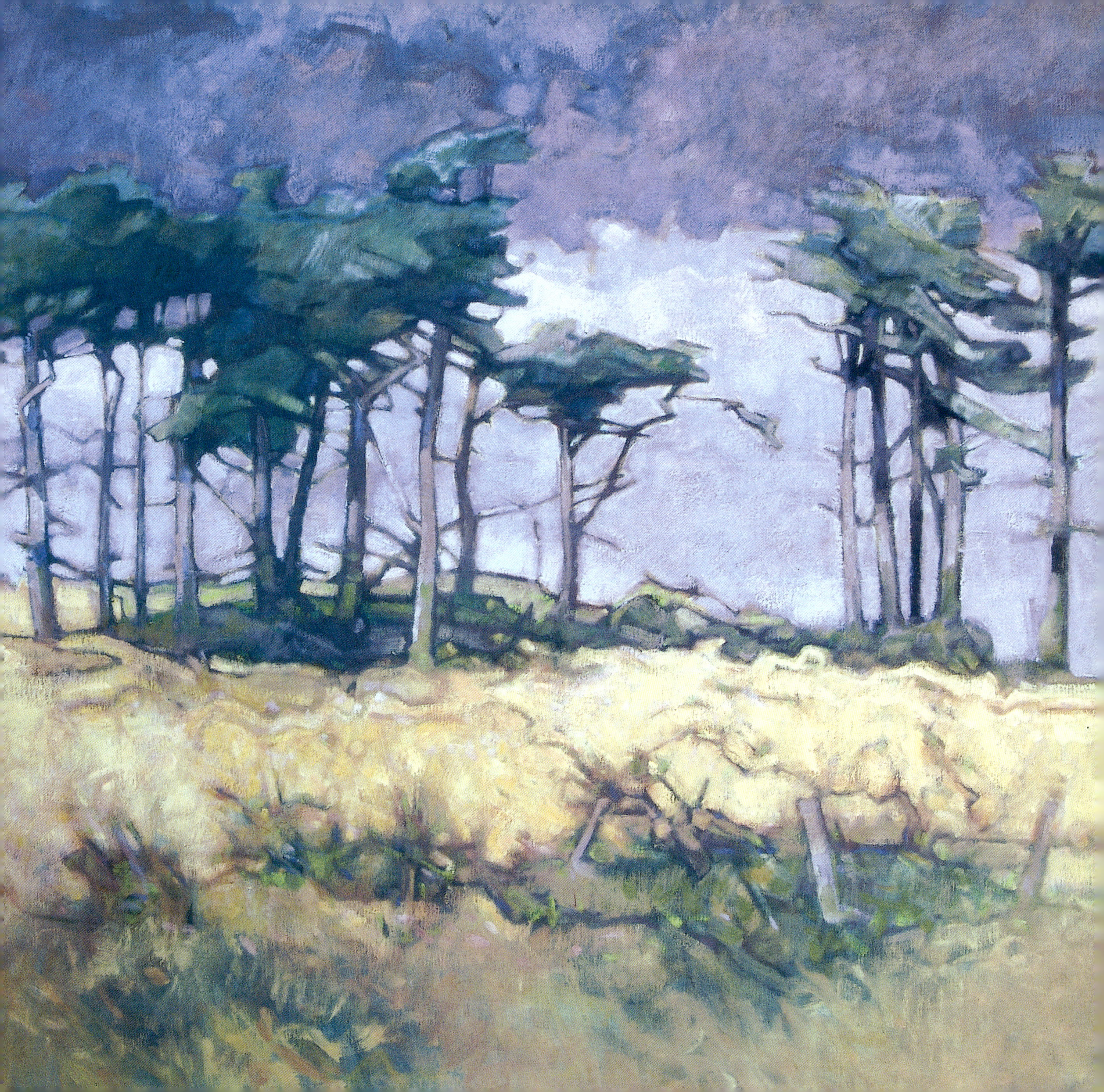

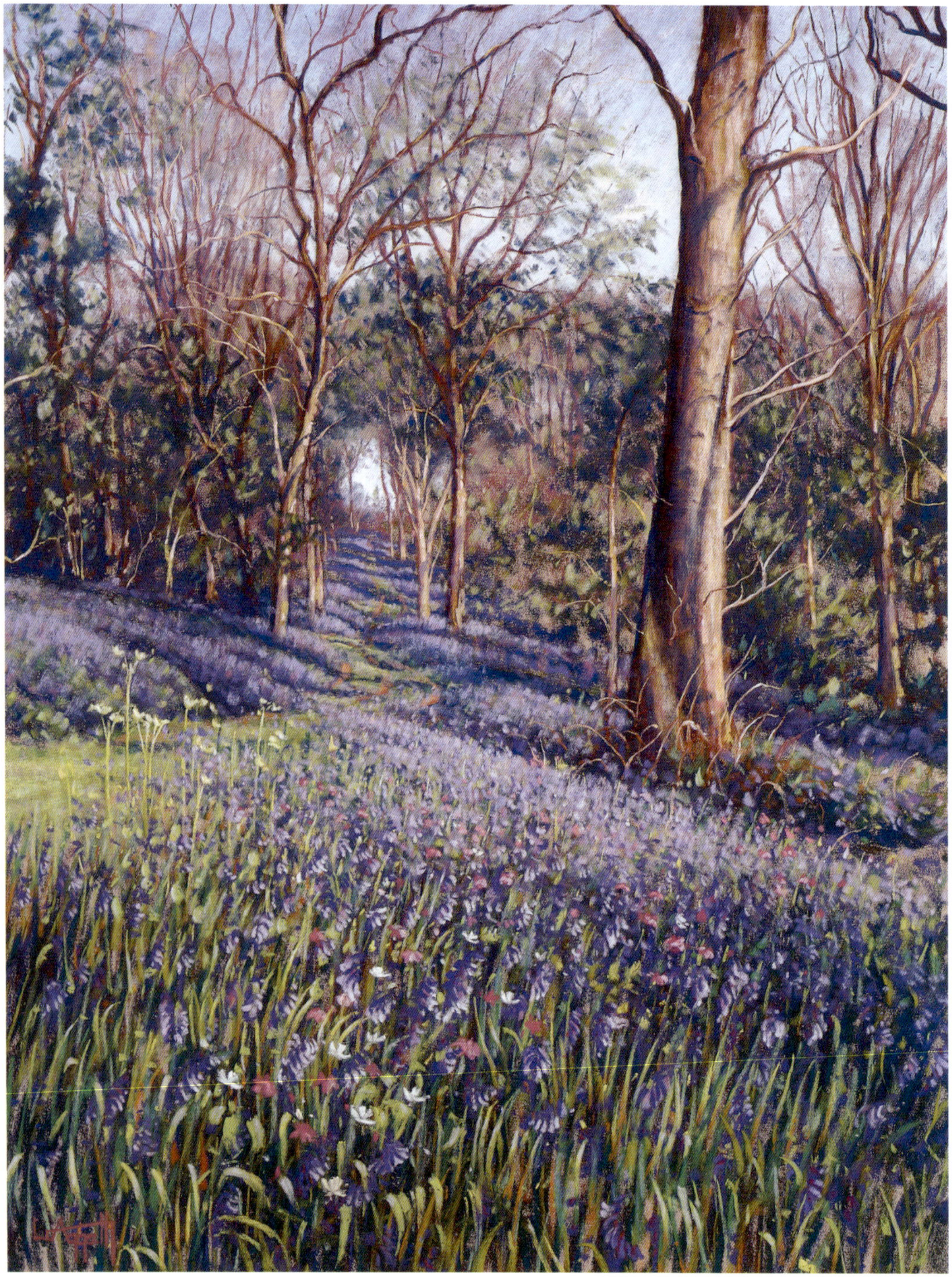

Lionel Aggett. *Chenson Woods*
Pastel 26x20in (66x 51cm)

The owners of Chenson Farm, between Lapford and Eggesford, open their spectacular bluebell woods to the public every spring. The intense blue carpet beneath the burgeoning canopy is an absolute joy to behold and is a subject I have painted many times.

Alan Cotton.
Devon – Barley Field with Teasels and Thistles
Oil 36x40in (92x102cm)

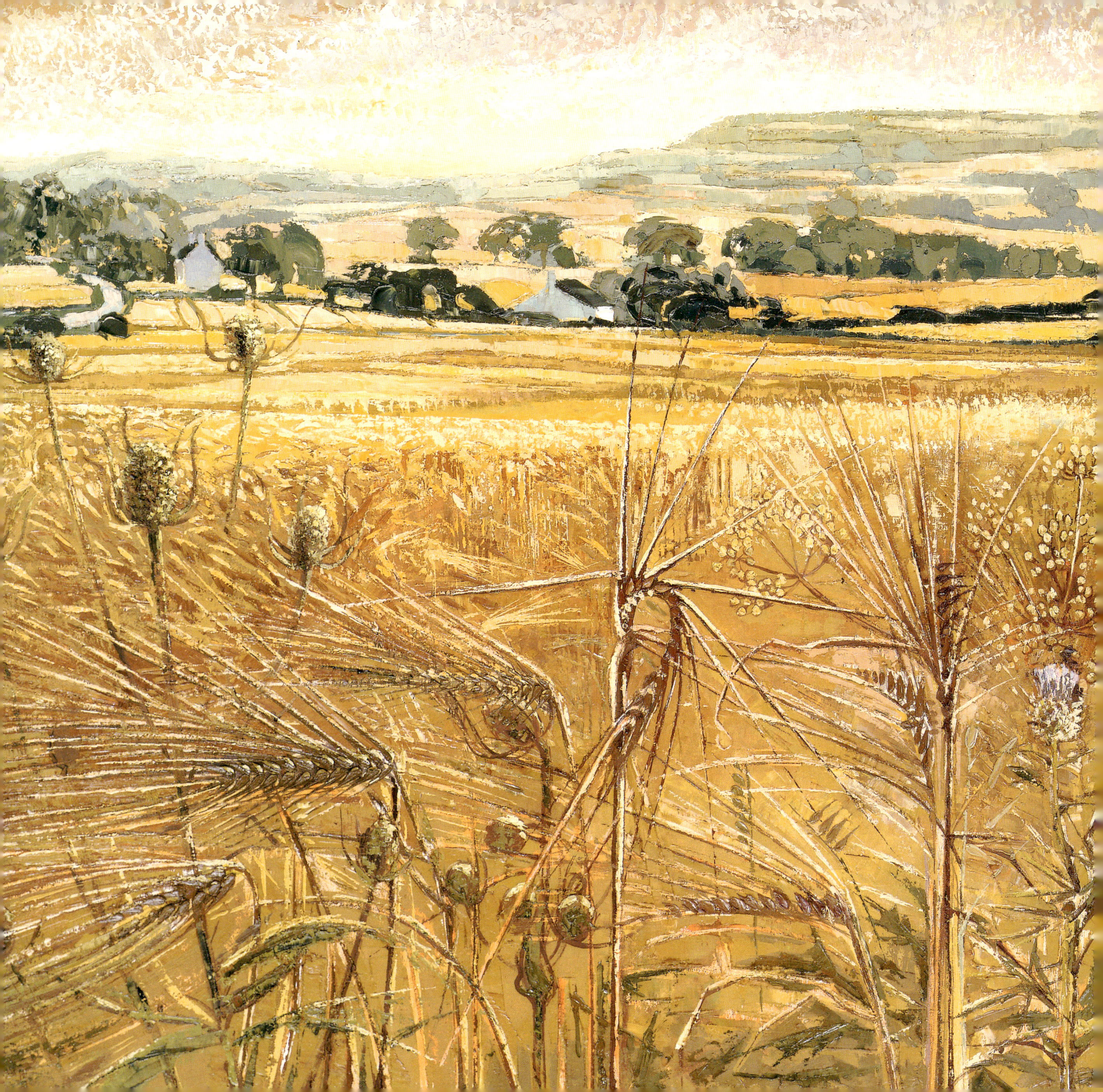

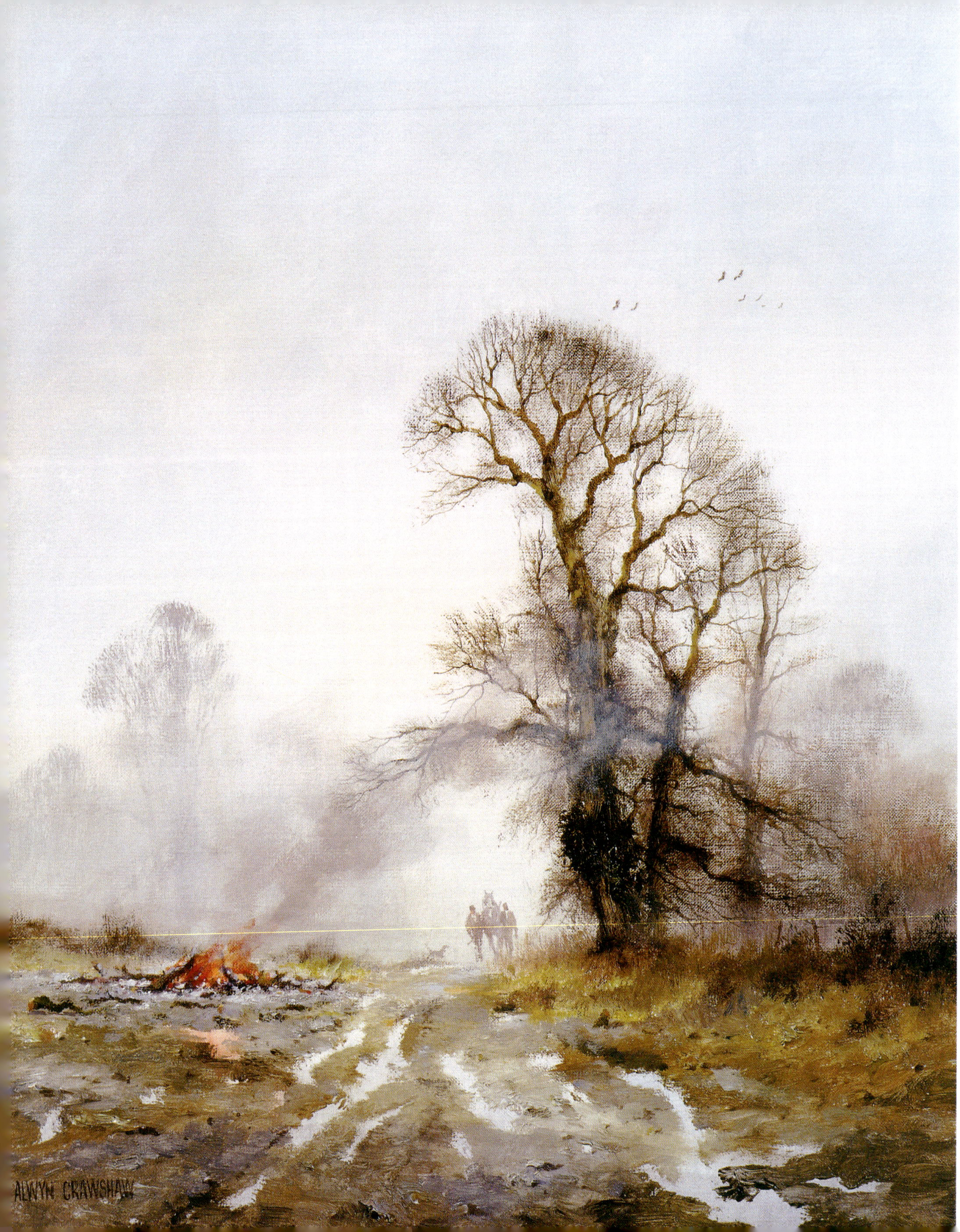

Alwyn Crawshaw.
Late Afternoon, Otter Valley
Acrylic 16x12in (41x30cm)

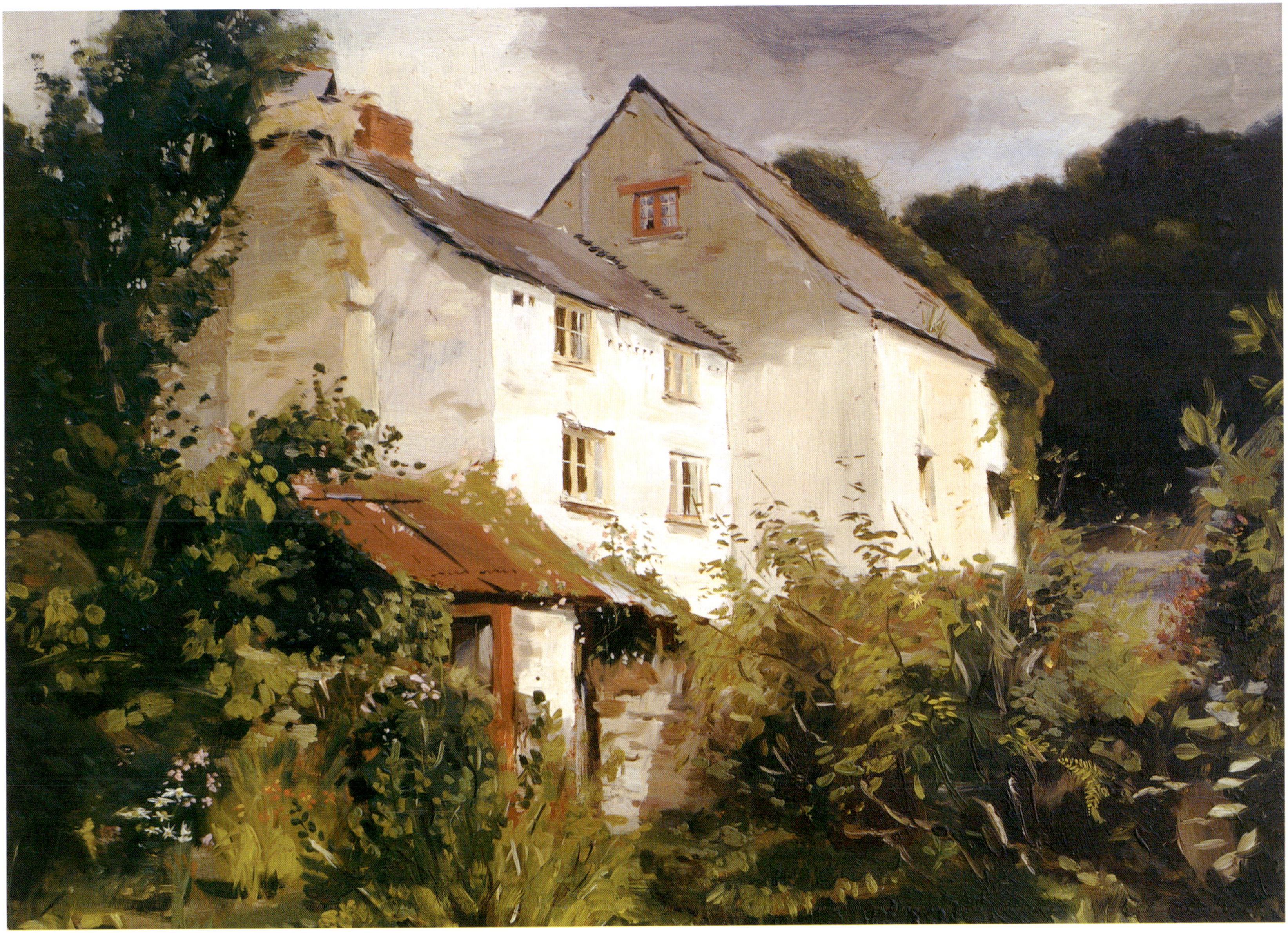

Barry Watkin. *Old Mill, Slapton*
Oil 17x23in (43x58cm)

I came across this gem years ago. I couldn't squeeze the paint on to my palette quickly enough. What a subject, strong tonal contrasts, textures, rusting corrugated iron and wild garden. Perfect, except for the weather. It took three mornings, dodging showers and drunken wasps to complete.

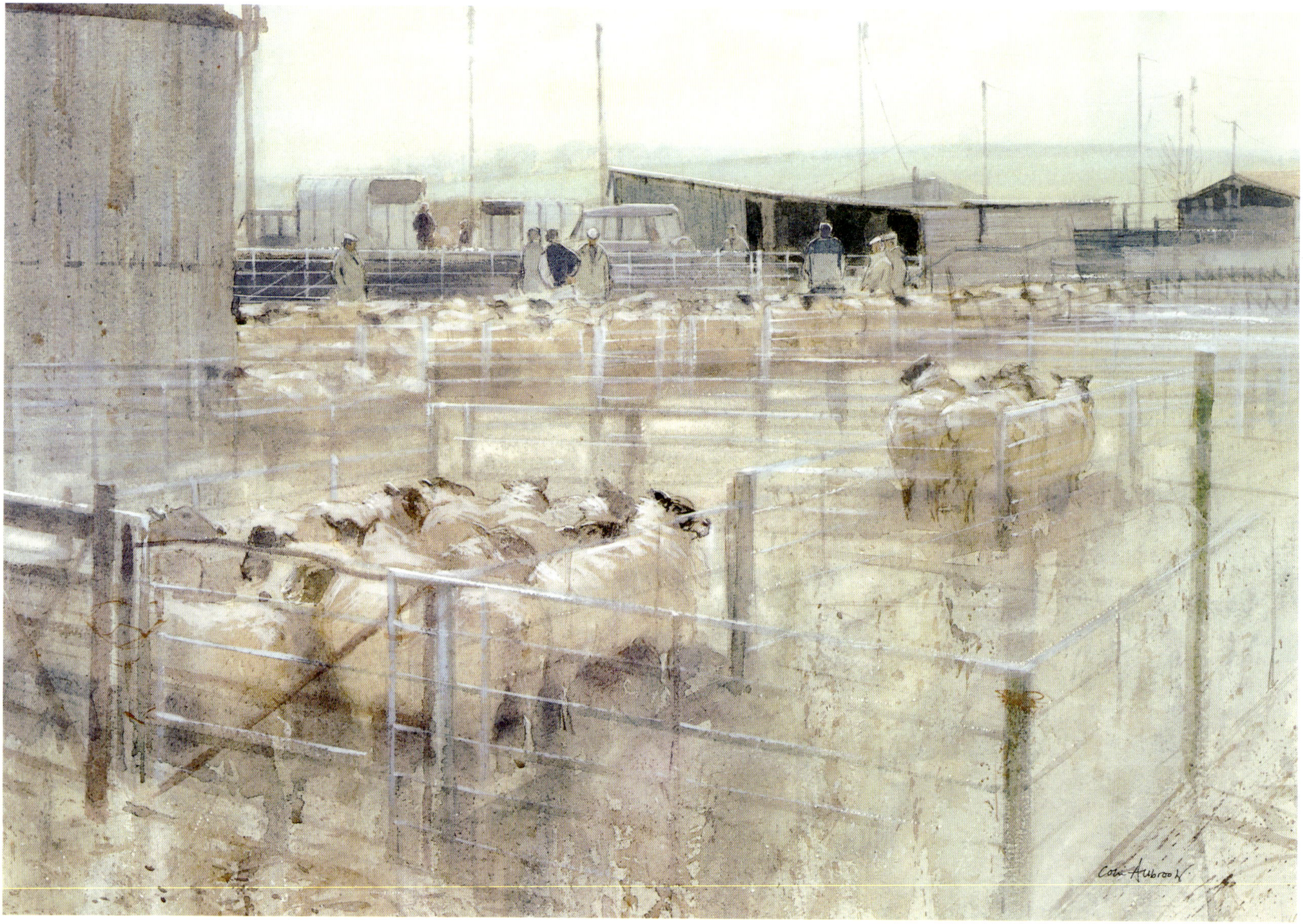

Colin Allbrook. *March, Blackmore Gate*
Watercolour 20x28in (51x80cm)

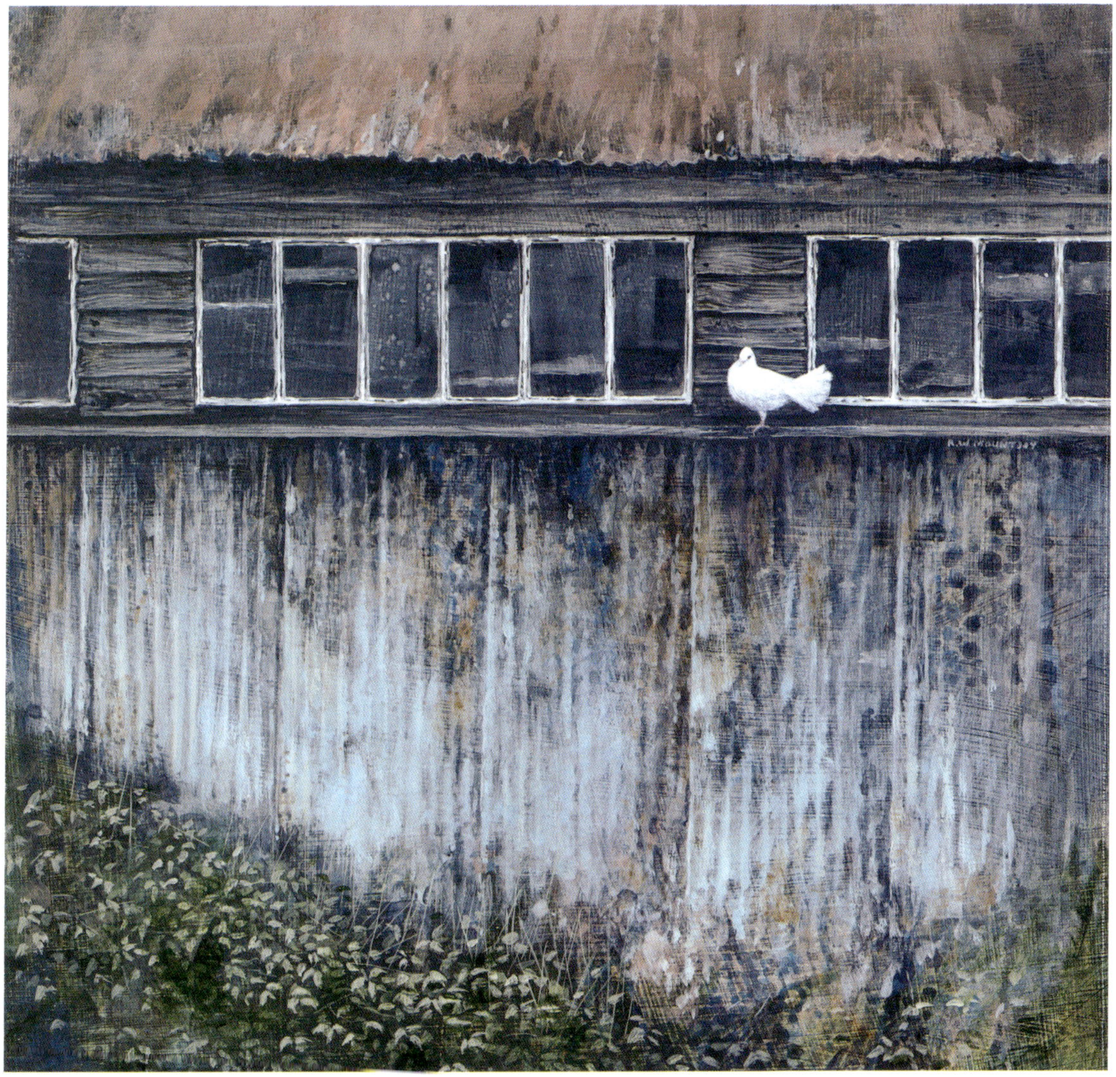

Bob Mountjoy. *Visitor in the Yard*
Watercolour 9x10in (23x25cm)

This West Devon garage and yard was falling into disrepair, but it provided a rich source of material. Sadly it was about to reach its peak when the site was developed. Here a white dove from the other side of the village contrasts with the dirty glass and rusting iron sheets.

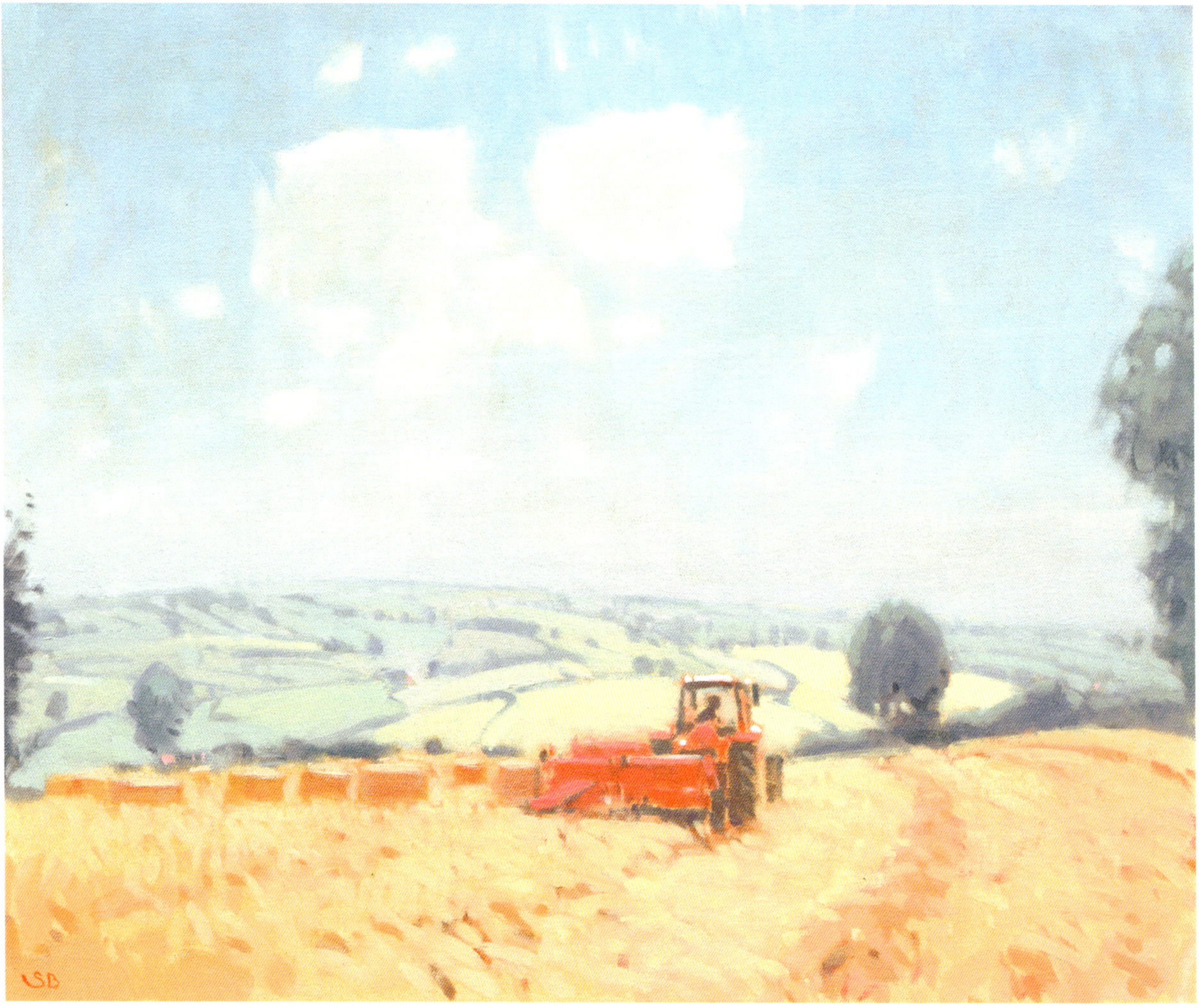

Stephen Brown. *Farm Scene, South Hams*
Oil 16x20in (40x50cm)

There are still some old weatherbeaten tractors working in Devon and I am always on the look out for them, as their faded colours provide the perfect foil to the greens, blues and yellows of the landscape.

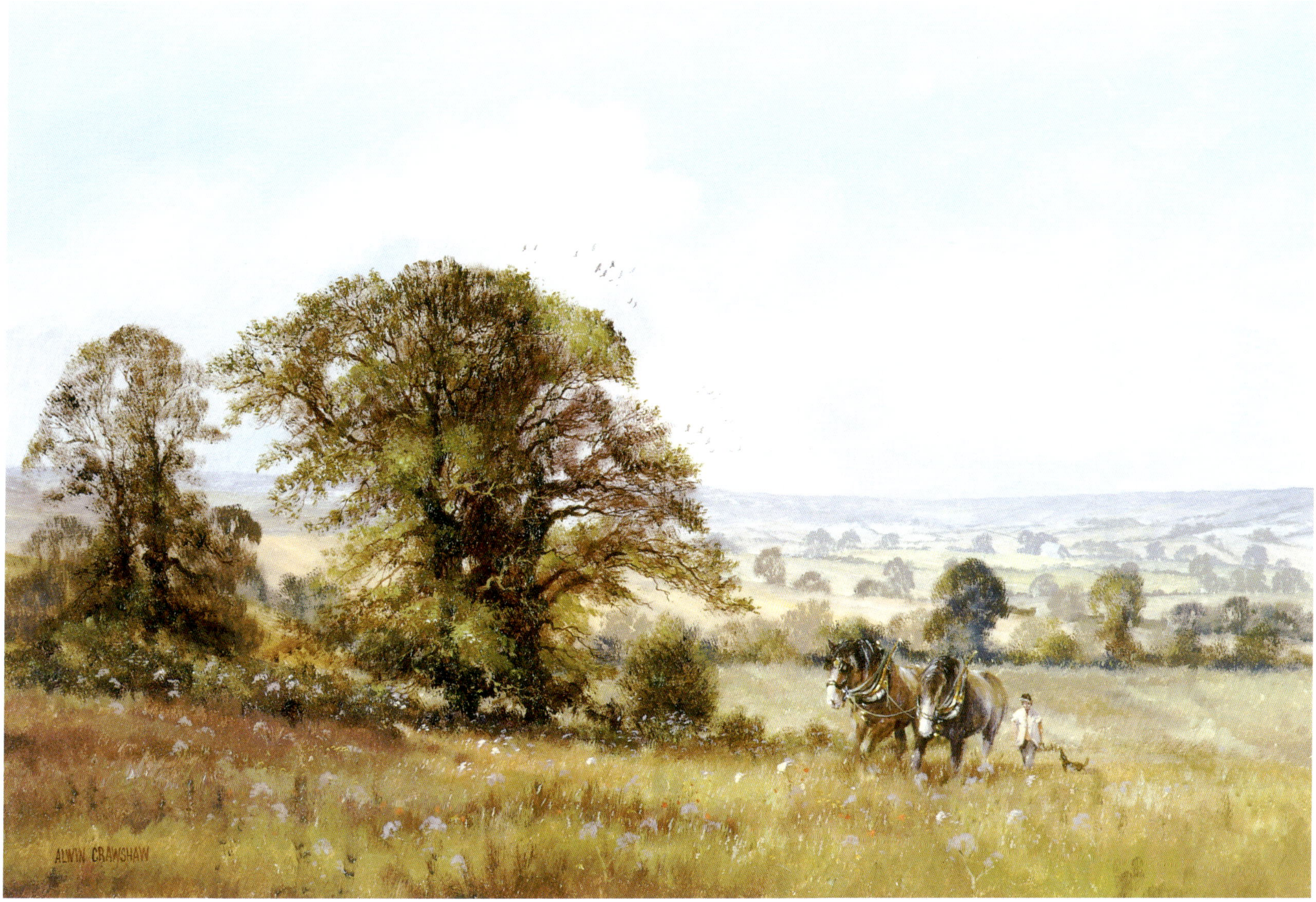

Alwyn Crawshaw. *In the Shade, Otter Valley*
Acrylic 20x30in (51x76cm)

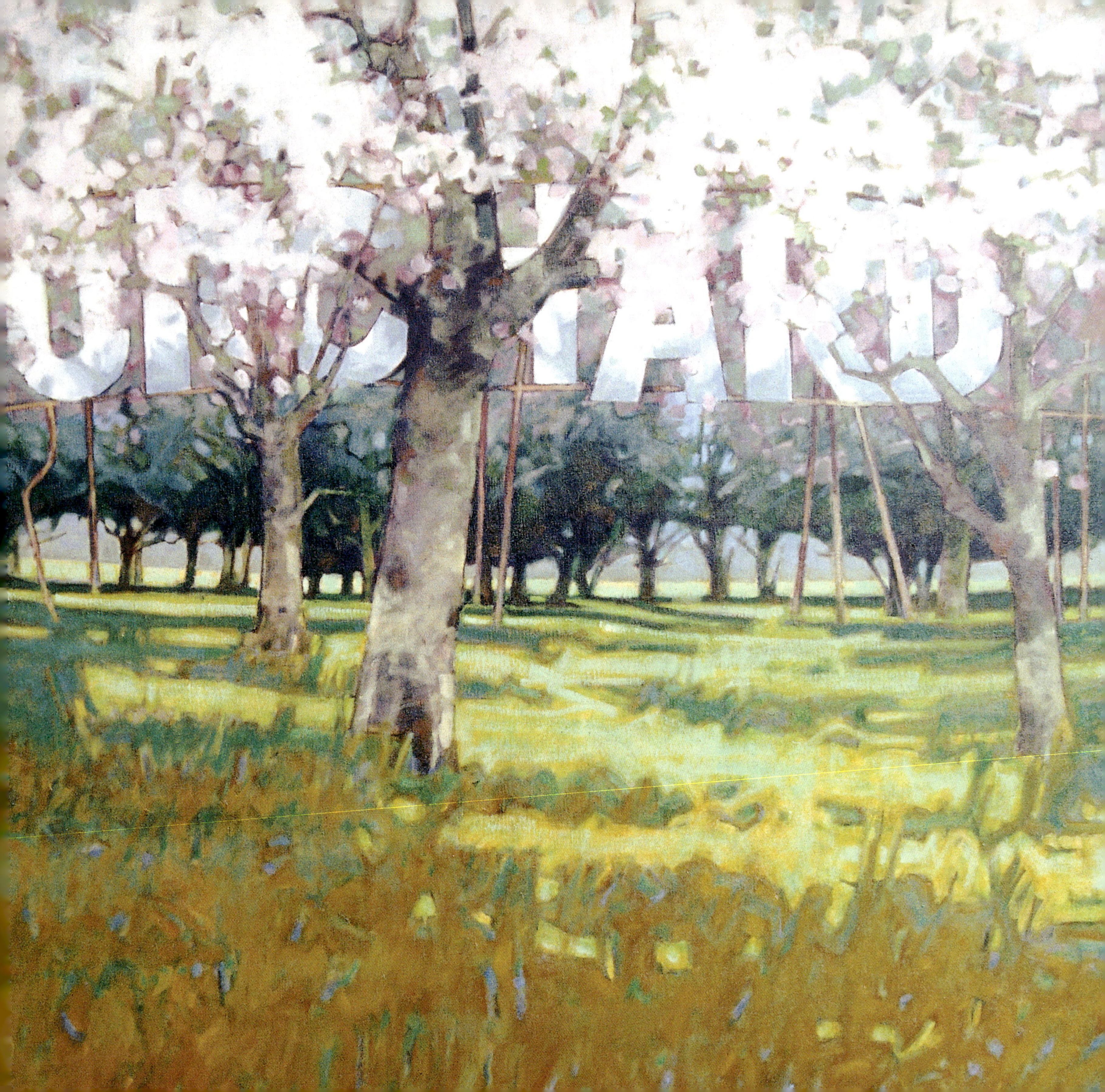

Colin Allbrook. *Barn Calves*
Watercolour 20x14in (51x36cm)

Barns are intriguing places often littered with equipment, some livestock, straw and dust, and full of luminous light and deep shadows, interesting places to draw and paint. When I first went to draw in a friend's barn she offered to tidy and clean up a little, something I managed to quickly dissuade her from doing. Another farmer, after seeing his farm reproduced in my paintings, replaced some fences and gates after realizing how much bailer twine he had used around the place.

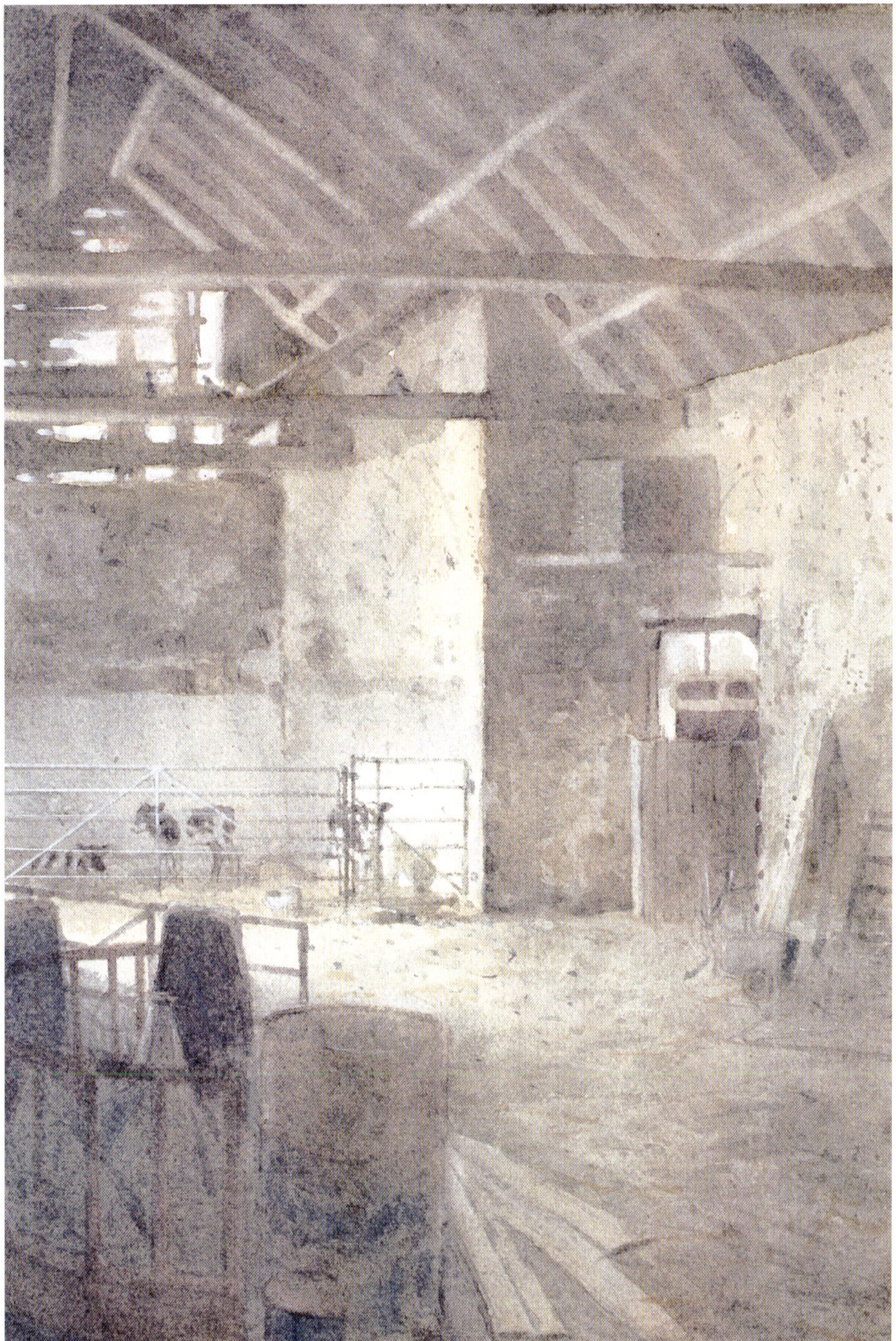

Opposite page:
Robert Jennison.
In Memoriam, Whiteway's Cider Orchard
Oil 36x36in (92x92cm)

Once apple orchards predominated in the landscape, now sadly the huge letters that emerge from among the apple trees advertise a local antique dealer rather than Whiteways Cider, as when this was painted.

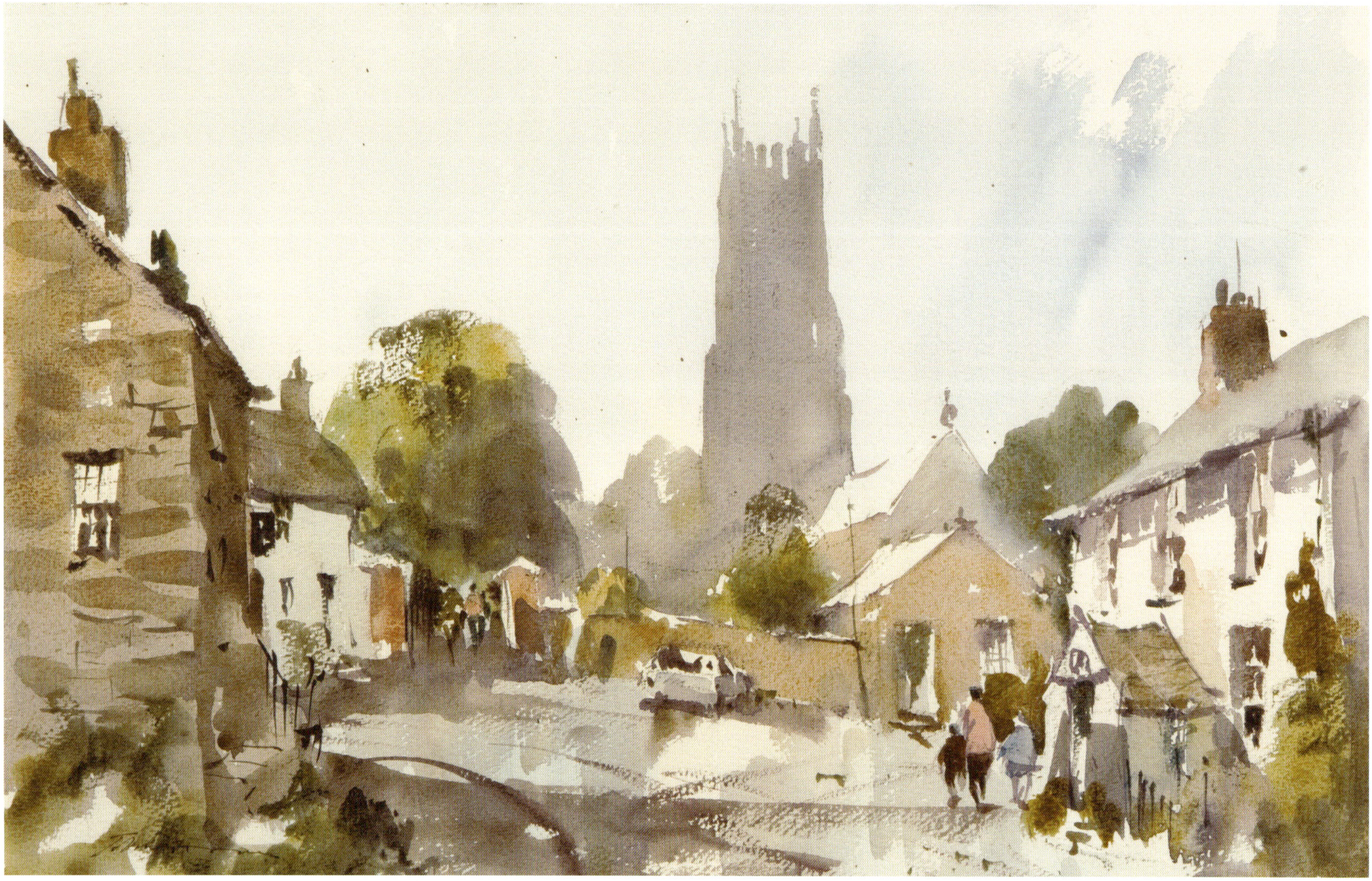

John Hoar. *Hartland*
Watercolour 12x18in (30x46cm)

Ray Balkwill. *Mist in the Valley, Ashton*
Oil 10x12in (25x30in)

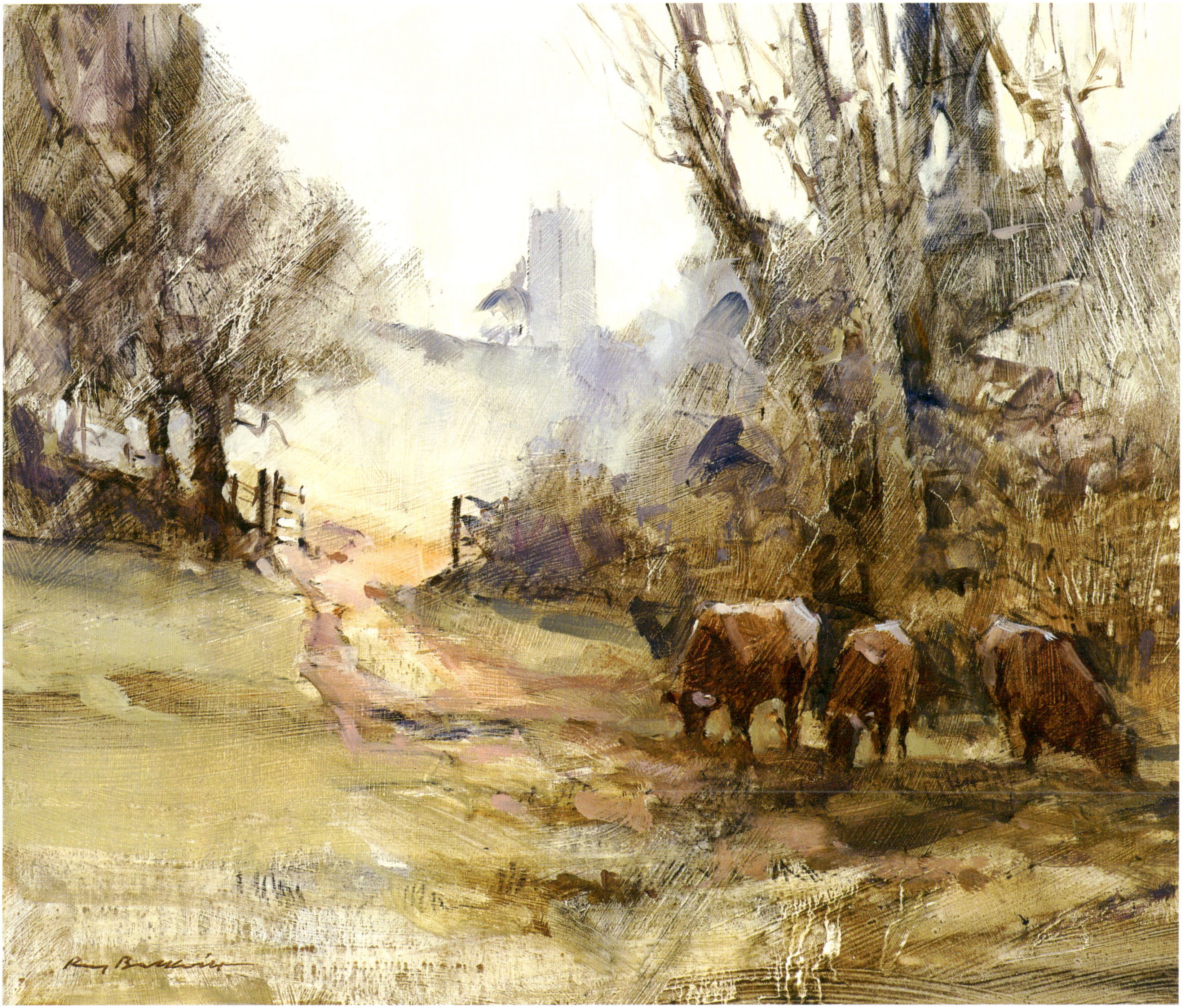

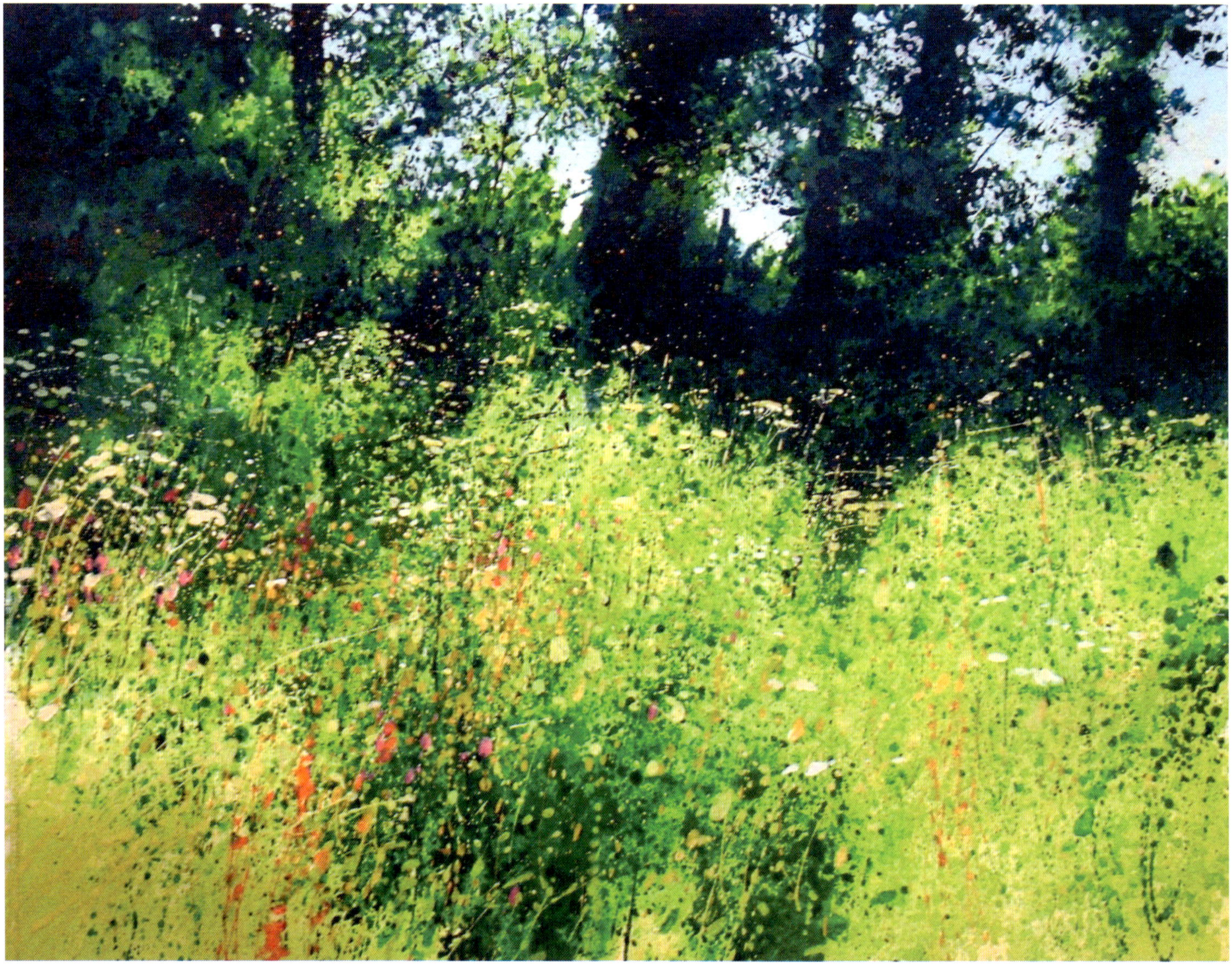

Richard Thorn. *A Corner of the Field.*
Acrylic 21x27in (53x69cm)

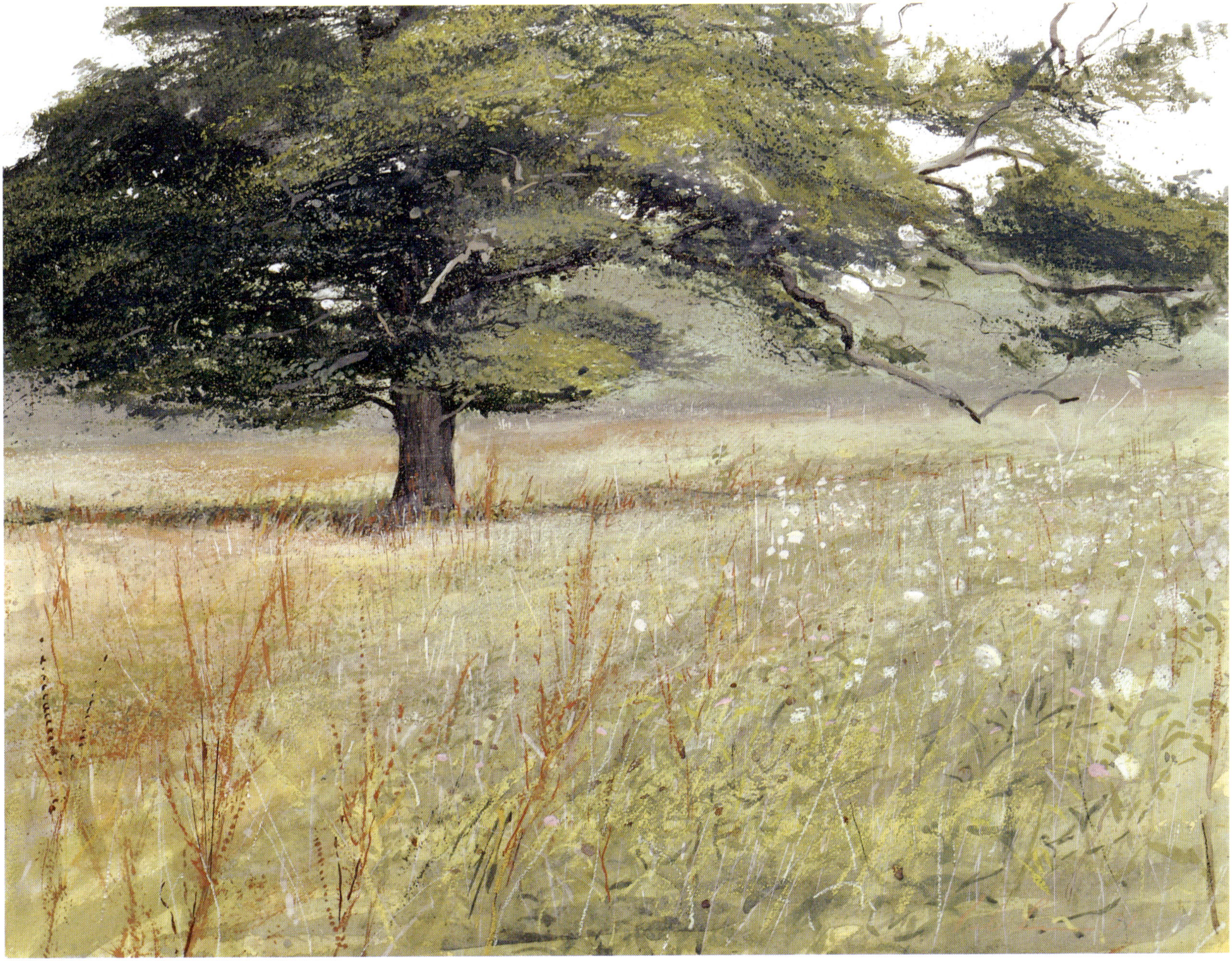

Paul Lewin. *The Abbotsham Oak, August*
Mixed Media 21.5x29in (55x74cm)

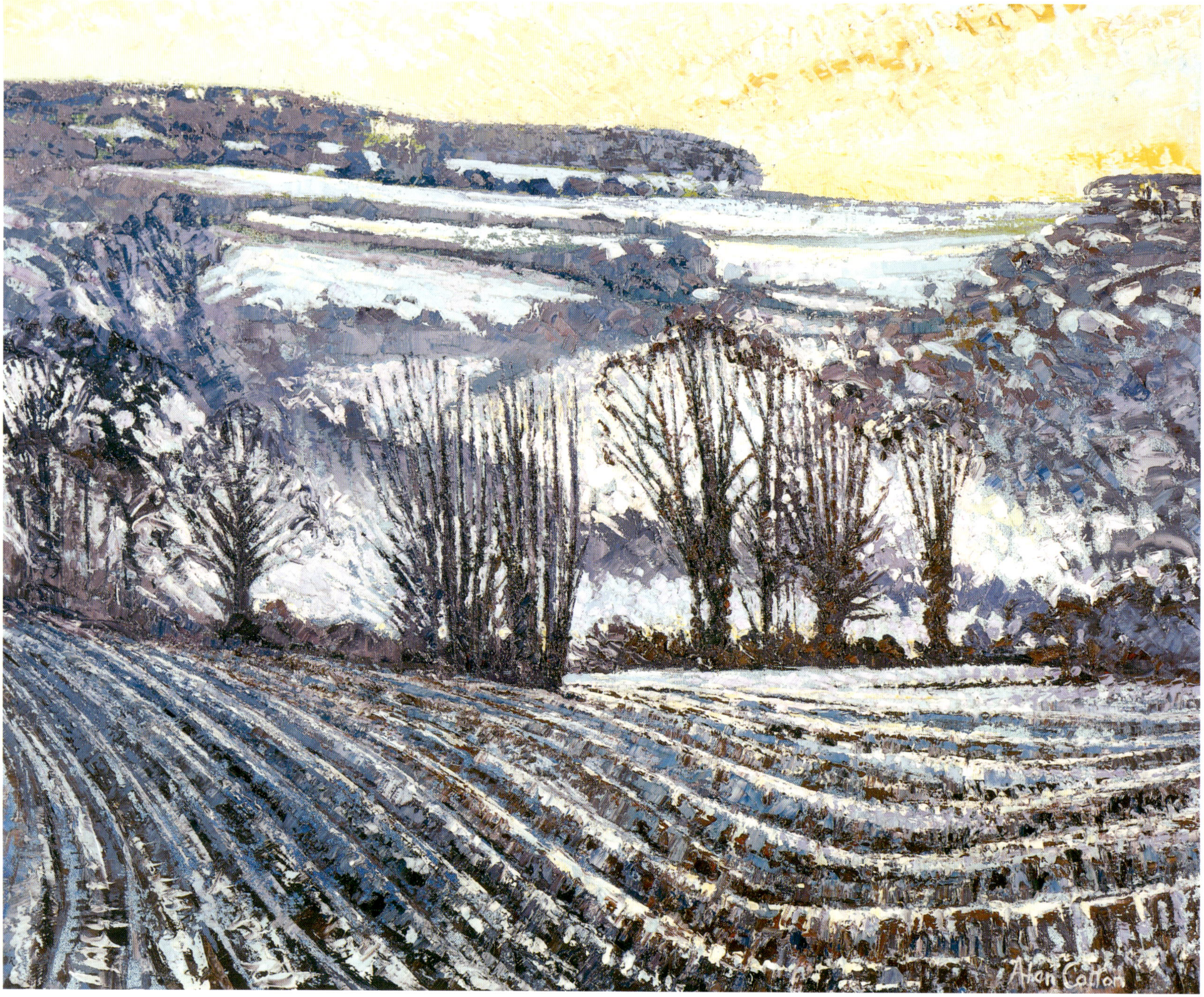

Alan Cotton. *Devon – Snow in the Otter Valley*
Oil 24x30in (61x76cm)

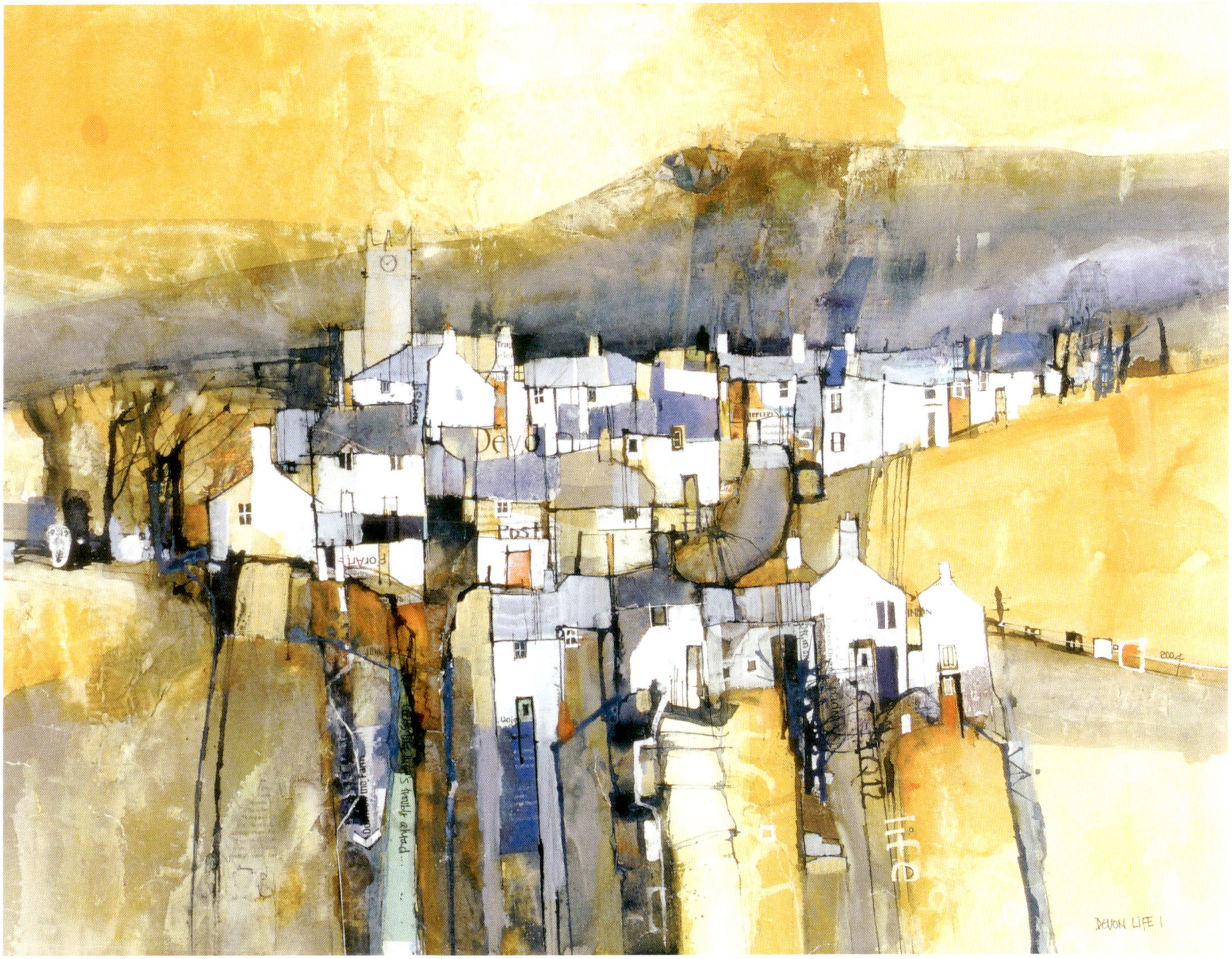

Martin Procter. *Devon Life 1*
Mixed Media 21x28in (58x71cm)

I have grown to love the 'backcountry' between the coastal strip and the south-eastern edge of Dartmoor. I walk our dog in this patch almost every day. This painting originates from some sketches of villages around where I live – Torbryan, Ipplepen, Denbury and amalgamates elements of all of them.

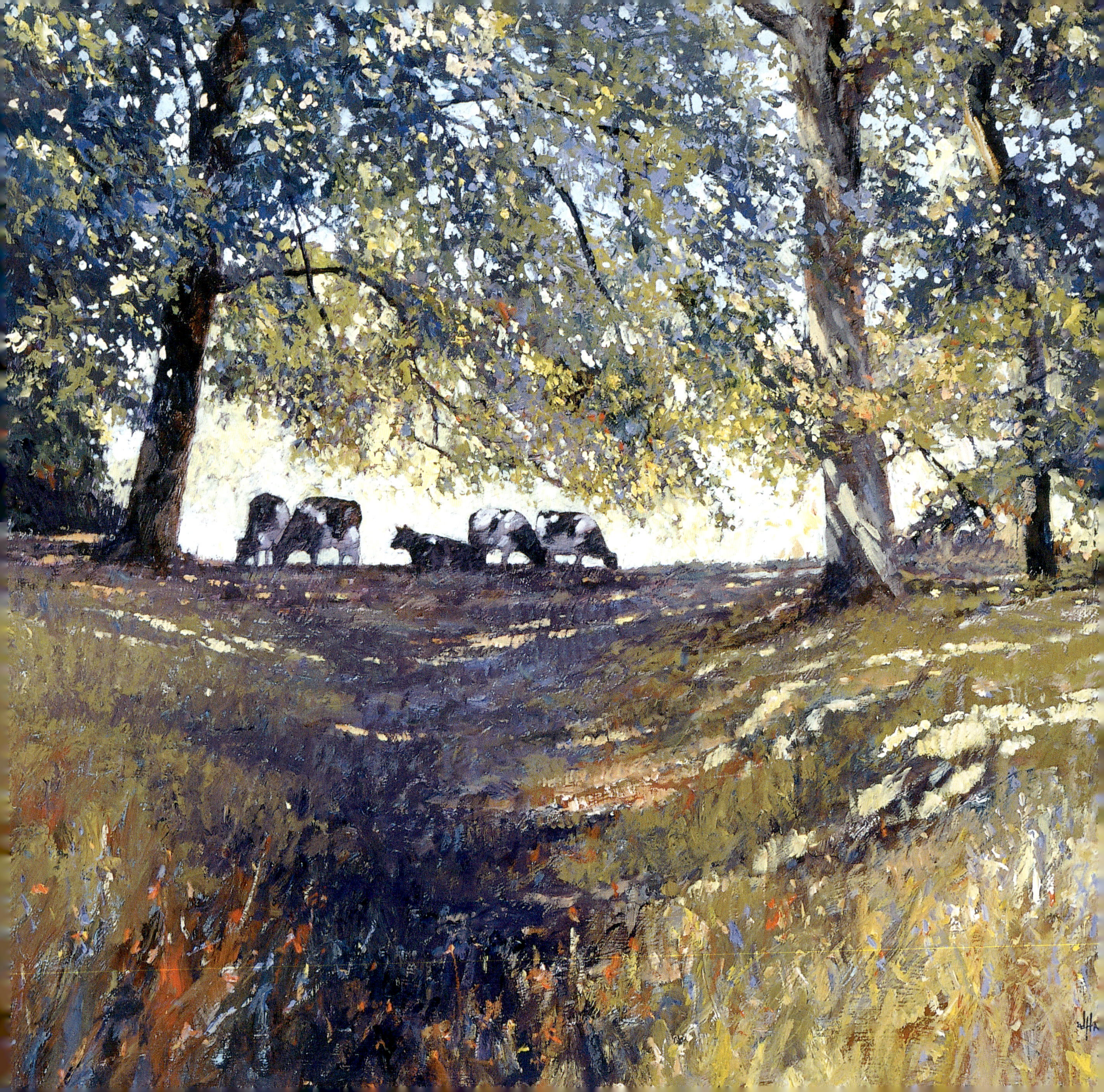

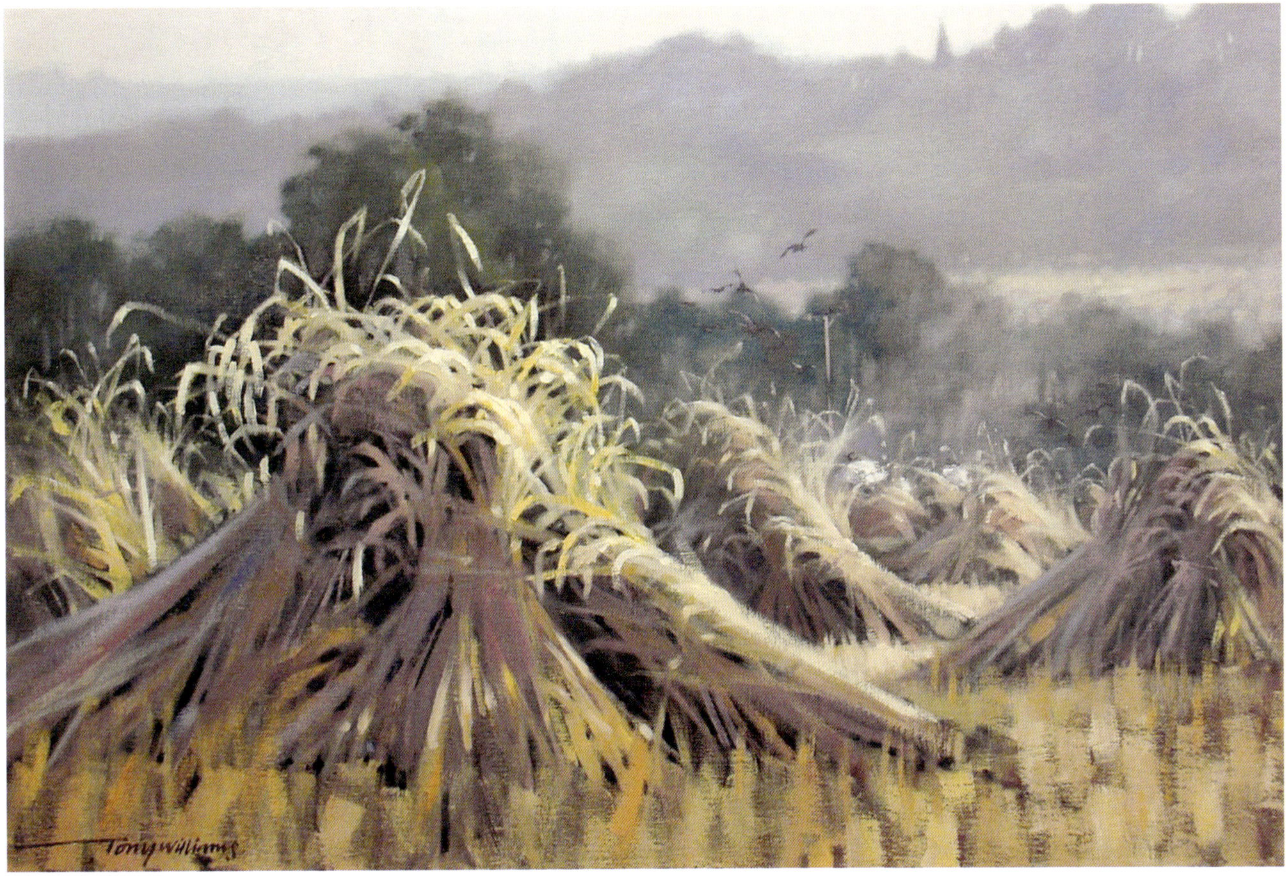

Tony Williams. *Stooks at Kings Nympton*
Oil 24x36in (61x91cm)

Straw drying in the evening sun near my home in North Devon. This must rank as one of the most tranquil and evocative sights in our rural landscape and can be seen here in late summer.

John Hammond. *Woodland Gathering*
Acrylic 22x24in (55x61cm)

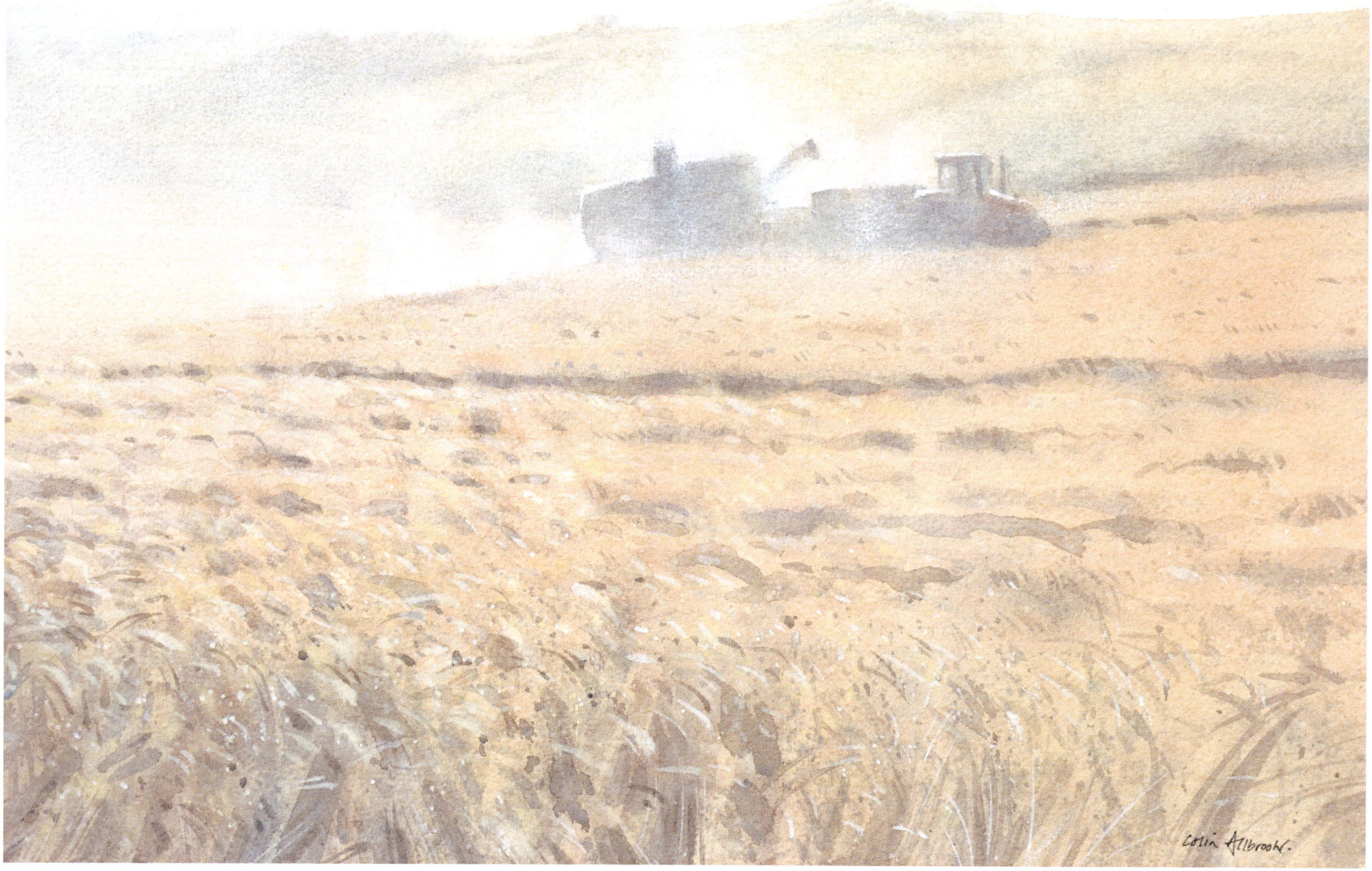

Colin Allbrook. *Heat and Dust*
Watercolour 14x20in (36x51cm)

This painting was done in the late afternoon as the sun started to dip, a favourite time of mine as the colours intensify, and after a rather frustrating day for the farmer. The combine had broken down twice already resulting in long delays and was about to again for the final time, finishing all harvesting that day.

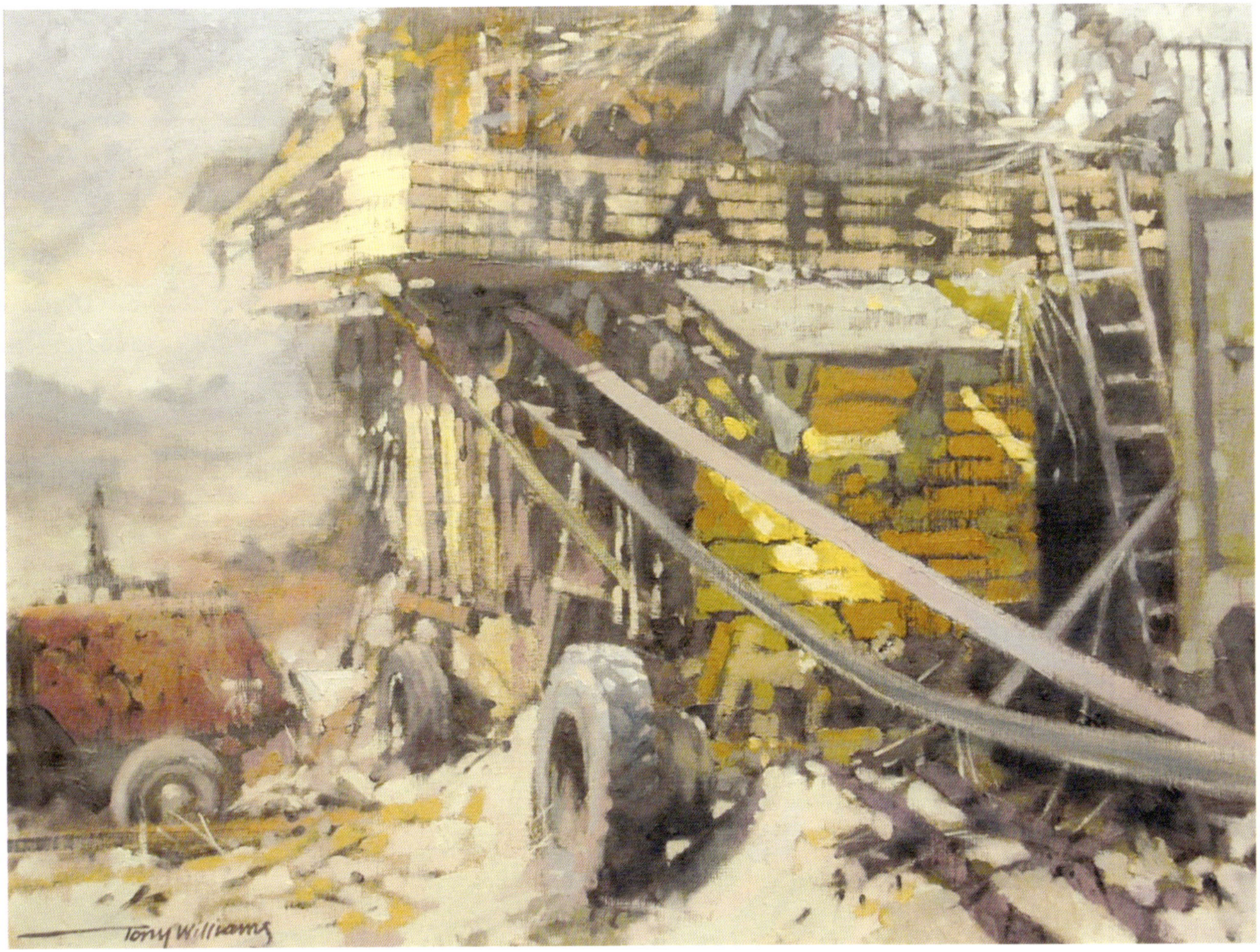

Tony Williams. *Reed Combing*
Oil 18x24in (46x61cm)

This marvellous old threshing machine dates from about 1940 and is being used here for reed combing amid clouds of dust, swaying drive belts, chattering cogs and the shouts of workmen on top.

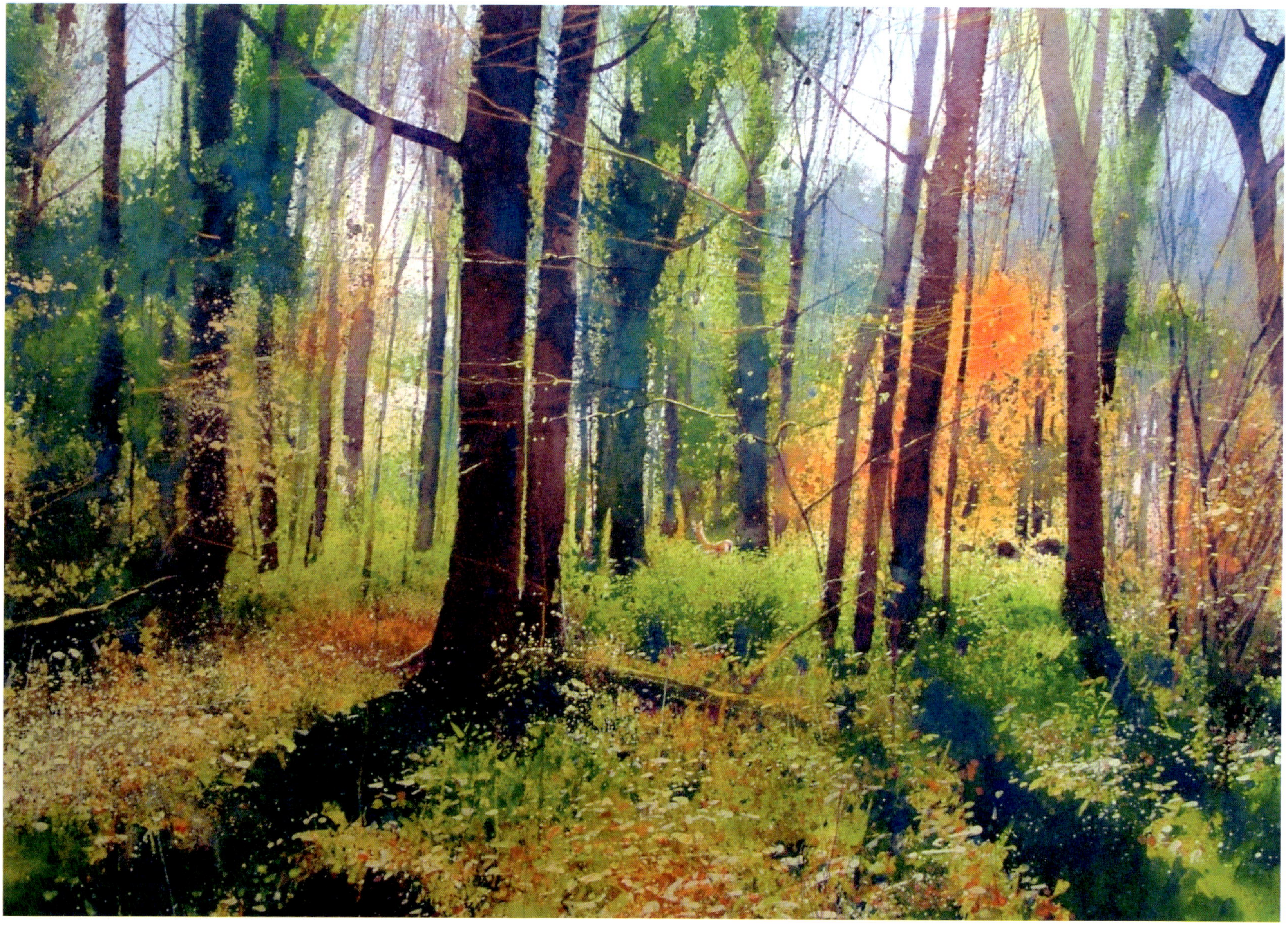

Richard Thorn. *...And There's a Fawn!*
Mixed Media 22x28in (56x71cm)

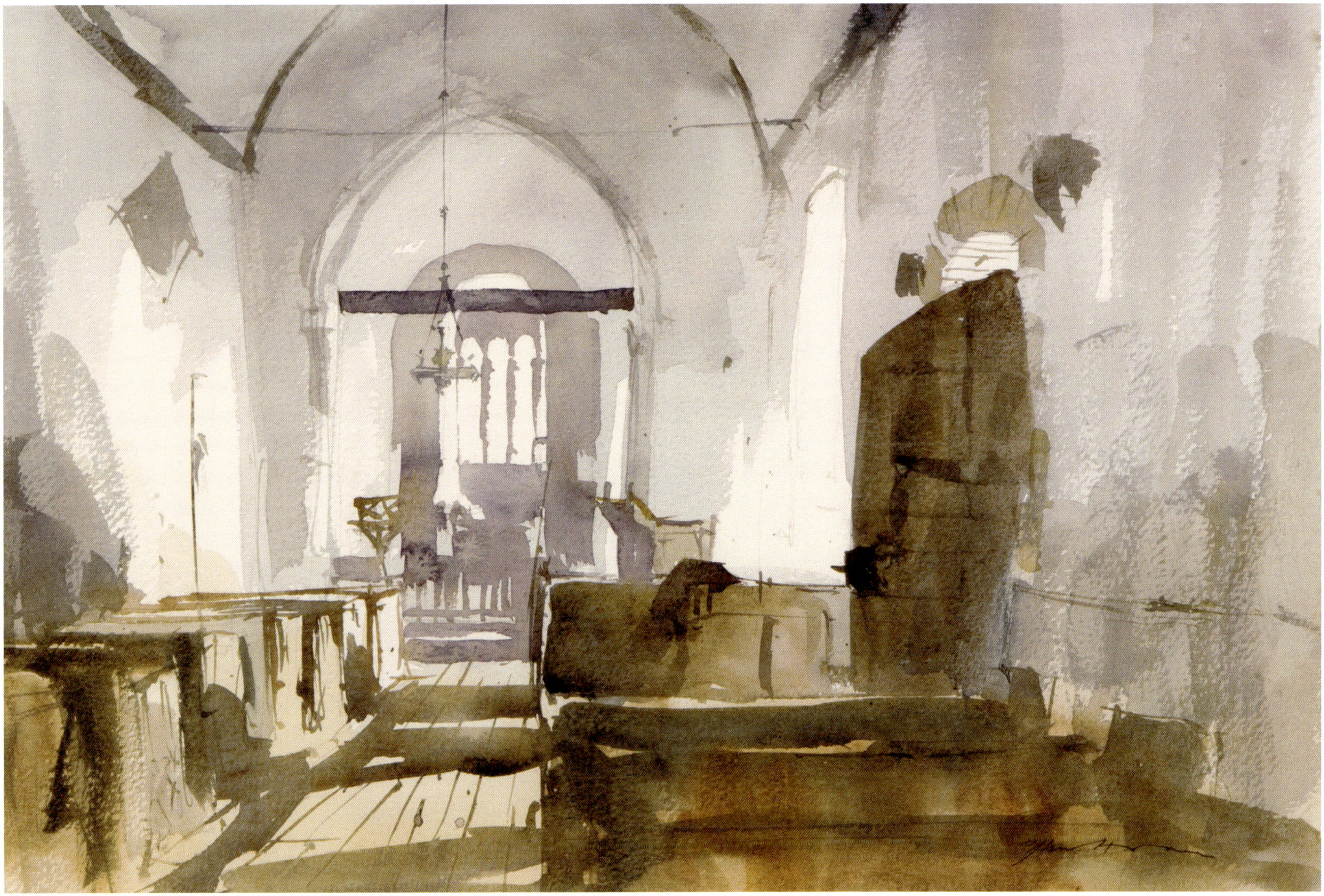

John Hoar. *Honeychurch*
Watercolour 12x18in (30x46cm)

This is a fascinating and beautiful tiny church on the fringes of Dartmoor in a hamlet of four farms. The sun streams through the plain glass windows lighting up the medieval pews and whitewashed walls.

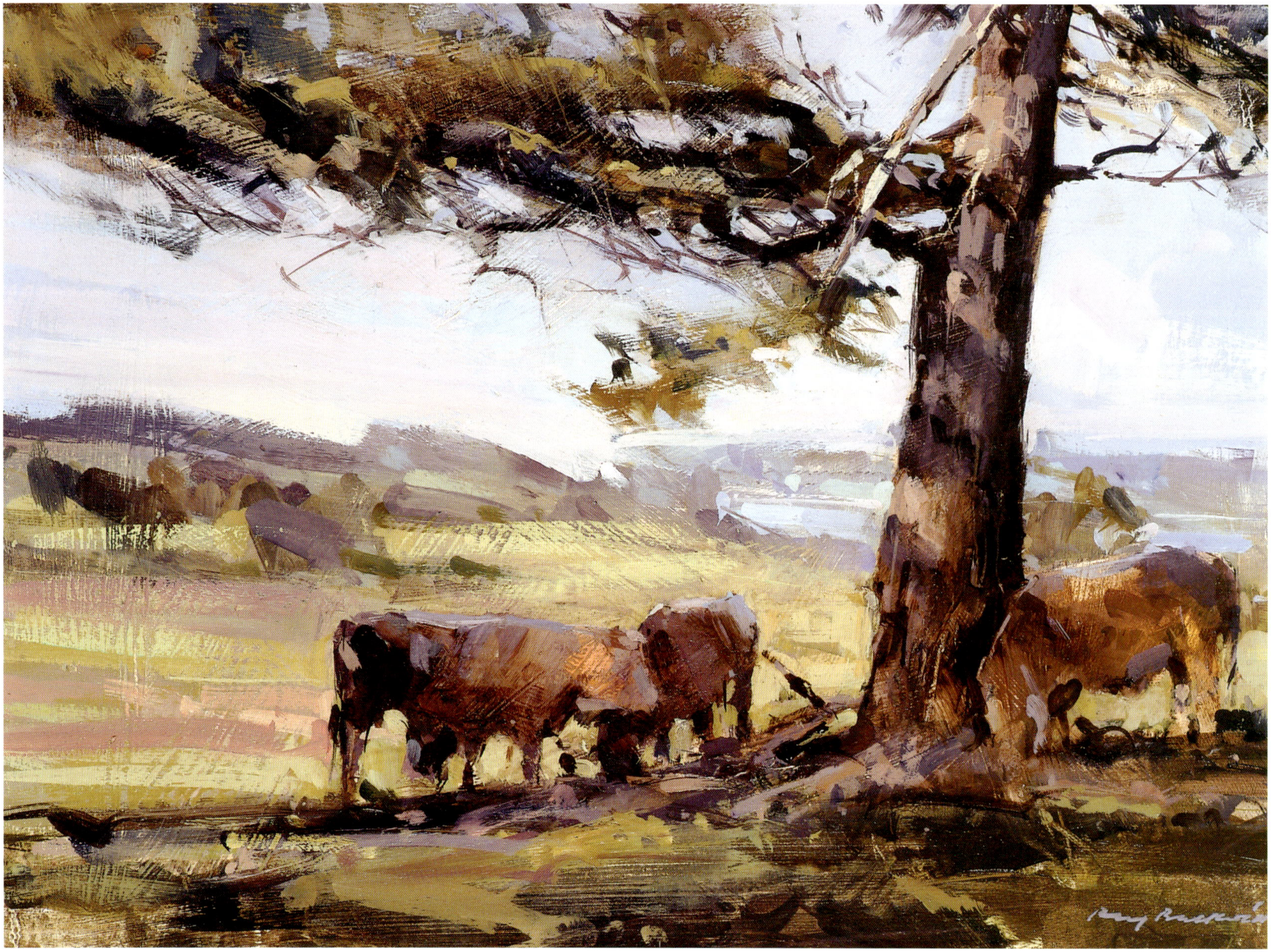

Ray Balkwill. *Welcome Shade, Pigeon Vale, Powderham*
Oil 8x12in (20x30cm)

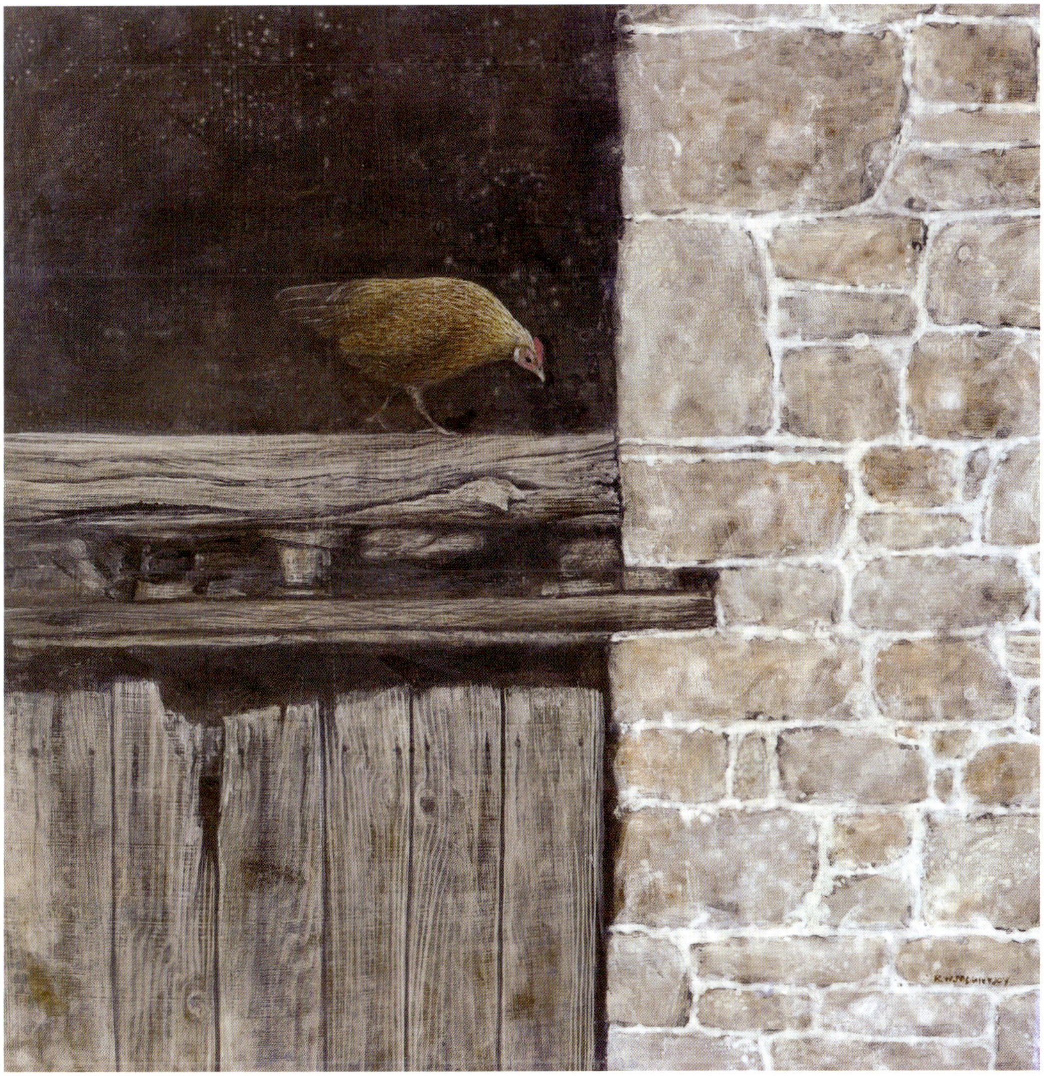

Robert Mountjoy. *Leaving the Loft, Jacobstow*
Watercolour 10x11in (25x28cm)

A road diversion forced me into unknown lanes where I found this combination of old timbers and stone in an old out building.

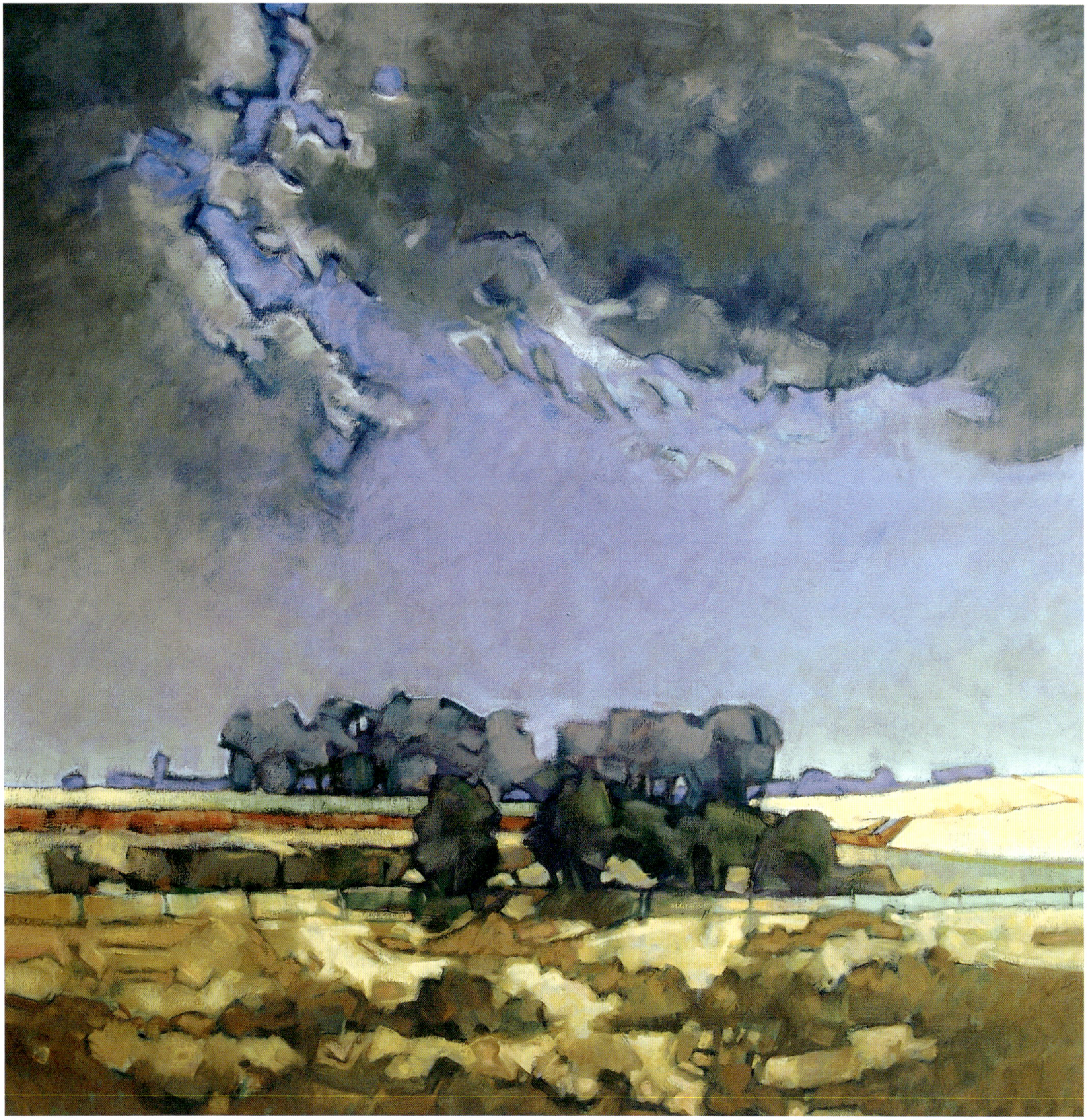

Robert Jennison.
Cloud over High Ground
Oil 36x36in (92x92cm)

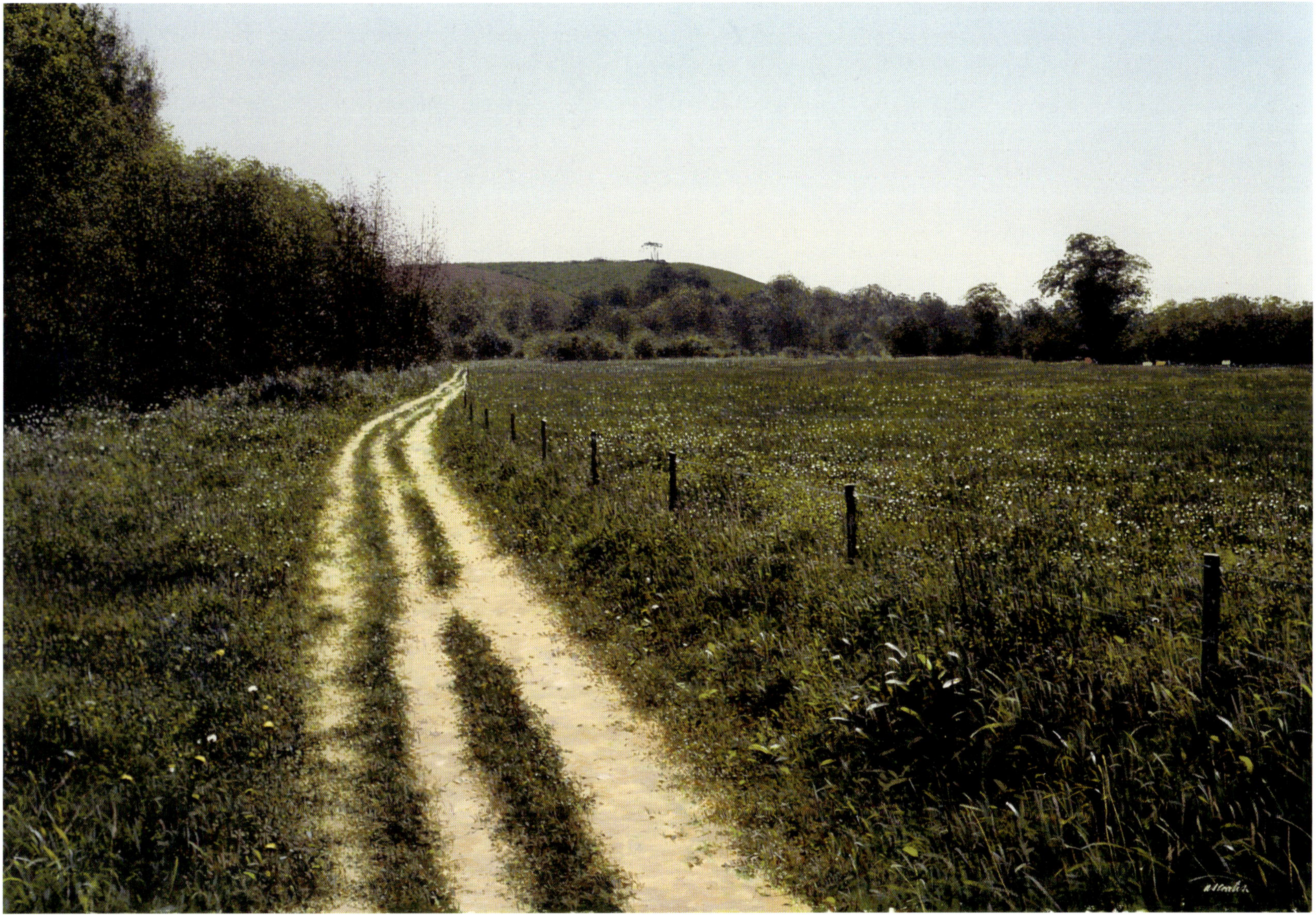

Andrew Coates. *Otter Meadows*
Oil 16x24in (41x61cm)

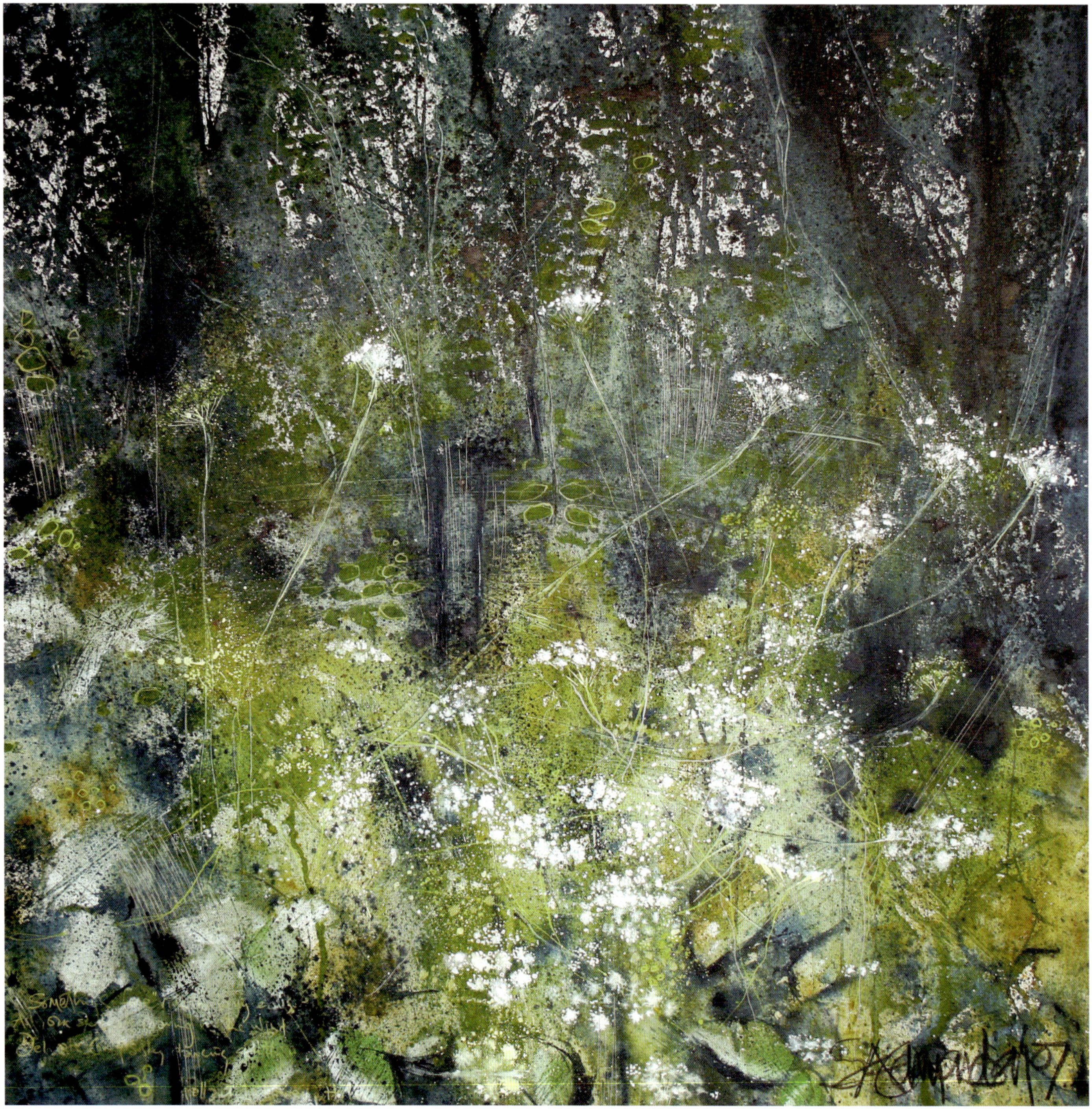

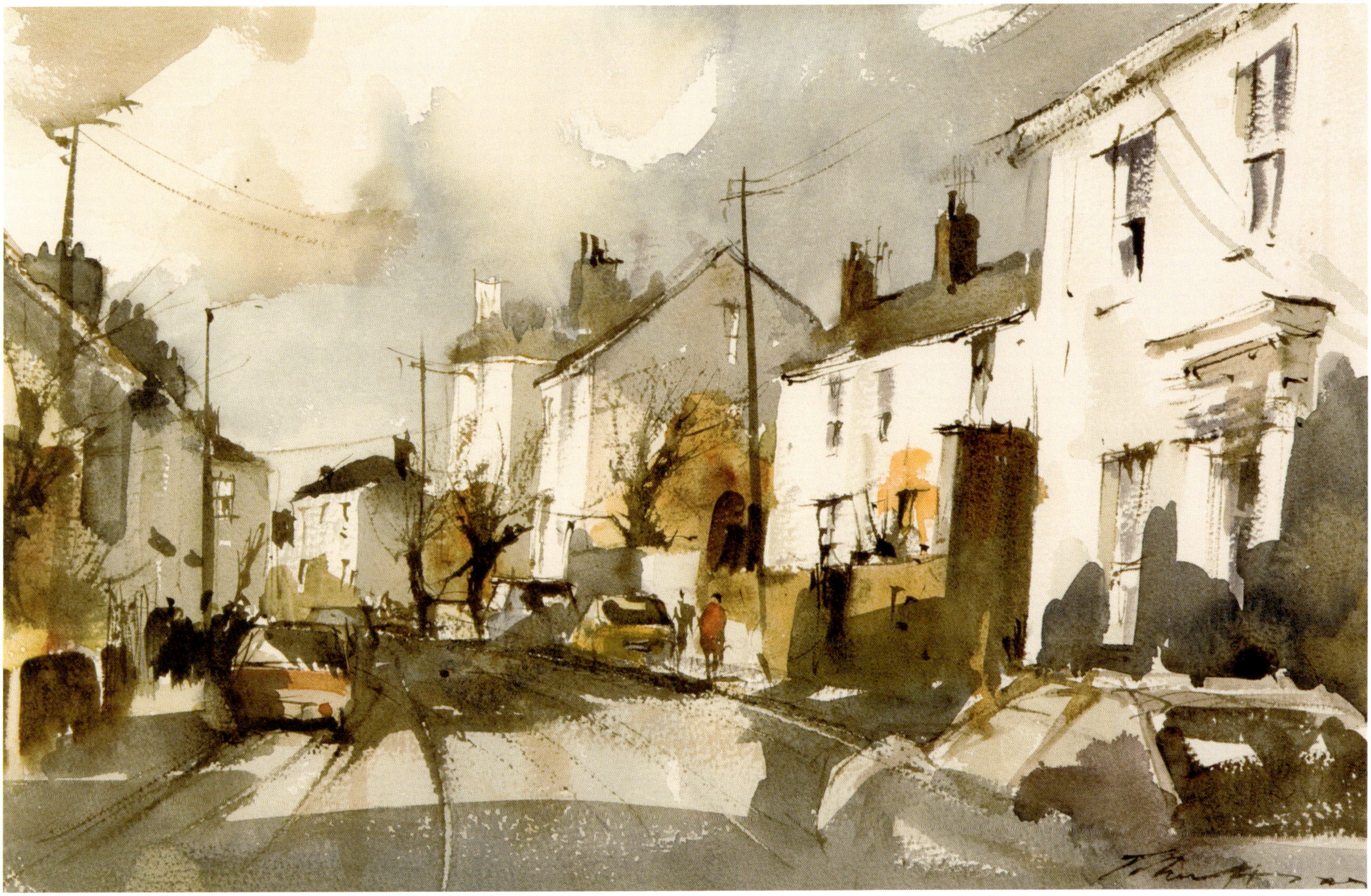

John Hoar. *Winter Light, South Molton*
Watercolour 12x18in (30x46cm)

Stewart Edmondson. *Something So Fine – Cow Parsley, Gallant Le Bower, Holne*
Mixed Media 27.5x27.5in (70x70cm)

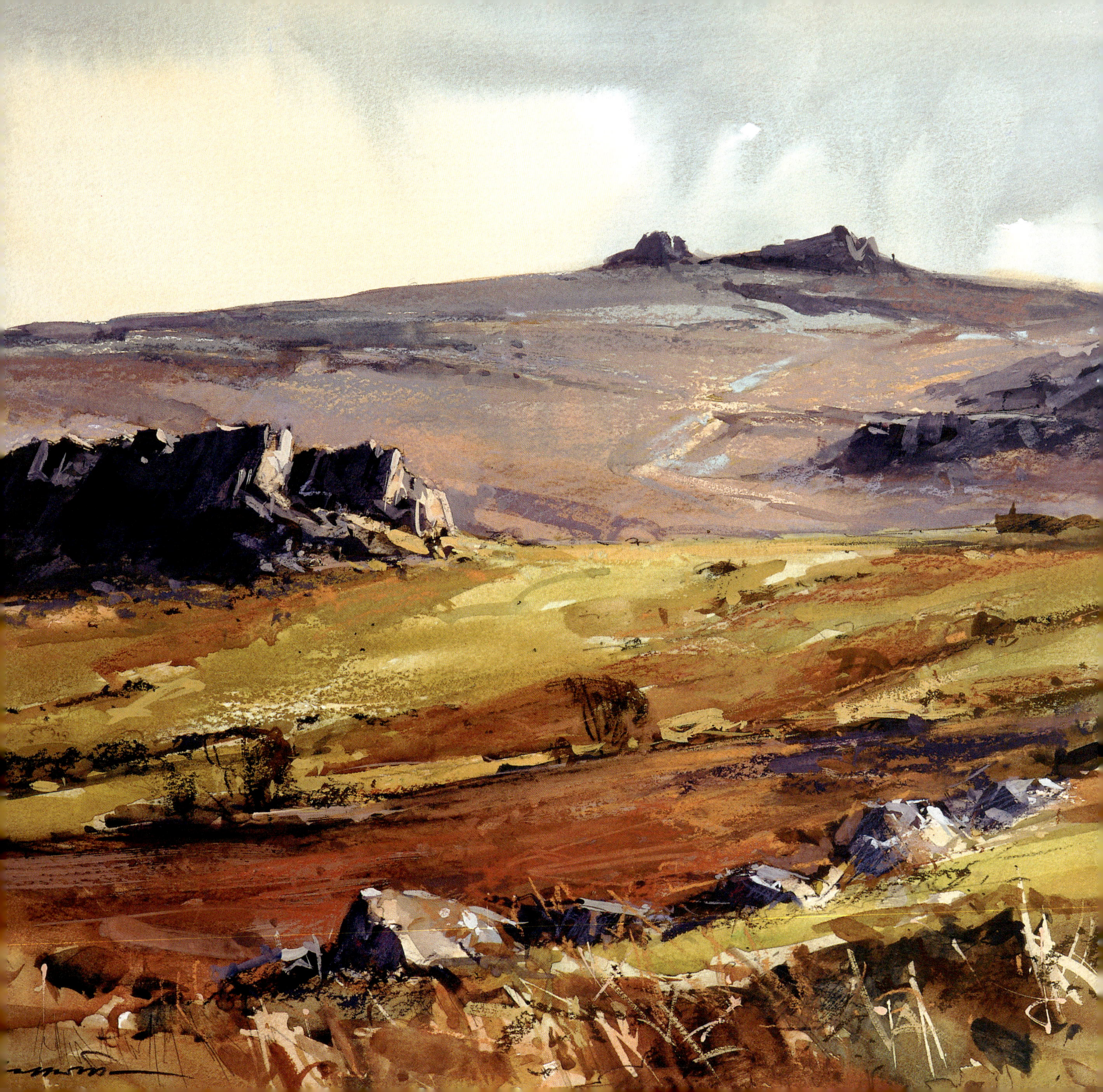

CHAPTER TWO

From wild rugged moorland to heather-clad combes...

'Those who have once set foot upon Dartmoor, who have climbed its giant tors, have listened to the plaintive music of its streams or have passed into its solitary places, where the cry of the curlew alone is heard, will, if they be true lovers of Nature, ever feel a longing to revisit it.'
This is how William Crossing described the moor in his book *Gems in a Granite Setting*, published in 1905.

Dartmoor has always been a special place for me and these words encapsulate the true 'spirit' of the moor, both remembered as a child growing up in its shadows and more recently returning to paint it. Here the elemental forces in nature with the erosion of its ancient stones, or the shaping of its wind-sculptured trees touch everything. The changing seasons also bring many different moods. Painting on the high moor in summer can be an exhilarating experience, with its stark granite tors set against vivid blue skies and great billowing cumuli clouds. Experiencing freedom as they race across the skies, their shadows creating great planes of light and shade across the vast open landscape. I find autumn a most inspiring season with its mists hanging eerily over the tors. As R.D. Blackmore wrote: 'Dartmoor, many fountained Dartmoor, a mother of a myriad streams, and wet nurse of a million mists.'

The unpredictably of Dartmoor's weather has always presented severe problems to its painters, as conditions on the high moor can change extremely quickly. There have been occasions when it would seem as if the vagaries of each of the four seasons have been experienced in just one day's painting out on the moor. A lovely quote from a Dartmoor farmer in a documentary made in the early 1970s entitled 'Peter and Ruby' describes it very well. In his rich Devonshire burr, Peter Hanniford says: 'Why do I like Dartmoor? Well Dartmoor is very healthy. The weather is a bit tantalizing sometimes – snow! We get nine months winter out here – and three months wet weather!' This is included in Tom and Barbara Brown's highly acclaimed 'This Farming Life' Commissioned by Beaford Arts. It is a fully integrated show that brings together archive film material and live performance, each medium supporting and illuminating the other.

Devon is fortunate in having not one, but two National Parks, in Dartmoor and (part of) Exmoor, and each have their own identifiable character. Dartmoor covers over 360 square miles and lies at the heart and soul of Devon, both geographically and, with many of its painters, spiritually too. Exmoor on the other hand, is far less rugged than Dartmoor and seems to have attracted fewer painters. Its softer rocks have weathered down to form deep combes and valleys. On its northern edge, Exmoor sweeps dramatically down to the sea, where in many places trees, heather and gorse grow almost down to the shore. Their differing qualities have not only inspired great artists, but many poets and writers too, including Ted Hughes, R.D. Blackmore and Henry Williamson. Each evoke an empathy with the hidden spirit of the county and their love of both moors is evident in their writing.

One painter who also epitomised the bracing breath of Dartmoor was **Frederick John Widgery** (1861–1942). He was born in Exeter and lived most of his life there. Although best known for his evocative

Ray Balkwill. *Towards Hay Tor, Dartmoor*
Mixed Media 13x16in (33x41cm)

studies of Dartmoor he also loved to paint the estuaries, beaches and cliffs around his native county. Unlike his father William, 'F.J.' as he was affectionately known benefited from an extensive art education. He was an accomplished painter in oils, watercolours and gouache and he also exhibited at the Royal Academy, the Royal Institute of Oil Painters and the Royal Institute of Painters in Watercolour. He also led an active life in public service and as well as being mayor, he was also awarded numerous civic honours. In fact, he was so involved in local politics in the city that it is a wonder that he ever found time to paint at all. But despite this, art was always important to him and in 1931 he bequeathed his entire collection of sketches and sketchbooks, amounting to six hundred in total, to the Royal Albert Memorial Museum. He thought 'they might be of use to students and of interest to the public generally' and 'was anxious to give to his native city some proof of his appreciation of the high honour accorded in having elected him Mayor and placed his name on the roll of honorary freemen'. The collection reveals his skills as a draughtsman in a variety of media including pen and ink, pencil, crayon, chalk, charcoal and watercolour. Like John Constable, he seems to have been moved by the ever-changing pattern of skies and made numerous studies of cloud formations and sunsets, many of which include written colour notes. Along with later acquisitions, they provide a comprehensive insight into his personal vision of the Devon landscape.

Michael Morgan, RI, SWAc has enjoyed two very different as well as distinguished careers. The first in teaching, becoming the Headmaster of Dartington Primary School in Devon in his late twenties, and later as Principal and CEO of the Froebel Institute in London. He remained at Froebel until moving on in 1985 to live in East Devon where he developed a second career as a painter in watercolours. His list of achievements in education make formidable reading, but it his meteoric rise in his painting career that is even more remarkable. It has rightly won him an international following and he has received many awards, including being elected a member of the Royal Institute of Painters in Watercolour in 2001. Although born in Bristol, his roots lie very much in Devon,

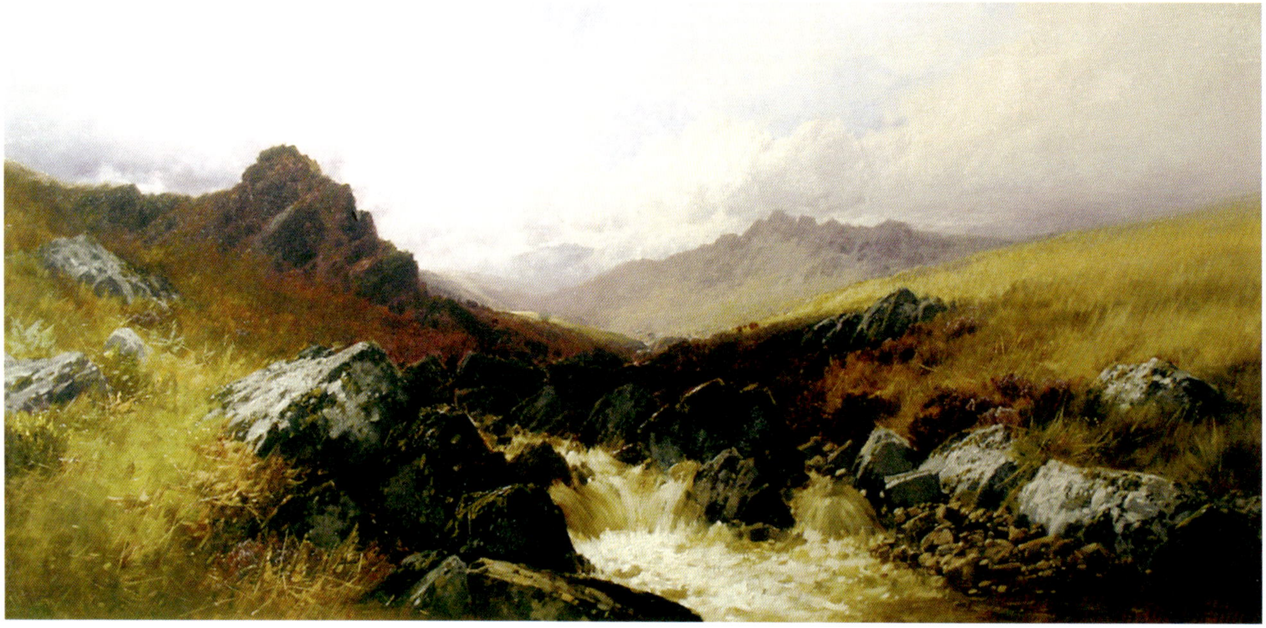

F.J.Widgery. *The River Lyd, Dartmoor*
Oil 19x40in (48x102cm) Courtesy of Elford Fine Art, Tavistock

Michael Morgan. *Davy's Farm*
Watercolour 12.5x12.5in (32x32cm)

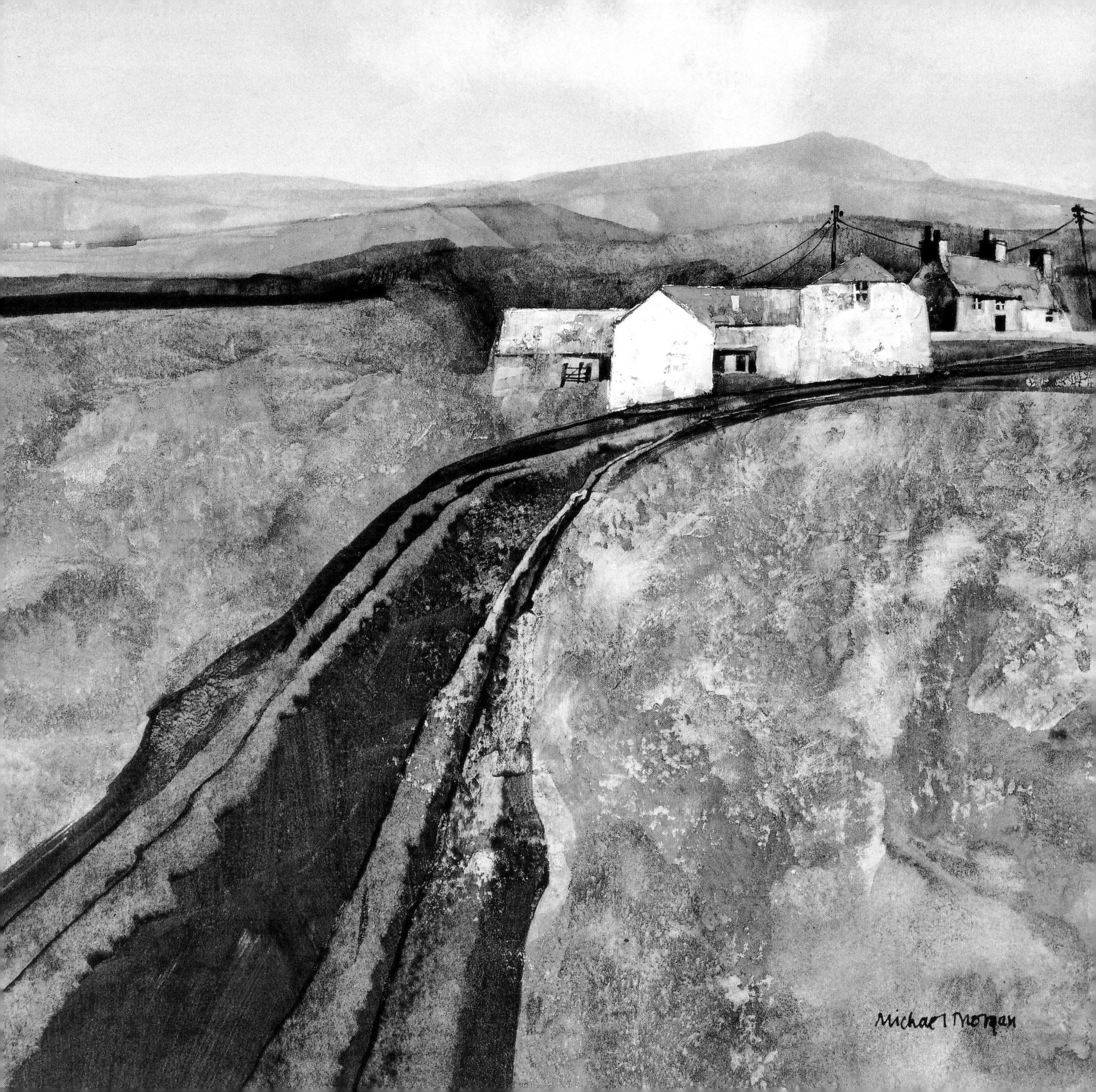
Michael Morgan

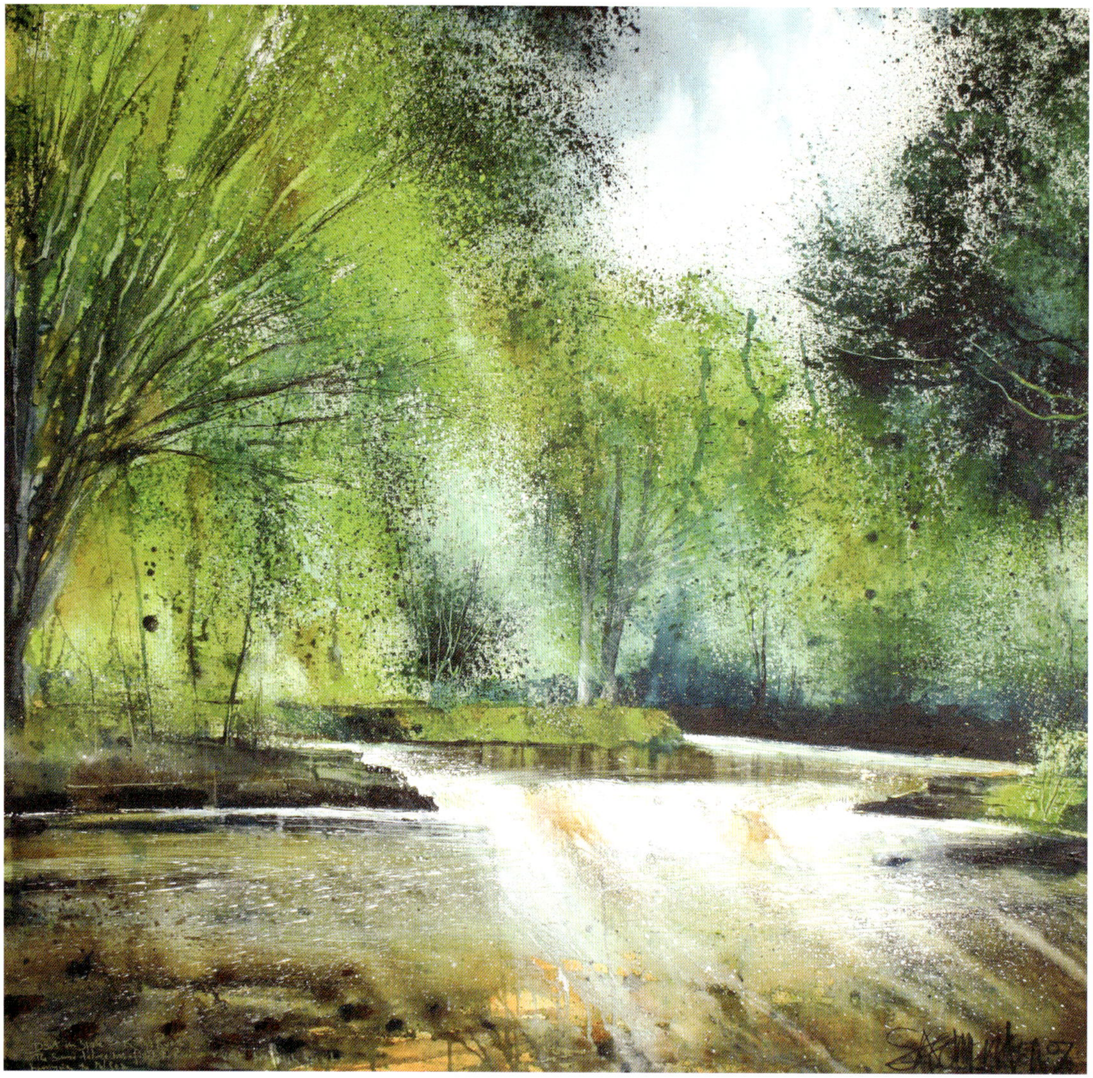

Stewart Edmondson. *The Dart in Spate at Katy's Rock*
Mixed Media 39.5x40in (100x102cm)

I paint along this section of the Dart a lot – the river between Newbridge and Dartmeet is just so alive – wild and kicking, big deep pools, huge rocks and the most beautiful trees.

being brought up in Exeter from the age of eight, as well as going on to train and teach in the city. He was also a Trustee and Founding Academician in the South West Academy of Fine and Applied Arts.

Michael has lived in East Devon for a quarter of a century and it was here that he began painting in the early 90s, when he was inspired and encouraged by John Blockley. His home is nestled snugly in a pretty valley near Axminster, which is far removed from the stark and primeval landscapes that he is drawn to. Dartmoor in particular, generates this emotional response and his adventurous approach and developed watercolour techniques reflect the brooding nature of the place.

He has based his approach to picture-making on Goethe's simple advice that the art of painting is to see beyond the everyday vision of things. His studio-based paintings are distillations of these landscapes; they are never fully representational and are not intended to infer a sense of place, but rather a sense of atmosphere. Even though there is the evidence of the hand of man – cottages, farmhouses, rutted tracks and ploughed fields for instance, you do not see them populated with people or sheep. Michael is unconcerned with these incidentals. His work lies somewhere between abstract and representational and his paintings have been described as 'like landscapes in a dream'. That is the paradox of his paintings, they are familiar yet unusual. Looking at his sketchbooks his passion for drawing is evident. His ideas are taken from these and from this sound foundation colourfully rich and textural paintings of the landscape are produced.

Another exponent of watercolour's wonderful properties of transparency, expressiveness and unpredictability is **Stewart Edmondson.** However, he is a painter in complete contrast to Michael in that he chooses to paint *en plein air,* searching for a more personal response to what he sees and feels. His subjects are all around him as he lives and works on the very edge of his favourite stretch of the Dart valley, in Holne, overlooking Sharp Tor. It is a beautiful and tranquil Dartmoor village, which was also birthplace of the author Charles Kingsley. It is a landscape rich in a raw, earthy vitality and it is these very elements of nature from which he gains his strength. Stewart told me that he loves to paint on location particularly when it is stormy. 'I have a fantastic pop-up shelter for when the rain pours, but sometimes this just collapses with the ferocity of the wind up on the moor There have been a number of occasions when my painting has been torn out of my hands and flung across the gorse bushes or rocks, usually with some pretty good effect for the painting.' His joy of working directly from nature is evident as he added 'I love the chaos of it, that takes some of the control away from you and lets the energy of the place come directly into the painting.' It is this physicality in his painting, mirrored by the untameability of the landscape, as the paint is expertly wrestled on to the paper that makes Stewart's paintings so exciting. It captures his real emotional involvement with the place.

East Devon painter **Judy Hempstead** is perhaps best known for her coastal work, but she has also found Dartmoor a place to set her ideas flowing. Her affinity to the moor is also strengthened by the fact that her great-grandfather lived on the edge of the moors. The resonance of this was in two diaries written by him in 1887 and given to Judy. She said: 'Not only was he a cobbler, lay preacher and market gardener, but also the local postman. In the diaries he talks at length about delivering

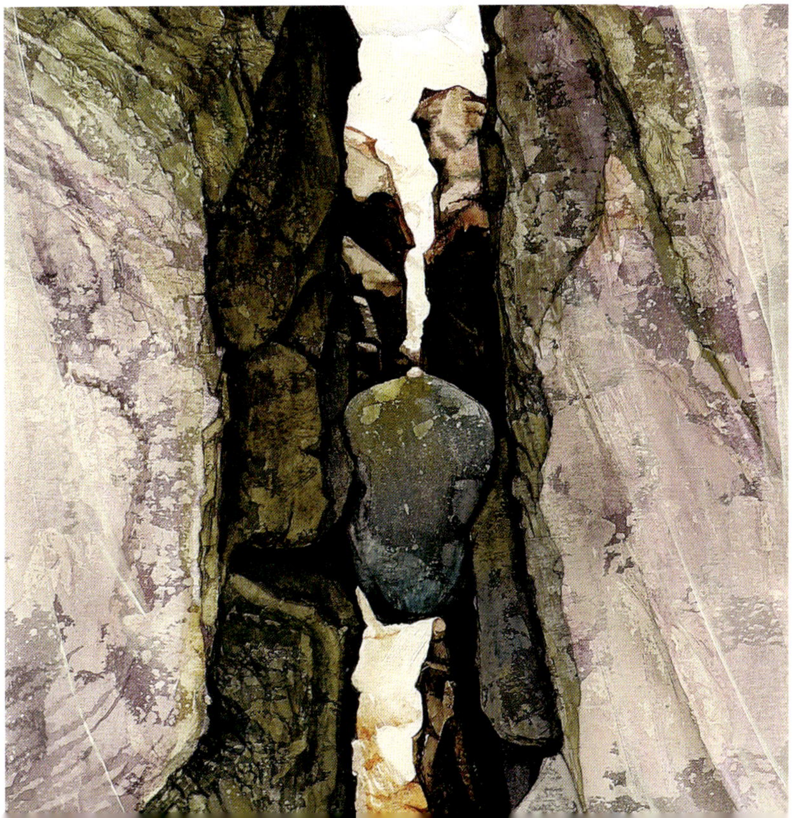

Judy Hempstead. *Looking Through 3*
Mixed Media 9x9in (23x23cm)

letters and parcels – presumably on horseback, or by pony and trap. Because so few people could read and write he often had not only to read a letter to the recipient, but also write a reply for them too.' It is the more intimate subjects of the moor that absorb her. She scrambles on to its rocky outcrops and glimpses the moor through its narrow clefts. Here she can study more closely the surface texture of the granite and the lichen and other plant life, which can be found in these enclosed spaces. The information she obtains follows in the tradition of Paul Nash and Graham Sutherland, who also examined minute forms that echoed the landscape. Attempting to capture a passing of time like the weathered granite rocks themselves, her paintings are a layering of tactile paint and materials creating a corresponding metaphor in paint. Words have an important resonance in her work too and she will often weave lines of poetry within its contours, echoes of the ancient moor's history.

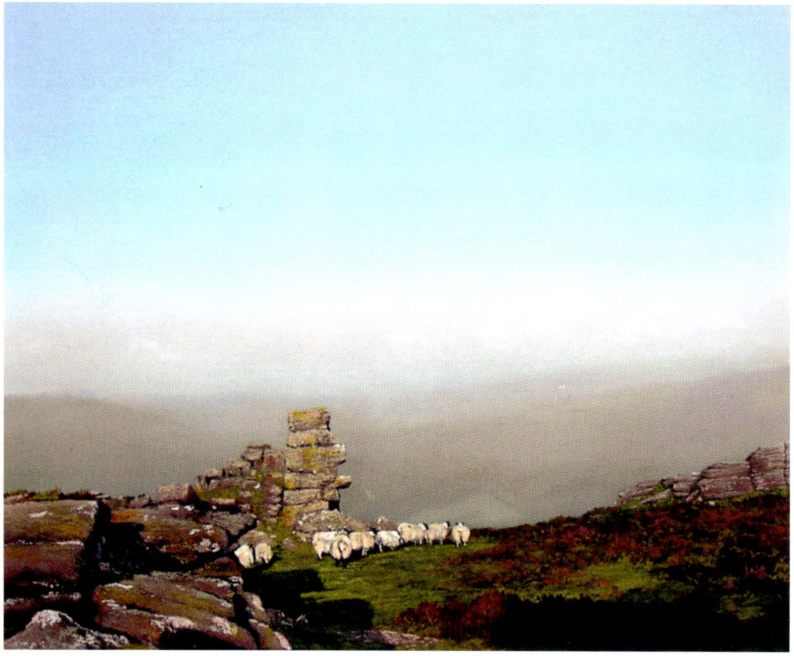

Keith Stott. *Looking North from Hookney Tor*
Pastel 14x18in (36x45cm)

Early on a Summer's morning when the breeze blows from the south-east, mist often forms over Hameldown, Hookney Tor and Shapley Common, tumbling down in the valley around Challacombe and Headland Warren. This is a favourite place to be as this magical light show develops.

Keith Stott follows closely in the tradition of past landscape masters such as F. J. Widgery and John Constable, where skies and the effects of weather on the landscape play a major role in their work. He has always had a passion for wild, desolate places. Much of his boyhood was spent in the Yorkshire Dales and the Lake District, then later he spent time in India and Pakistan treking the Western Himalayas. It is little wonder that when he moved to Devon in 1981 it was the wide vistas of the high moor that were to become his next passion. His pastel paintings are produced mainly in the studio, based on sketches and photographs, as well as a strong visual memory. The deep love and respect for the moor is apparent in his fine detailed paintings. In conversation he told me: 'In every corner of the moor there is evidence of man, from the settlements of prehistory through to tinners and miners. To walk alone on the moor is to walk with the ghosts of the 'old men' and they have a strong influence on my love of the place.'

Barry Watkin, FRSA was born in Yorkshire and is well known through his art instruction books, films and painting courses. After training at Bromley College of Art he pursued a career as a commercial artist and later as an art editor for a major publishing house. In 1988 he moved to Somerset where he and his wife ran successful painting courses from their farmhouse near Stogumber. More recently he moved to Crowcombe, a small village in the lee of the Quantocks. An oil painter for many years, he now works mainly in pastel because the medium enables him to capture the fleeting passages of light and atmosphere more effectively. He says ' I prefer the challenge of painting directly from nature and the advantage of pastels is that they are light and portable, and being dry, they provide an immediate effect, without the problems found in paints, primarily drying speed and colour mixing on the palette. Norman Battershill, whom he regards very highly, influenced his earlier work. It was he who showed me how to organise light and shadow in a subject to the best effect.' His love of the countryside, particularly the remote areas of Exmoor and the Quantock Hills, have been the main inspiration for much of his work. But occasional forays over the border into Devon have offered him an even wider range of subjects than his beloved Exmoor.

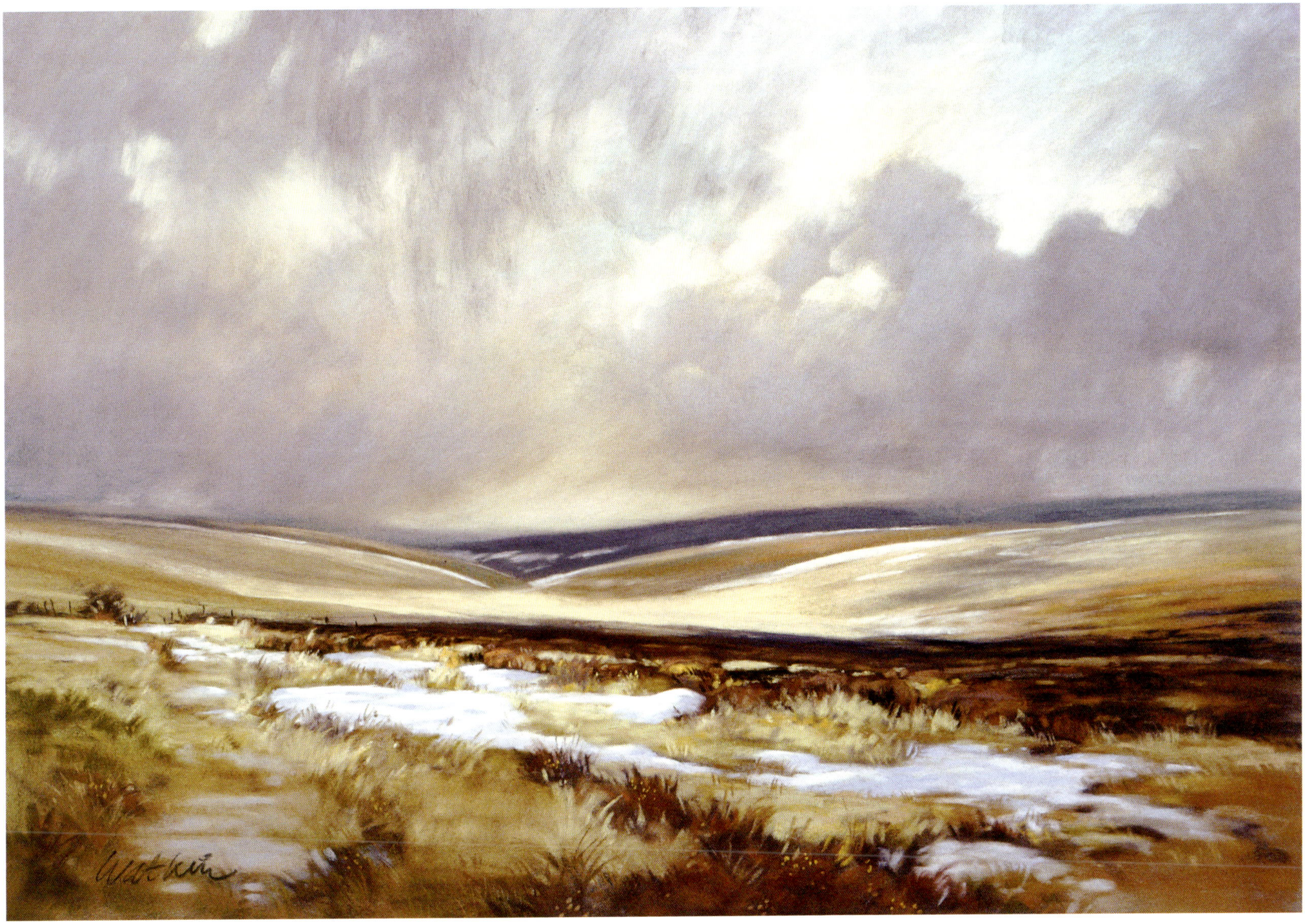

Barry Watkin. *Snow Shower, Doone Country*
Pastel 15x22in (38x56cm)

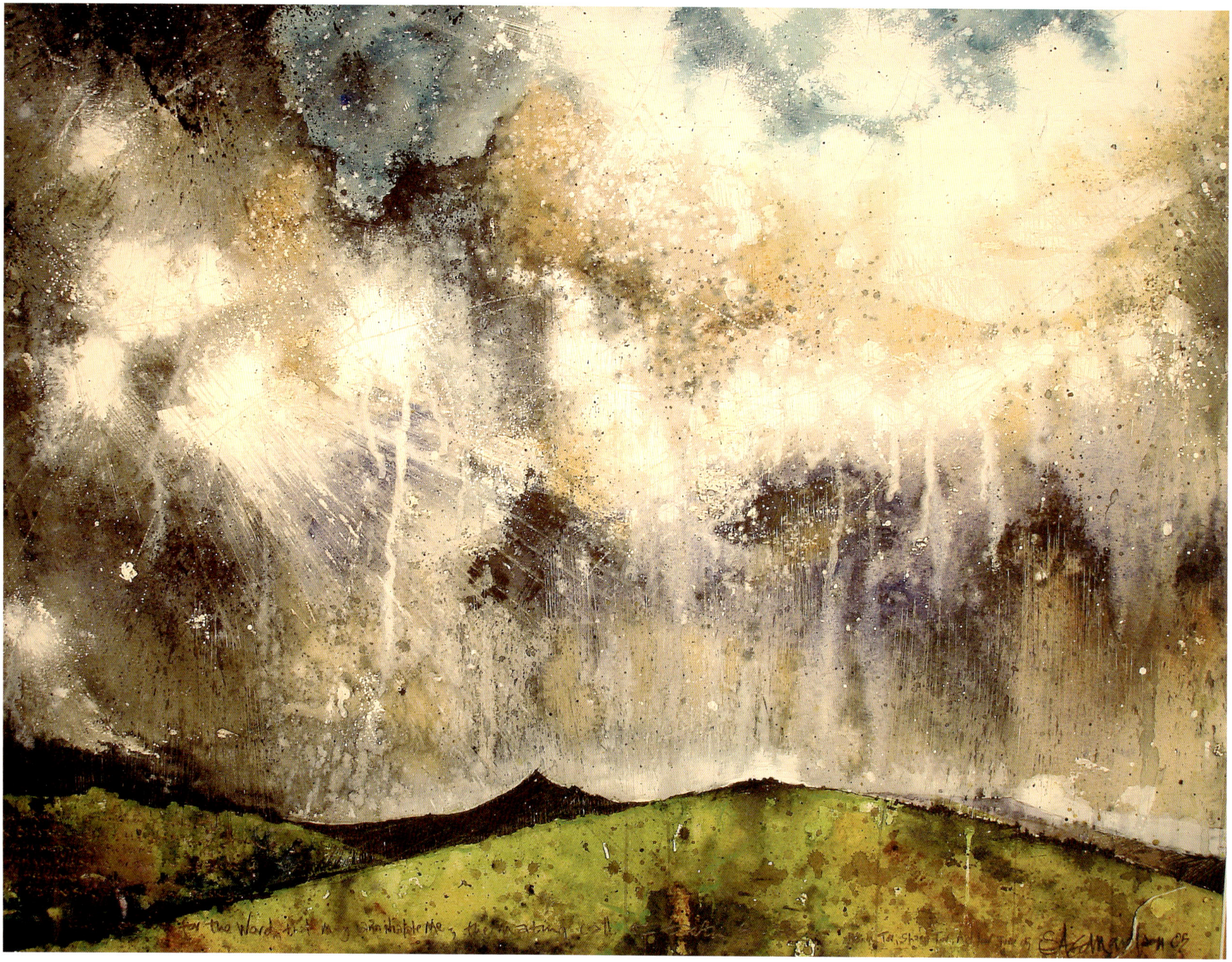

Stewart Edmondson. *Waiting for the Word – Storm over Sharp Tor*
Mixed Media 22x30in (56x76cm)

Stewart Edmondson. *Big Oak, Shutterford, Near Holne*
Mixed Media 22x30in (56x76cm)

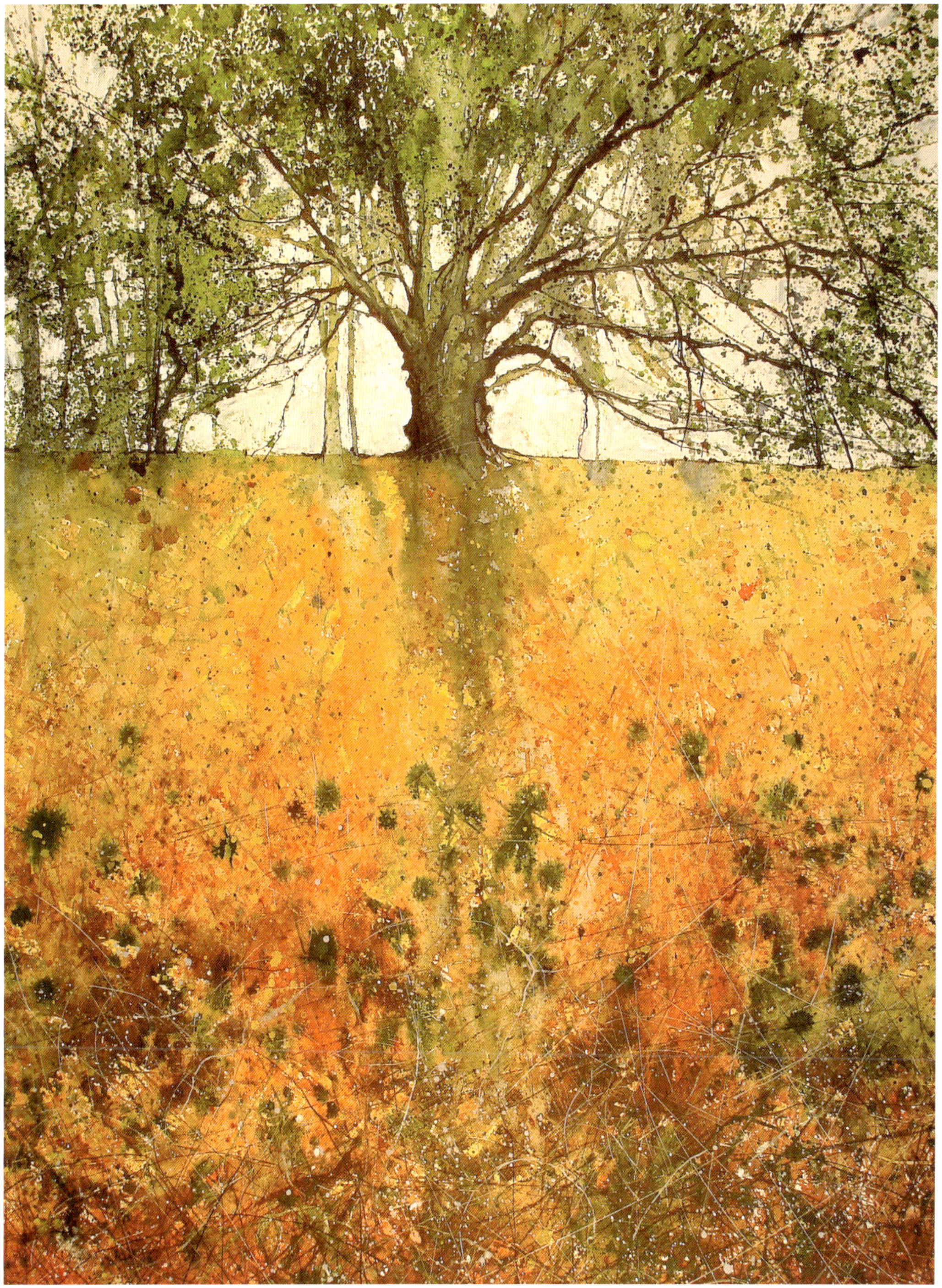

Opposite page: *This painting was inspired and in response to a poem by Daverick Leggett, and is painted from my home on the edge of the Dart valley where you can watch some fantastic stormfronts building up on the high moor. The caption on the painting is a small potent part of the poem:*

'There is rain coming. Everywhere knows it.
The birds sing the song of the approaching storm,
The moist wind teases the leaves
and already the seed swells for the rainsperm
and the tree dreams the deep drink
and the dry rocks suck the vapour from the sky
and I am waiting for the word
that may annihilate me
the mating call of earth and sky'

From 'Wild Land, Burning Hearts – Poetry and Paintings by Daverick Leggett and Stewart Edmondson.

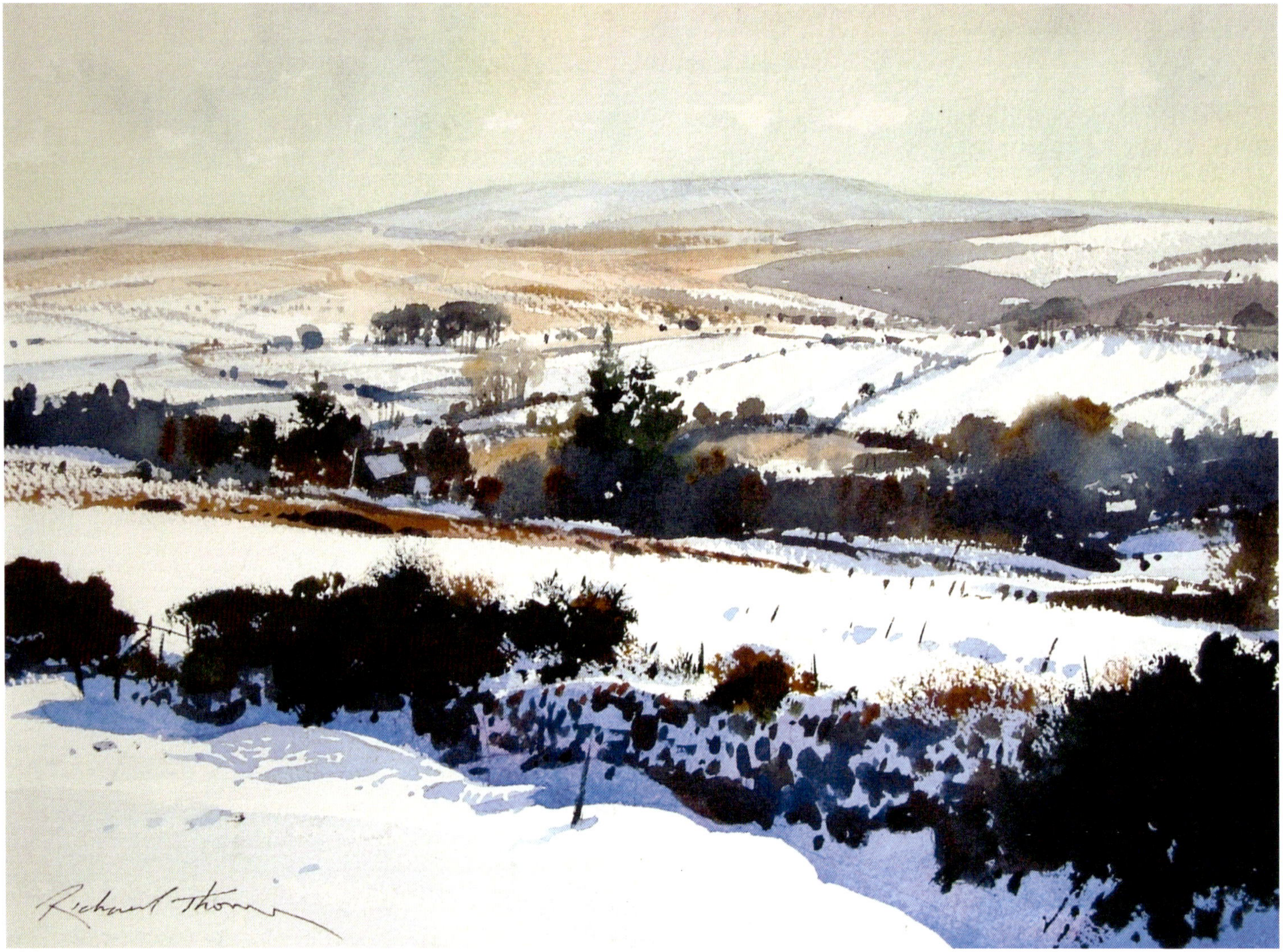

Richard Thorn. *Transformation*
Watercolour 12x16in (30x41cm)

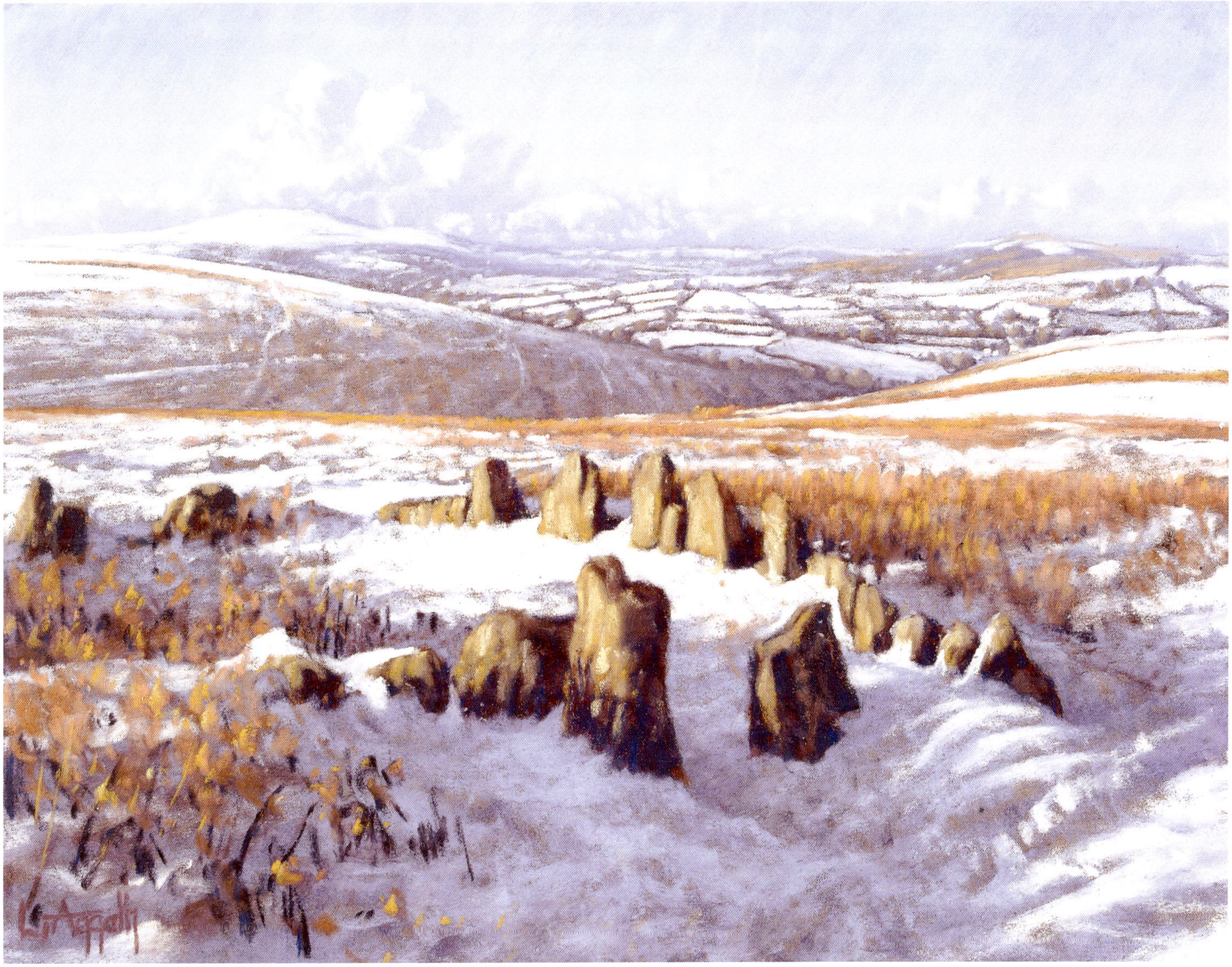

Lionel Aggett. *Winter, Dartmoor*
Pastel 10x13in (250x325)

Just into the moor from Leapra Cross lies Shapley Common with its numerous hut circles. Although I have painted extensively well into the moor, I also find the topography looking out from all sides fascinating, where the intricately detailed Devon landscape unfolds beyond the rugged moorland.

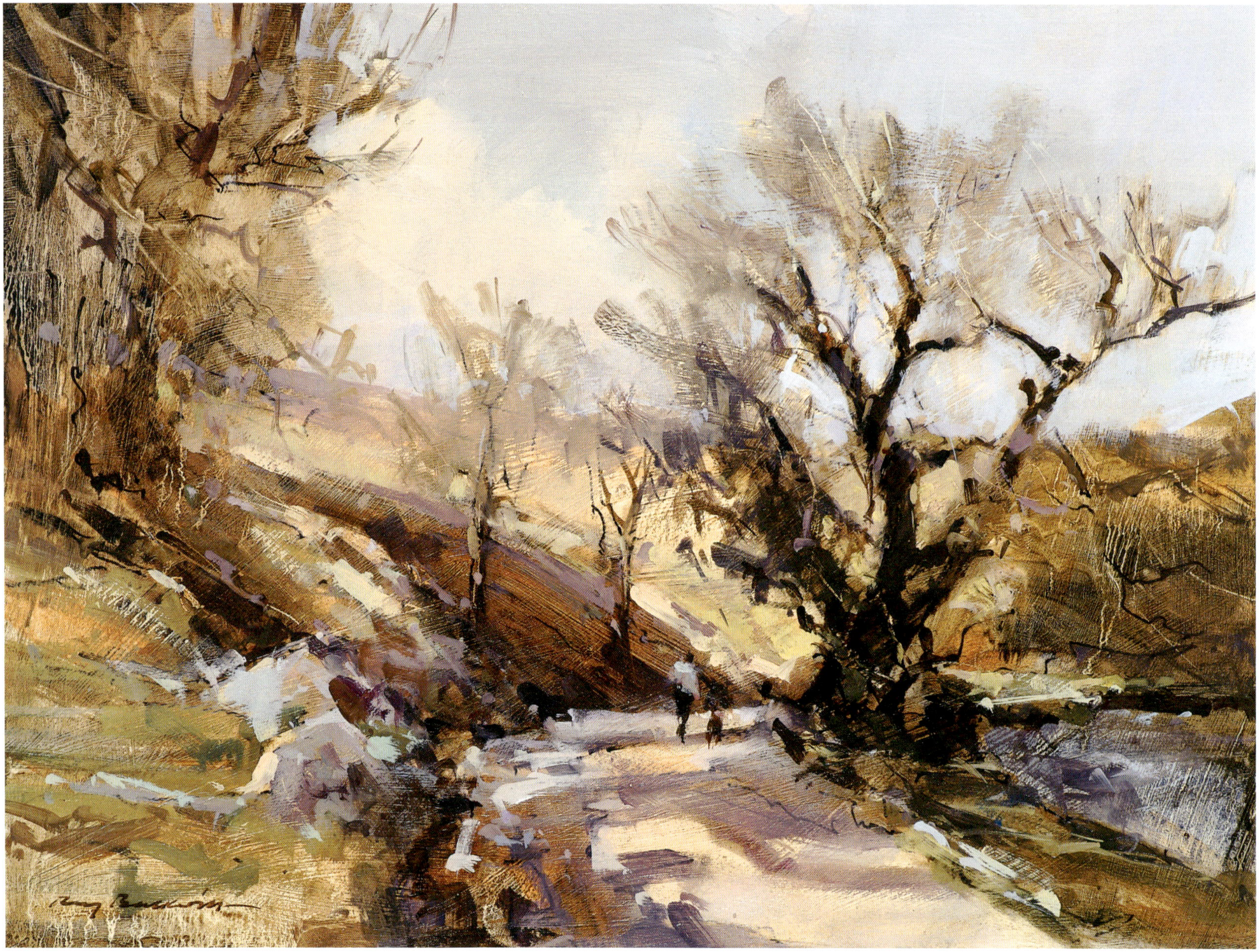

Ray Balkwill. *Winter Walk Beside the River Avon*
Oil 10x14in (25x36cm)

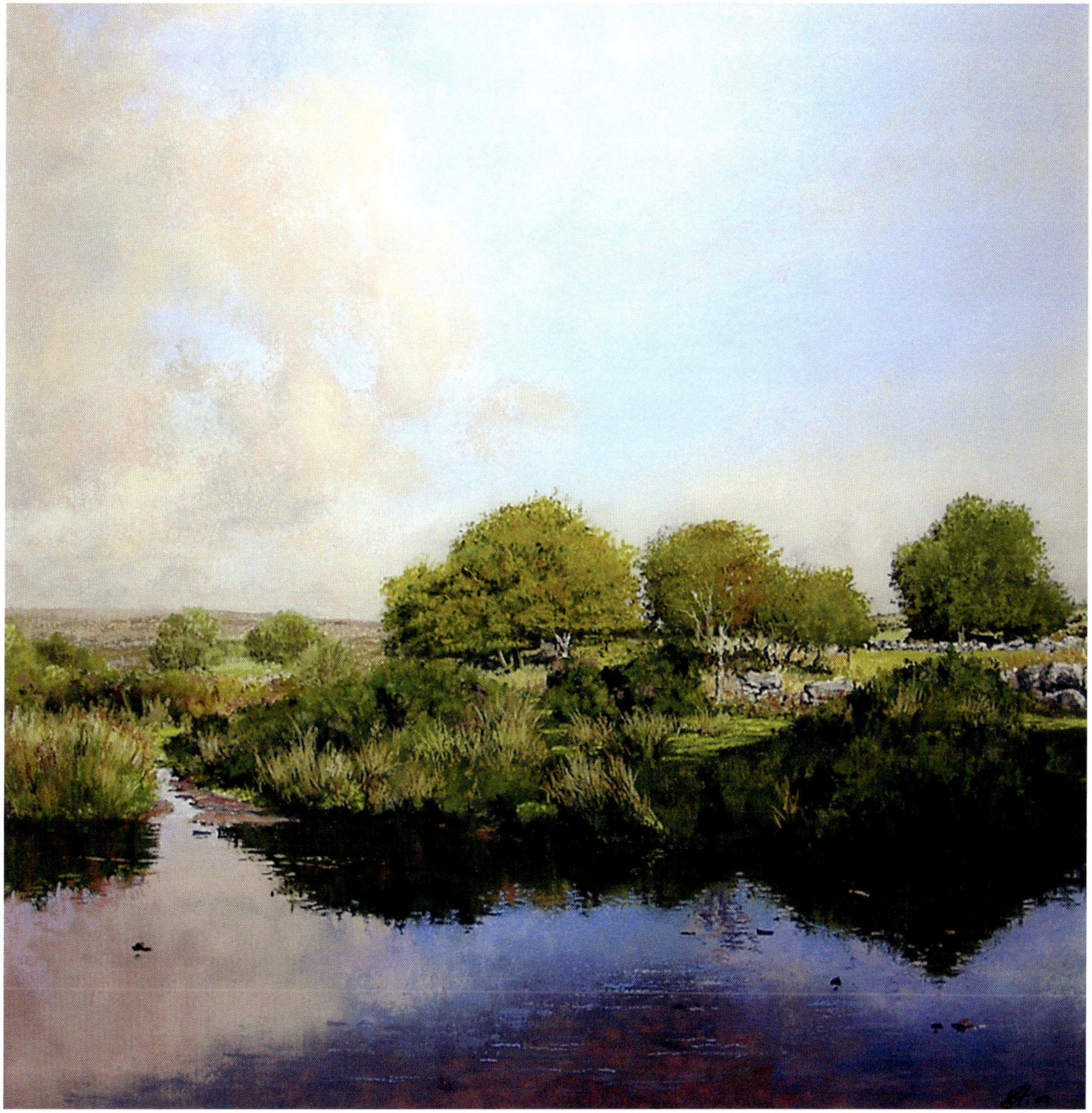

Keith Stott. *Autumn Morning, Swincombe*
Pastel 17.5x17.5in (45x45cm)

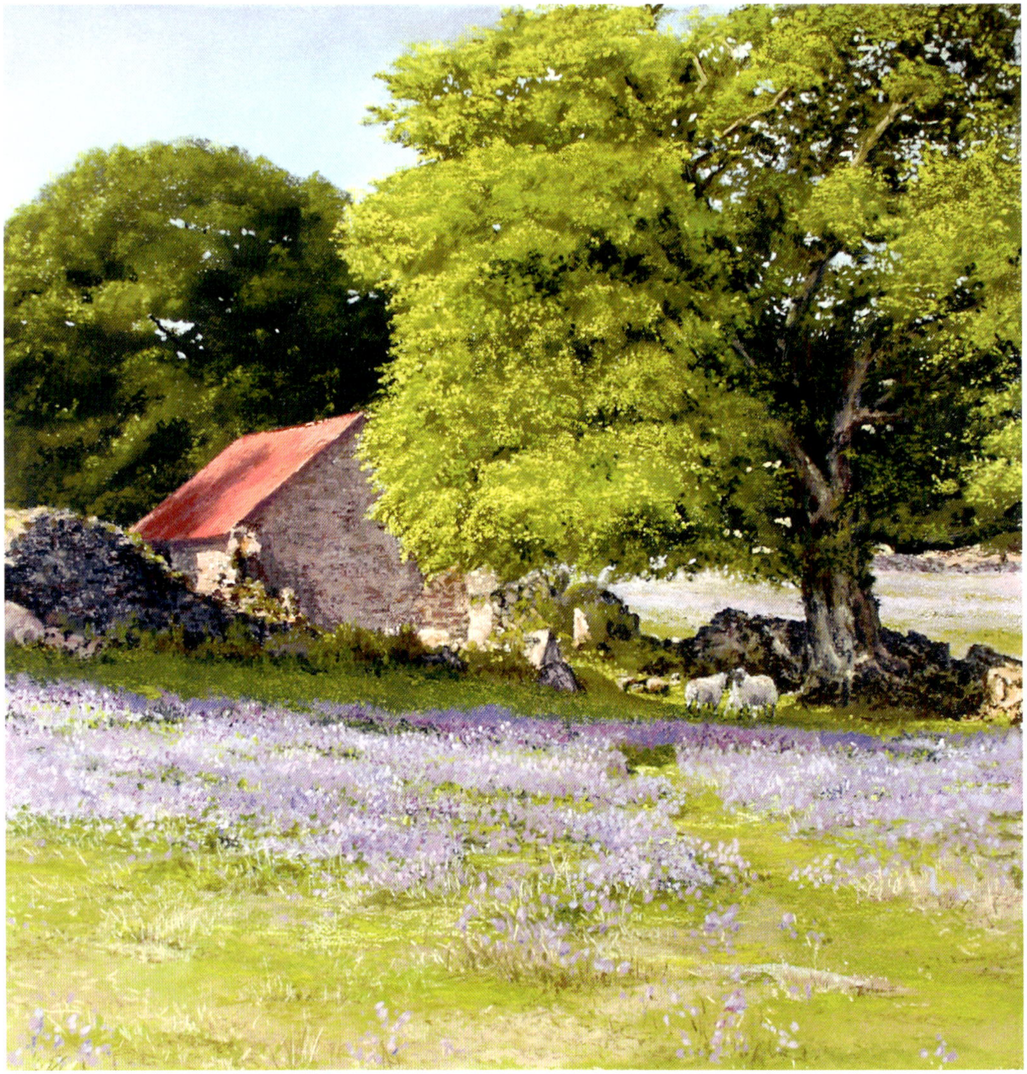

Keith Stott. *Emsworthy Spring*
Pastel 14.5x14.5in (37x37cm)

As I came over the top of Rippon Tor on a Spring morning, the middle distance was dominated, not by Saddle Tor or Haytor Rocks, but a blaze of blue around the old Emsworthy field system. The long shadows of early morning, the bright Spring green of the trees contrasting with the red of the barn roof and the different tones of the bluebells in the light and shade gave the scene an incredible vibrancy.

Ray Balkwill *Tavy Cleave, Dartmoor*
Mixed Media 20x16in (51x41cm)

There is a lovely story about William Widgery painting on the moor told by William Crossing in his book Dartmoor Worker *(1903). A passer-by who had a slight acquaintance with him stopped to look over his shoulder at his work. He could not recognise the view before him as that which the artist was painting. In the foreground instead of a marsh there appeared a rocky stream. 'Mr Widgery', said the visitor mildly, 'there is no river at the foot of that hill.' 'Isn't there?' returned the artist, without looking up, 'well there ought to be!'*

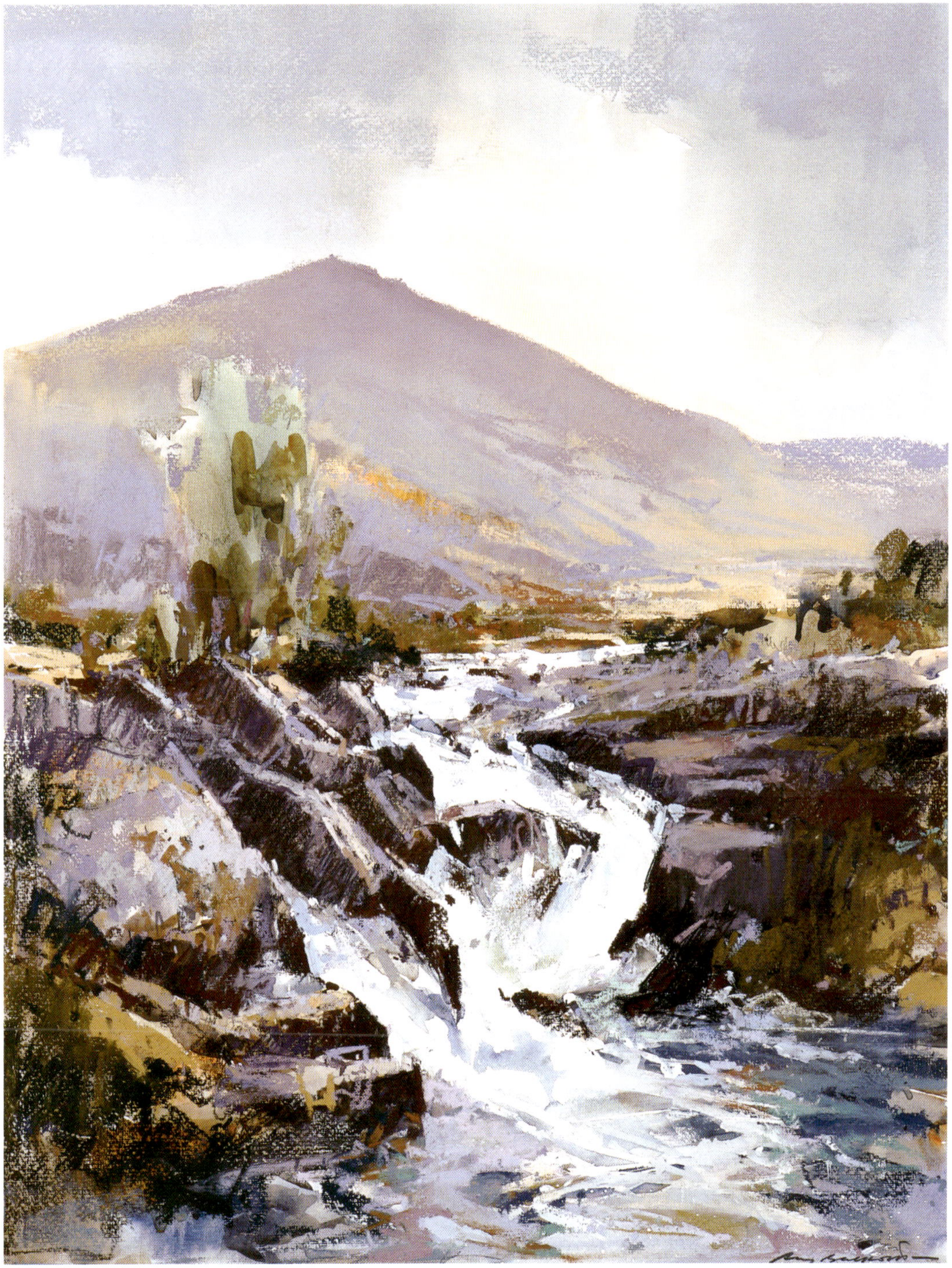

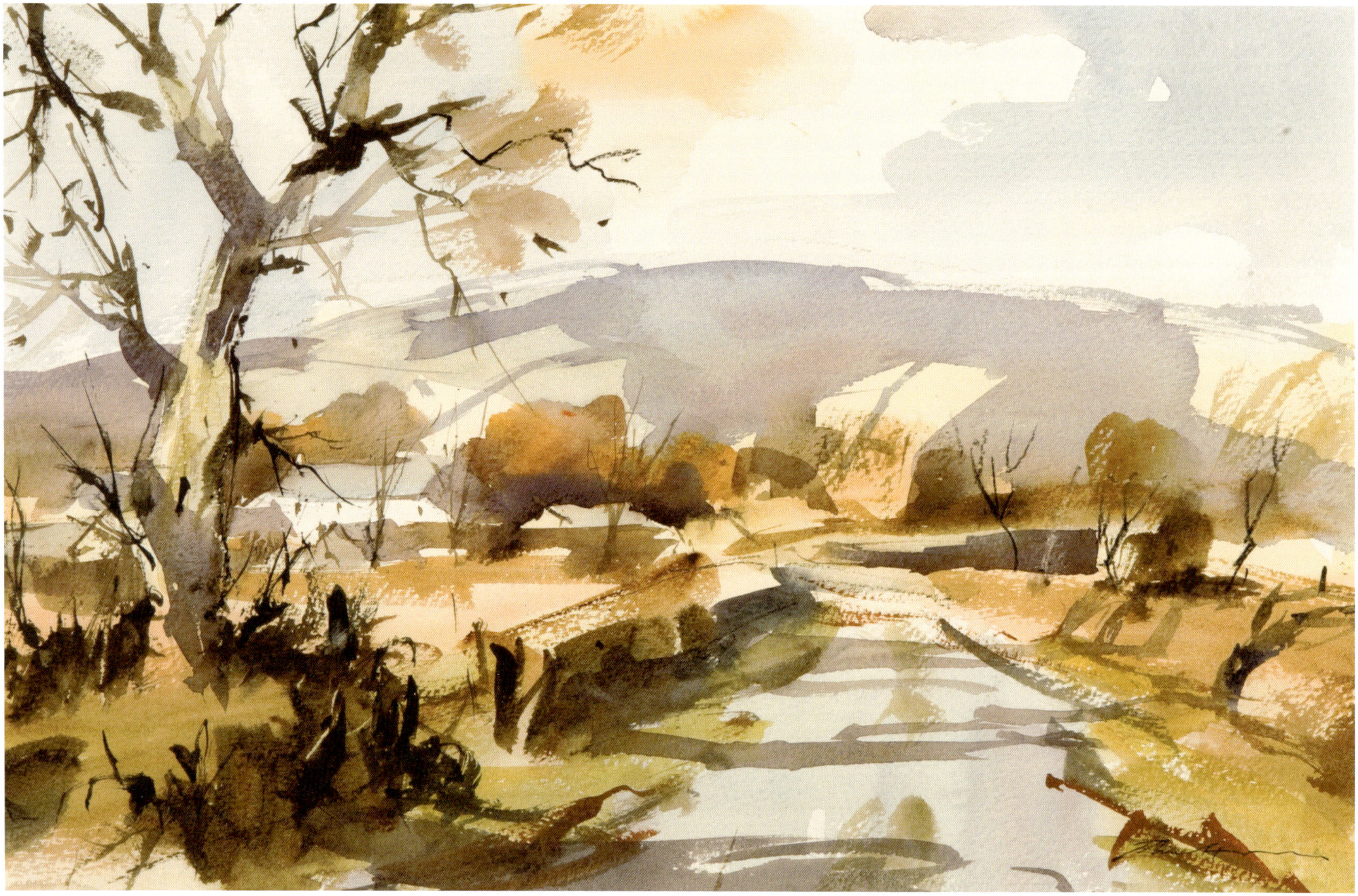

John Hoar. *Gated Road, Sandyway, Exmoor*
Watercolour 12x18in (30x40cm)

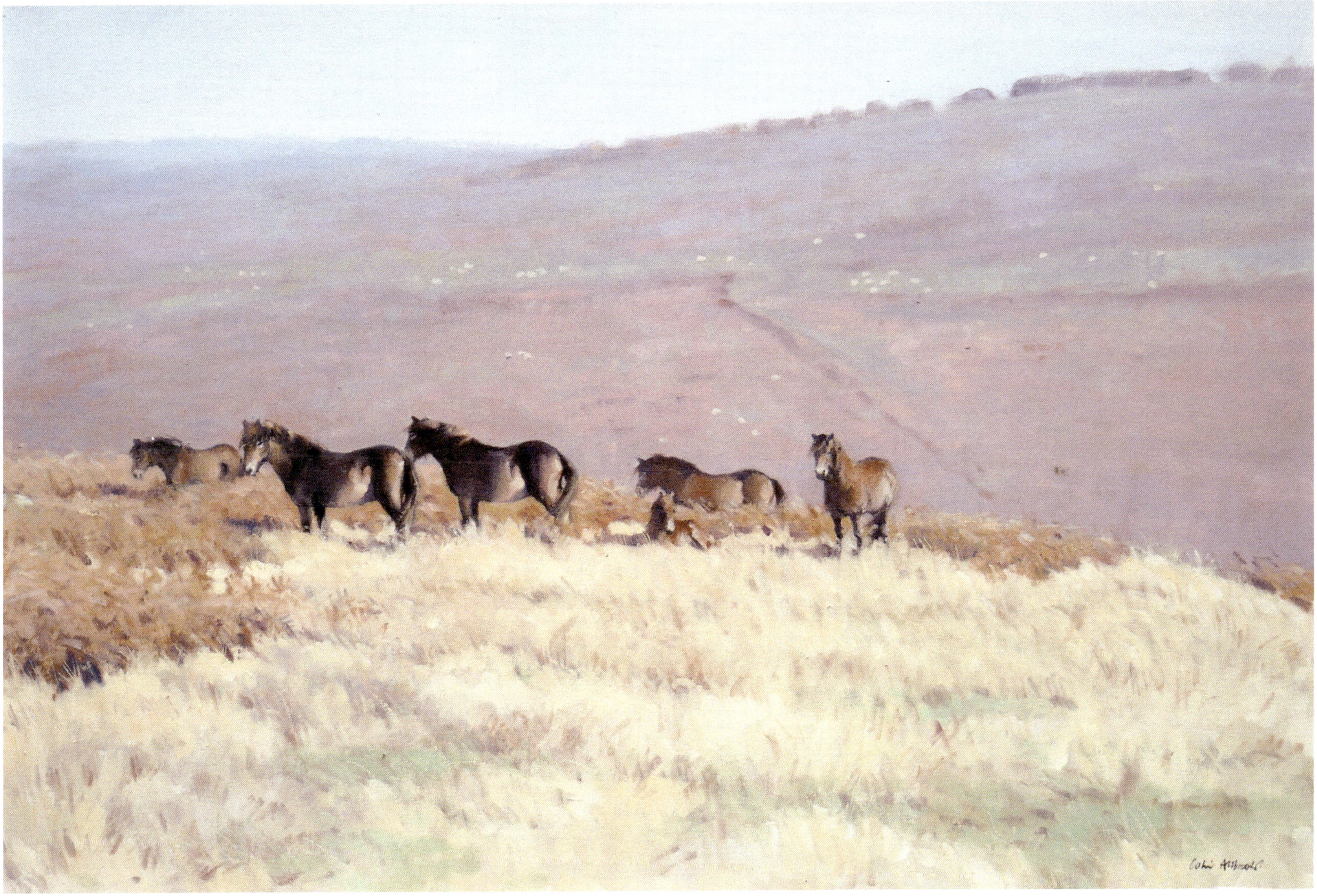

Colin Allbrook. *Exmoor Ponies*
Oil 24x36in (60x91cm)

I frequently seek out the ponies on the moor and this group I found just above Landacre Bridge on Exmoor. The September sun is lowering, bathing the horses in a warm light against the violet heather.

I have clambered over granite outcrops the length and breadth of Dartmoor, but the area, which holds the most interest for me, is that which lies behind the popular tourist attraction of Haytor. Walk north just a few hundred yards from here to find the peace and solitude of Holwell and a multitude of comparatively small but inspirational outcrops, which are easy to climb over and into. These paintings convey my love of the negative shapes between the boulders through which intimate glimpses of Dartmoor can be viewed.

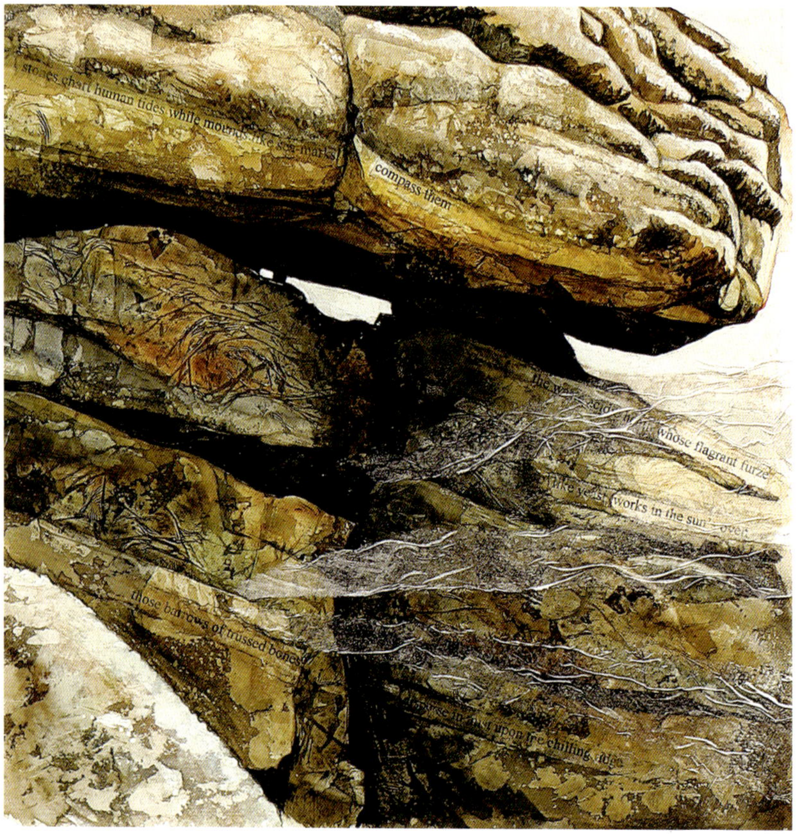

Judy Hempstead. *Dartmoor from Secret Places*
Mixed Media 9x9in (23x23cm)

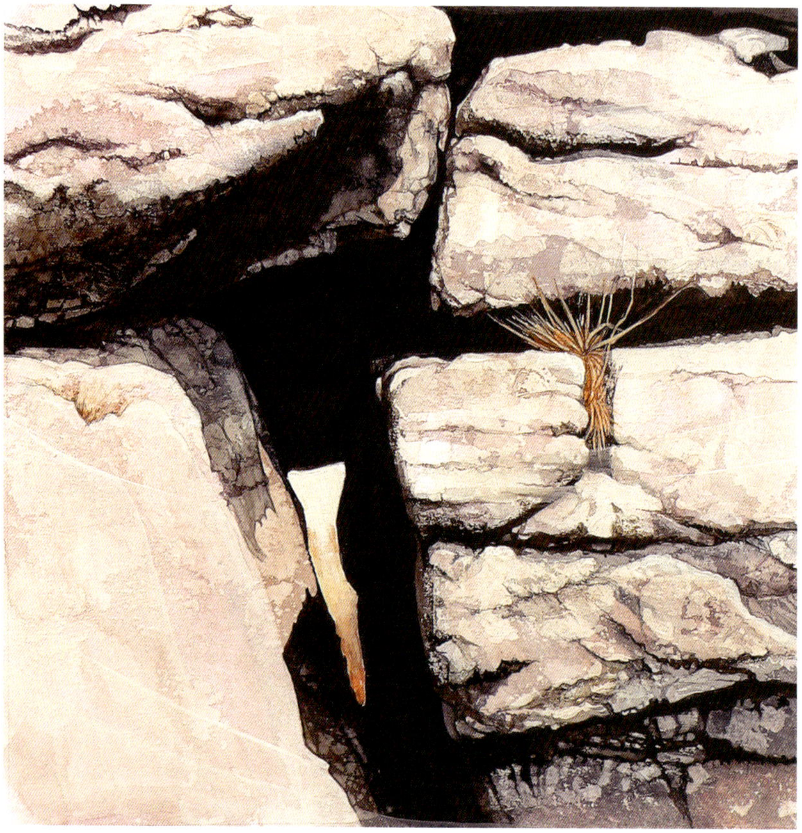

Judy Hempstead. *Looking Through 1*
Mixed Media 9x9in (23x23cm)

Michael Morgan. *Distant Dartmoor*
Watercolour 14.5x14.5in (37x37cm)

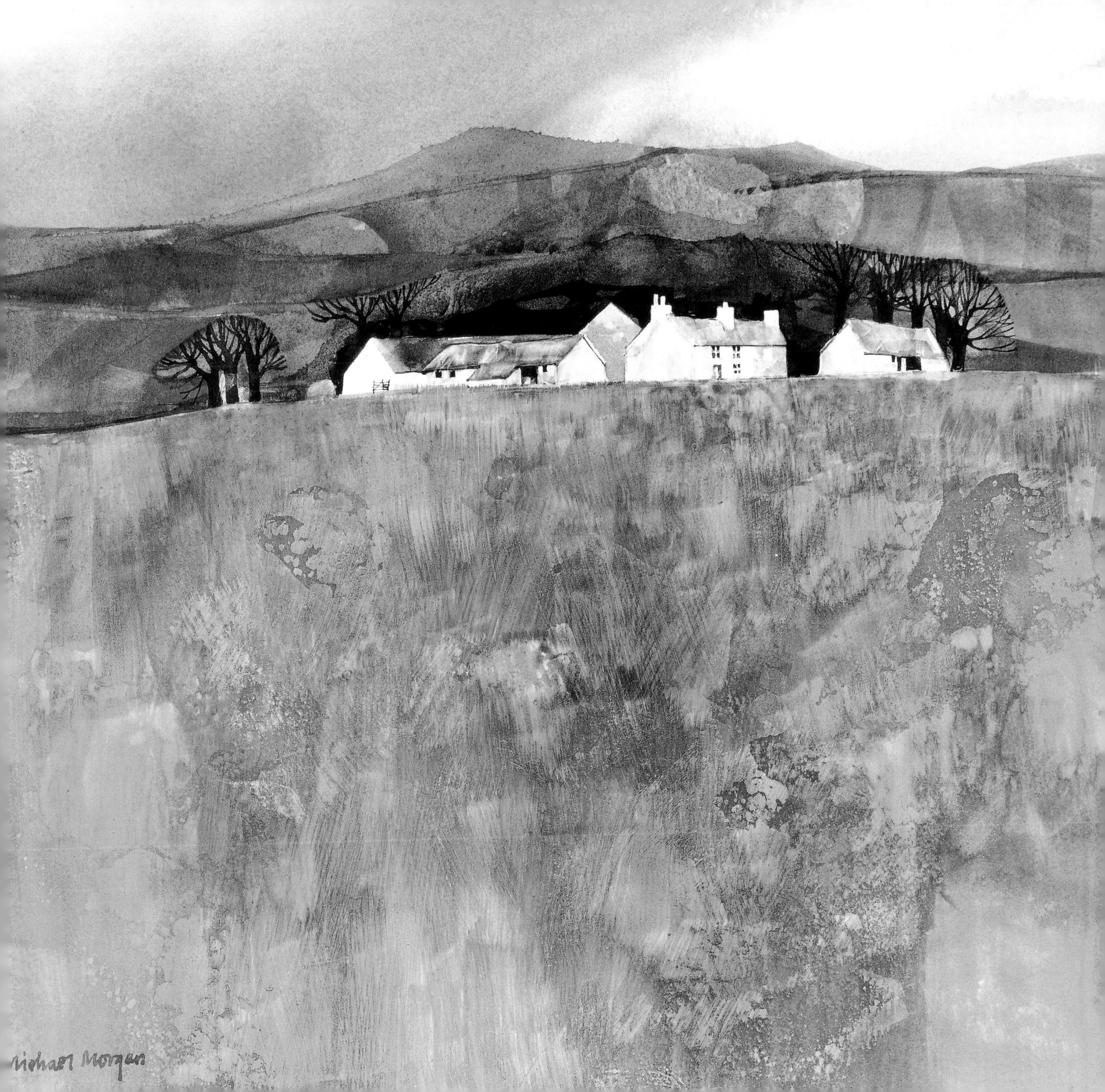

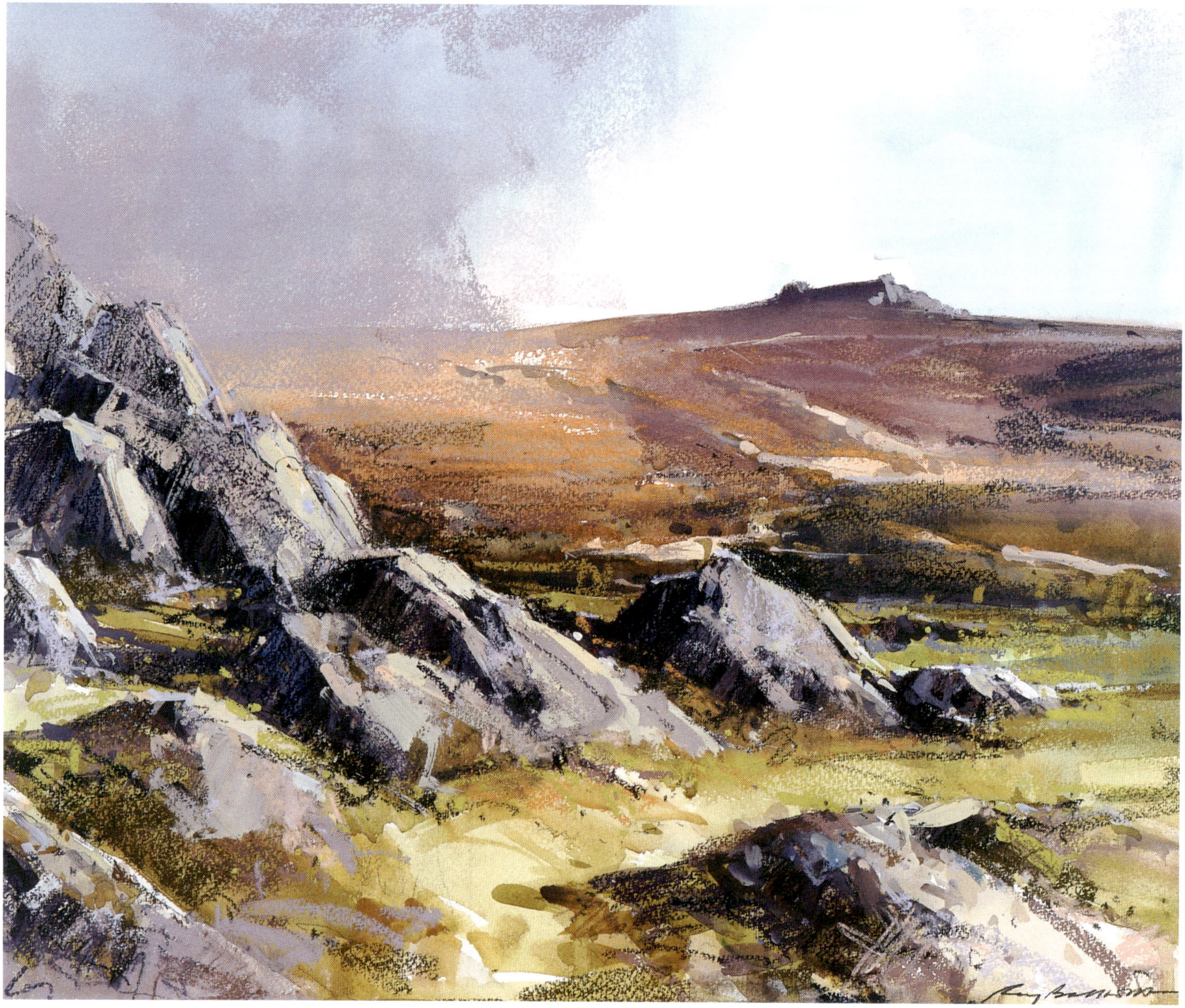

Ray Balkwill. *Passing Shower, Hay Tor*
Mixed Media 13x16in (33x41cm)

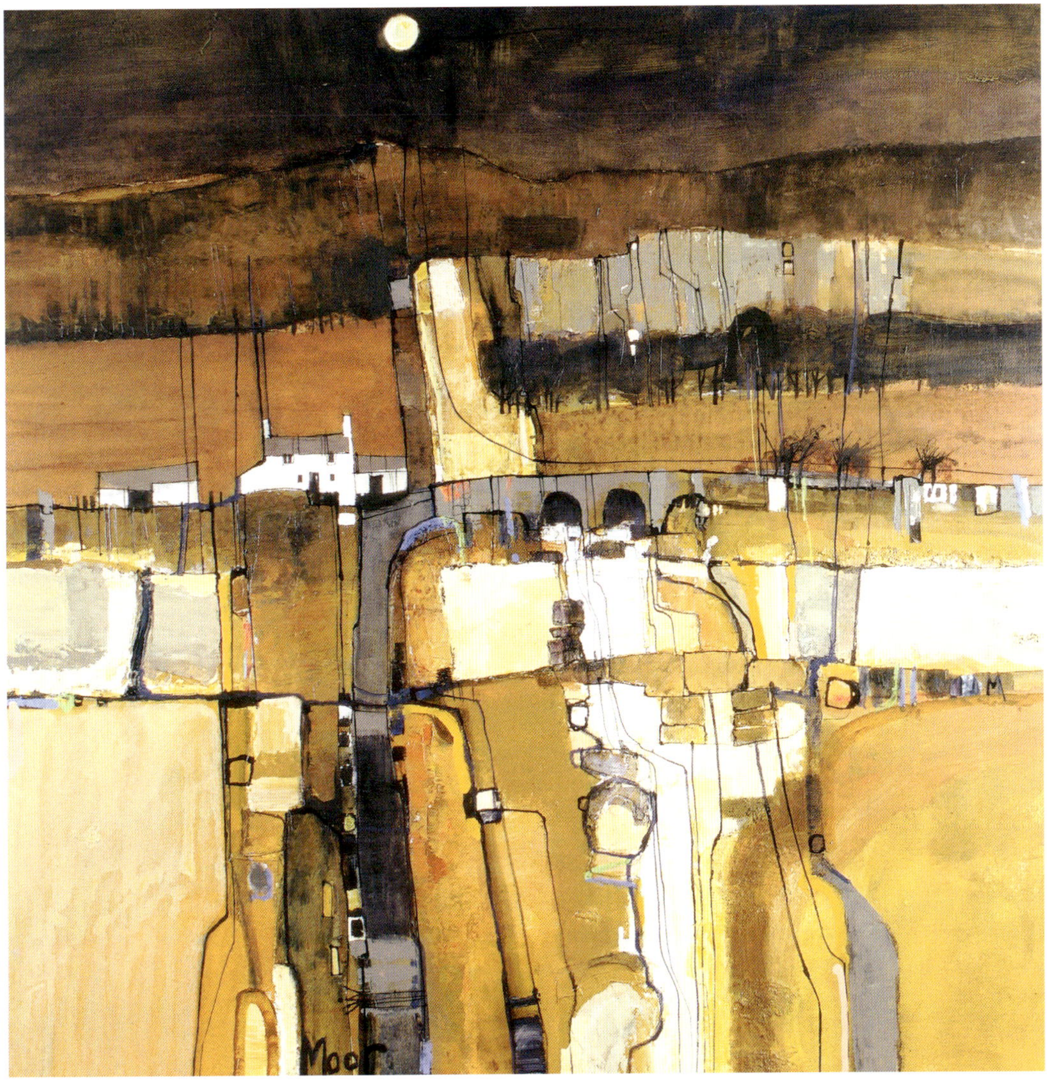

Martin Procter. *Moor 12*
Acrylic 40x40in 9100x100cm)

This painting forms part of a series and contains many of the iconic Dartmoor images; there are references to the granite tors and walls, the hill farms, the stone rows, the bridges.

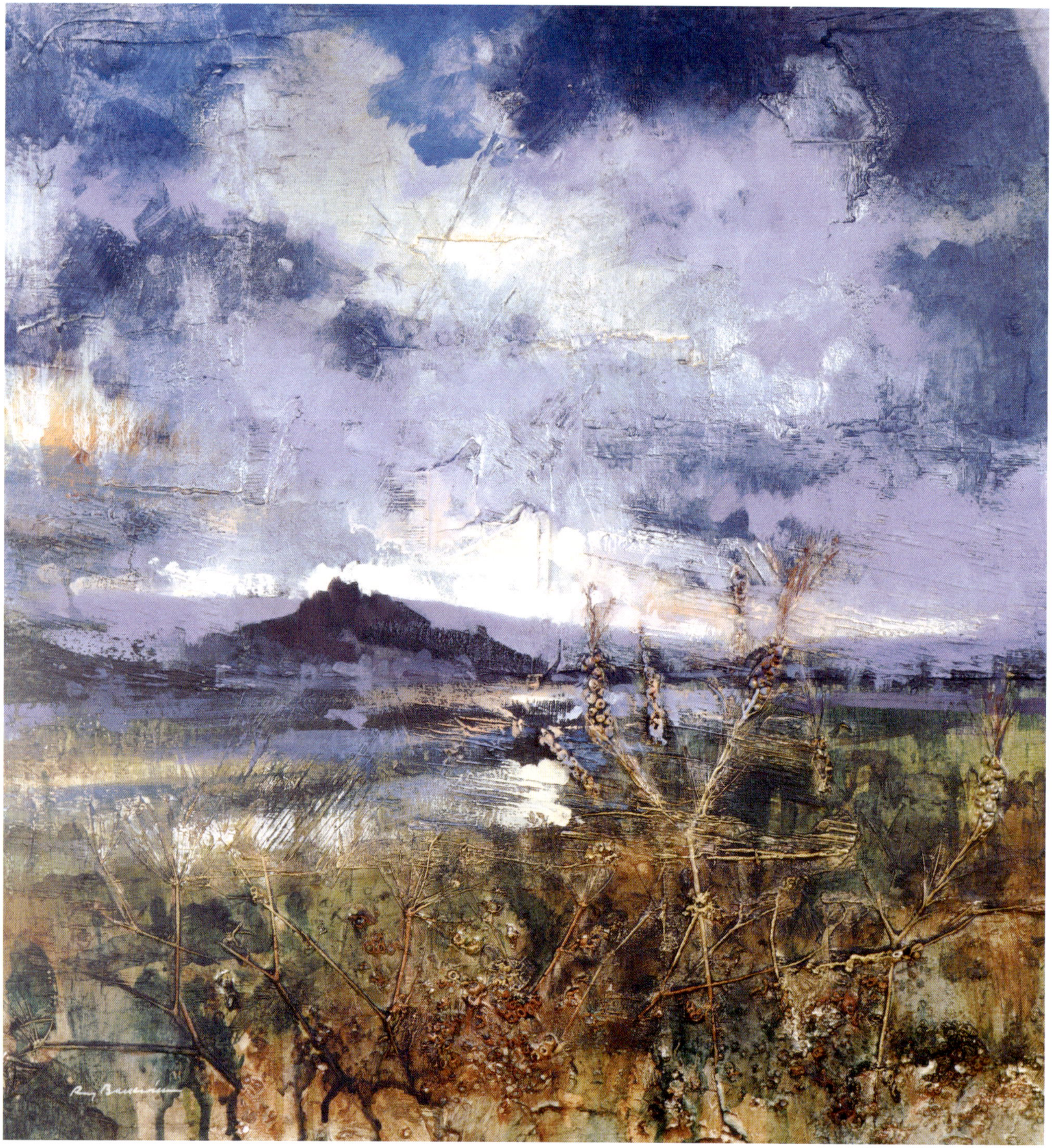

Ray Balkwill. *Distant Tor*
Mixed Media
18x18in (46x46cm)

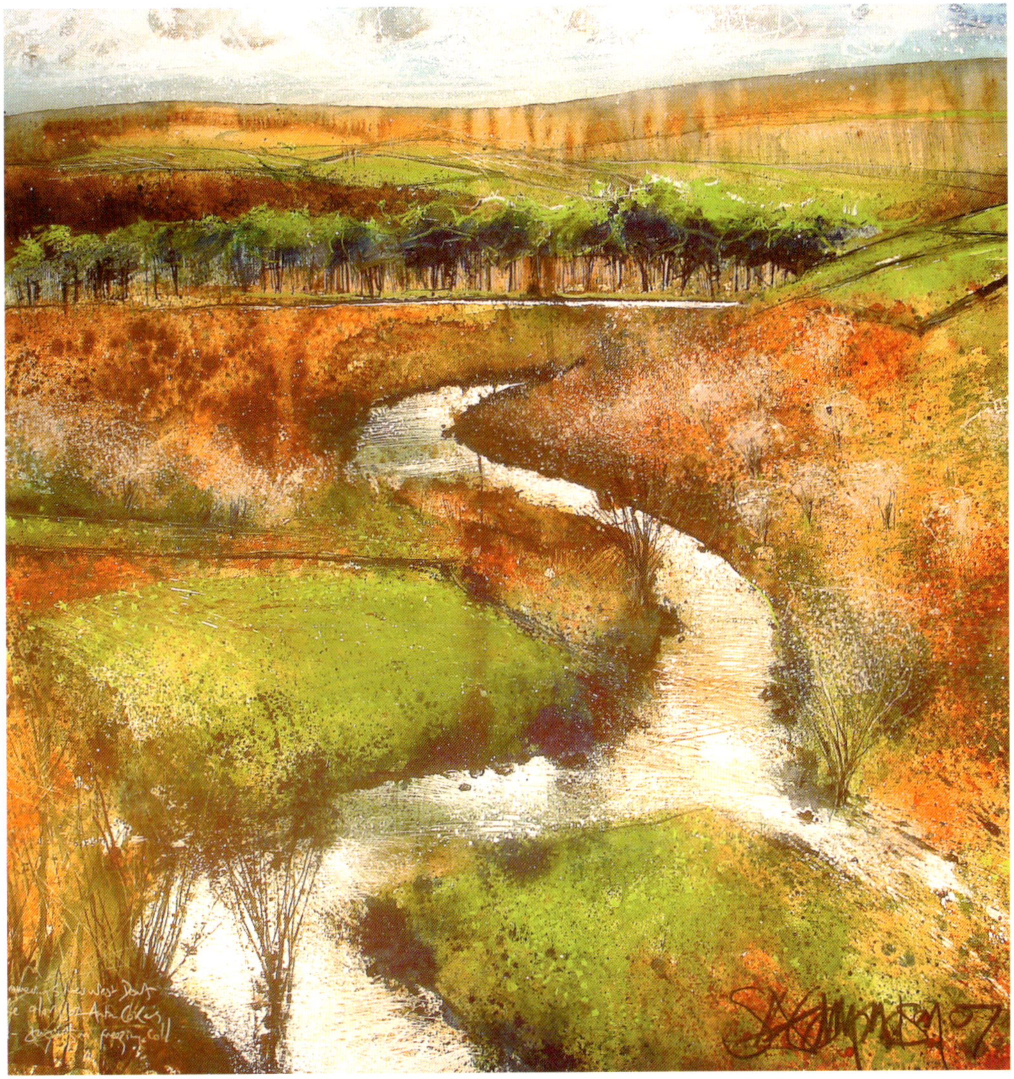

Stewart Edmondson *Shimmering Silver, West Dart*
Mixed Media 29.5x29.5in (75x75cm)

The West Dart near Dunnabridge winds its way through unforgiving open moorland, a real contrast to the lush, wooded valleys of the lower Dart. The bleak, bright openness of the moor here is just breathtaking.

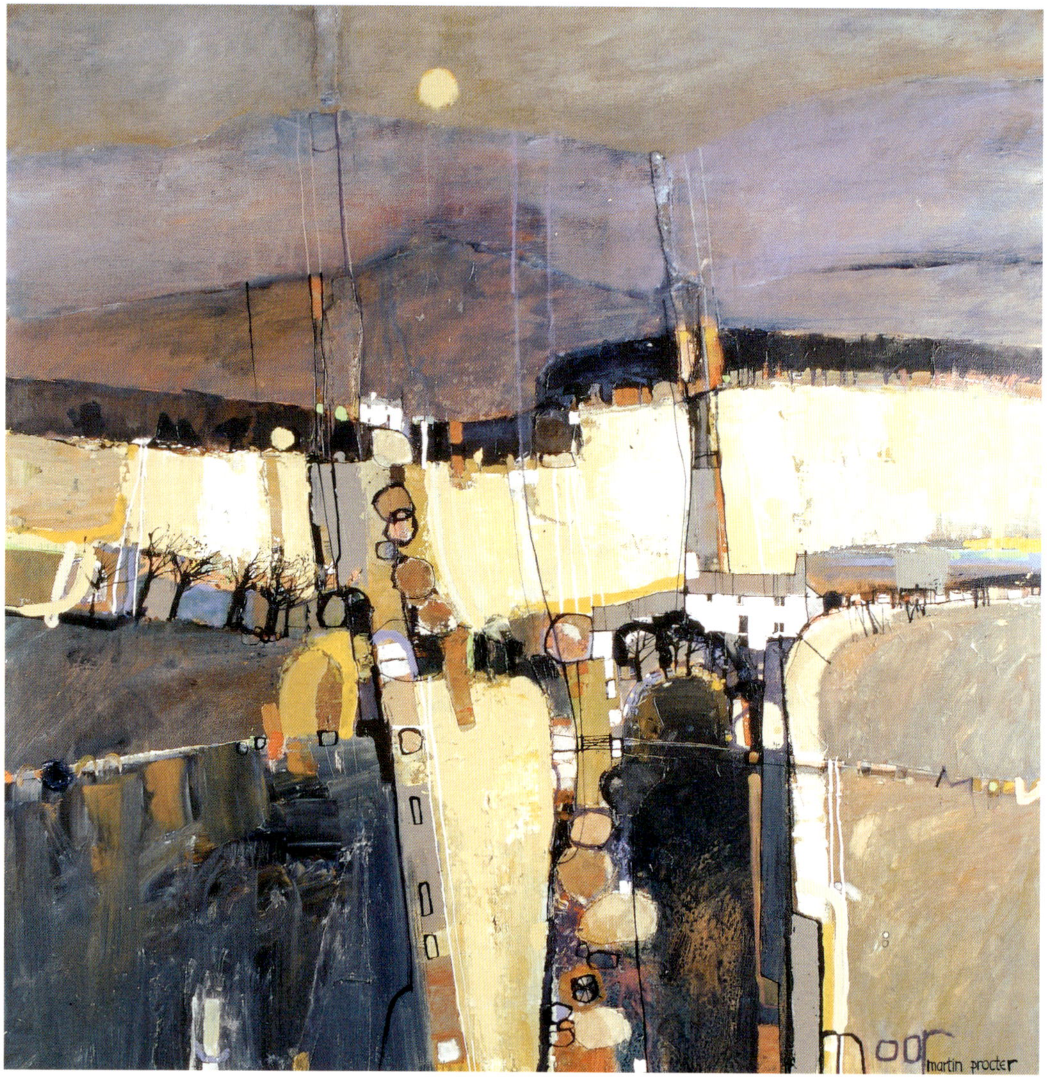

Martin Procter. *Moor 11*
Acrylic 40x40in (100x100cm)

I like to use recurring shapes to suggest the particular nature of Dartmoor – weathered granite boulders, stunted windblown trees, slotted granite gateposts, standing stones, newtake enclosures, livestock pens. My aim is to find a way of painting the moor as a fully abstract image, using my stored memories of this very special place.

Michael Morgan.
Isolated Farm Two
Watercolour
11x11in (28x28cm)

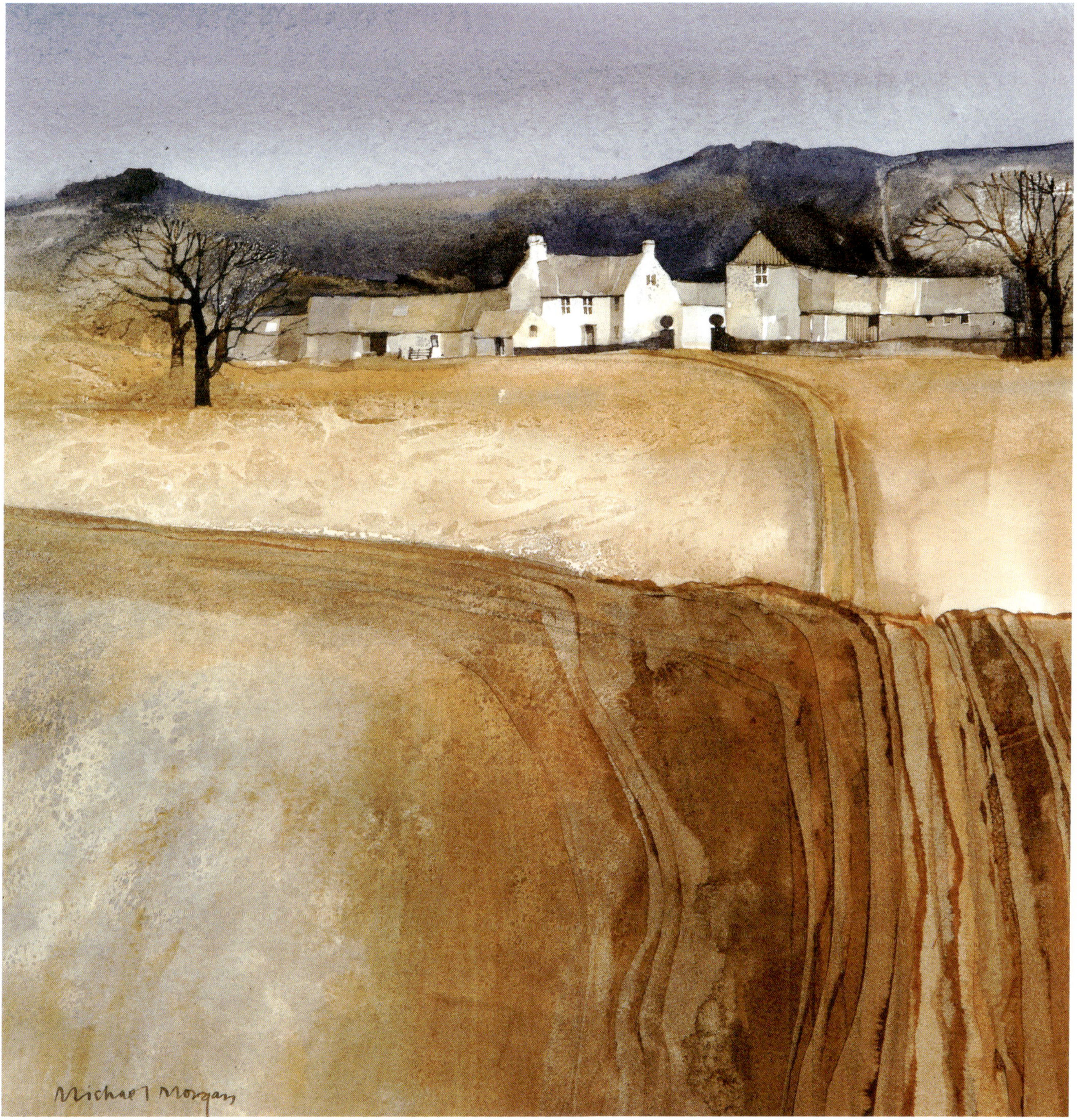

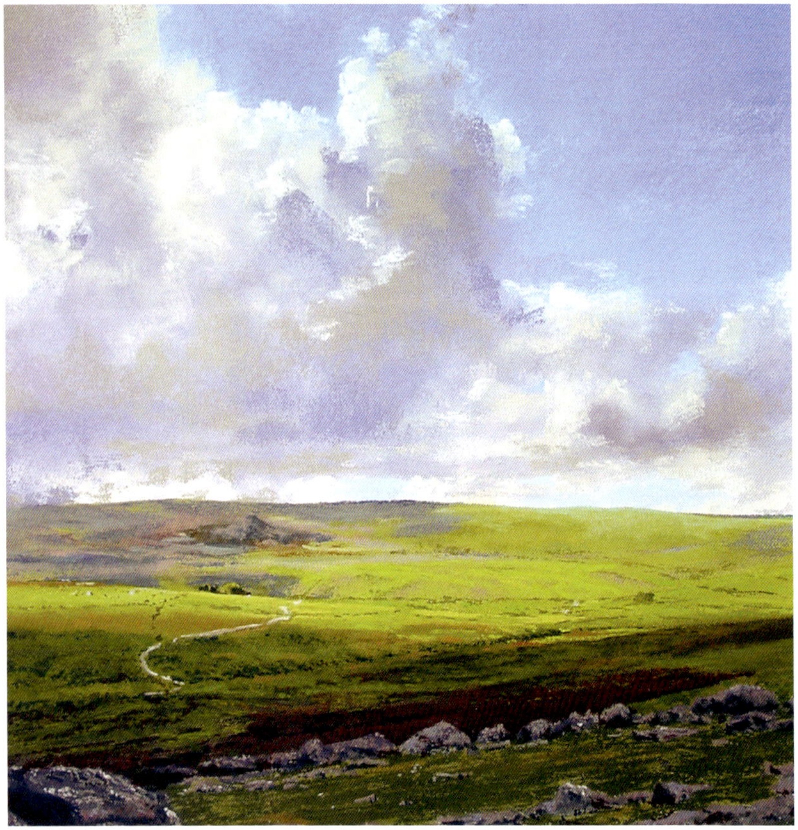

Keith Stott. *The Lane to Ditsworthy*
Pastel 15x15in (39x39cm)

A morning in late Summer, of brief bursts of sunshine between short, sharp showers. Standing on the summit of Gutter Tor, looking towards Hen Tor and Ditsworthy, the many-coloured cloud shadows chase each other down into the Plym valley.

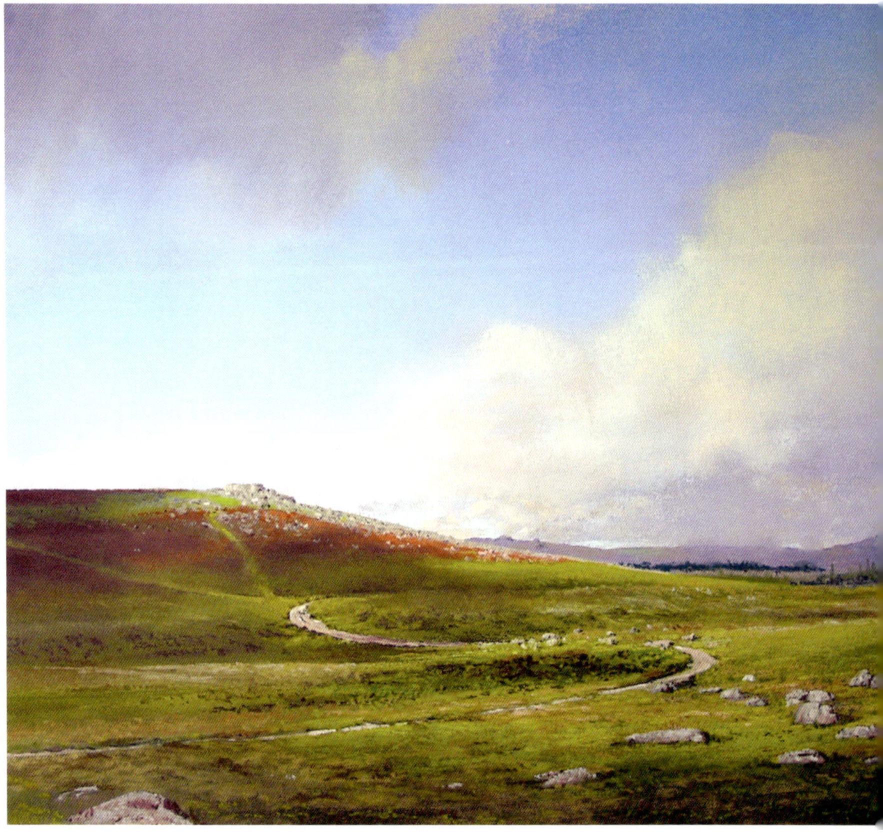

Keith Stott. *Cloud Shadows, Gutter Tor*
Pastel 18x22.5in (46x57cm)

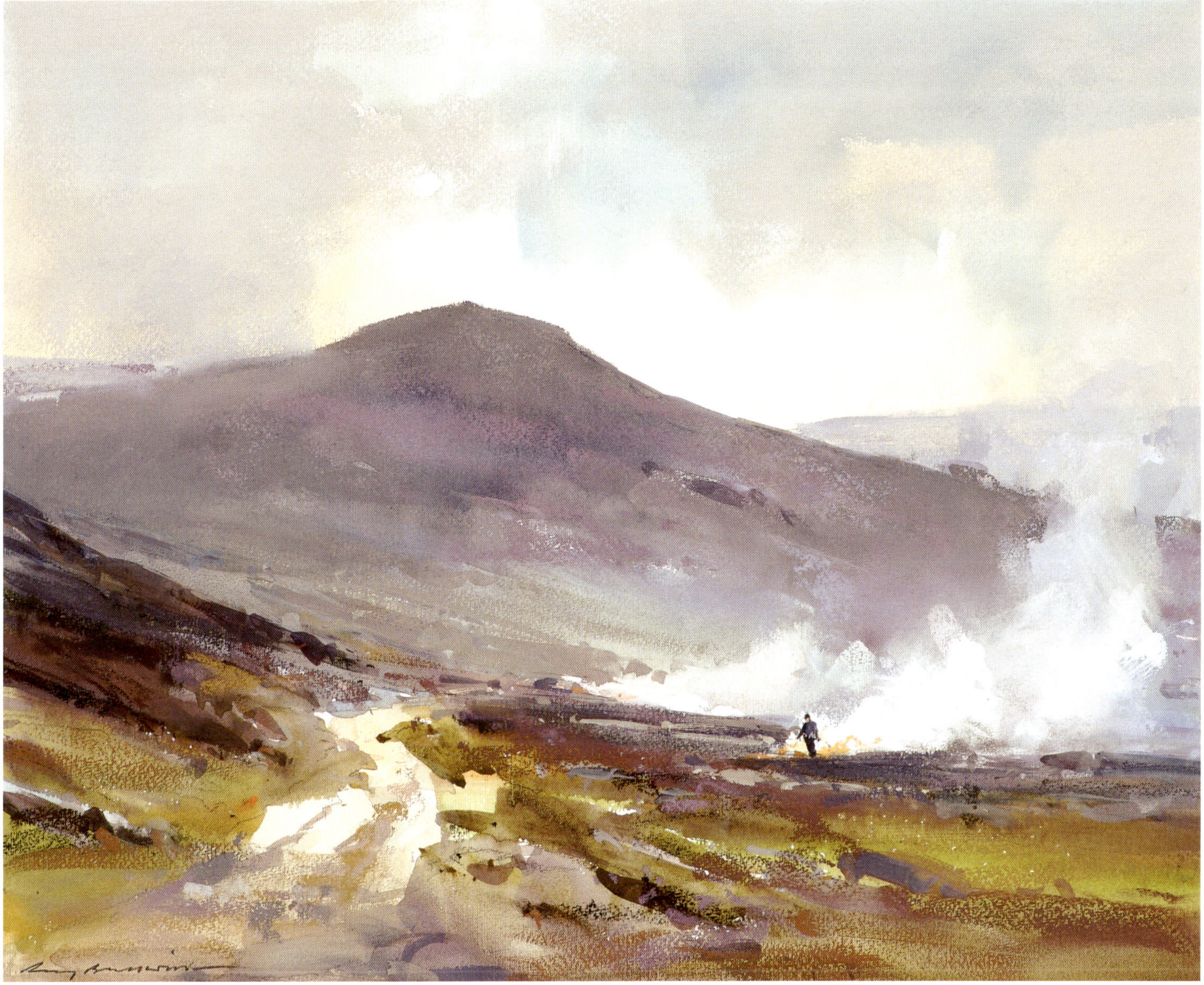

Ray Balkwill. *Swaling on Dartmoor*
Mixed Media 13.5x17in (34x43cm)

Swaling is the annual burning of the gorse and scrub in order to allow new grass roots to grow, thus providing grazing for the livestock. Swaling on Dartmoor has been carried on for centuries and it is thought the word is derived from 'Swaelen' an Anglo Saxon word, meaning to burn.

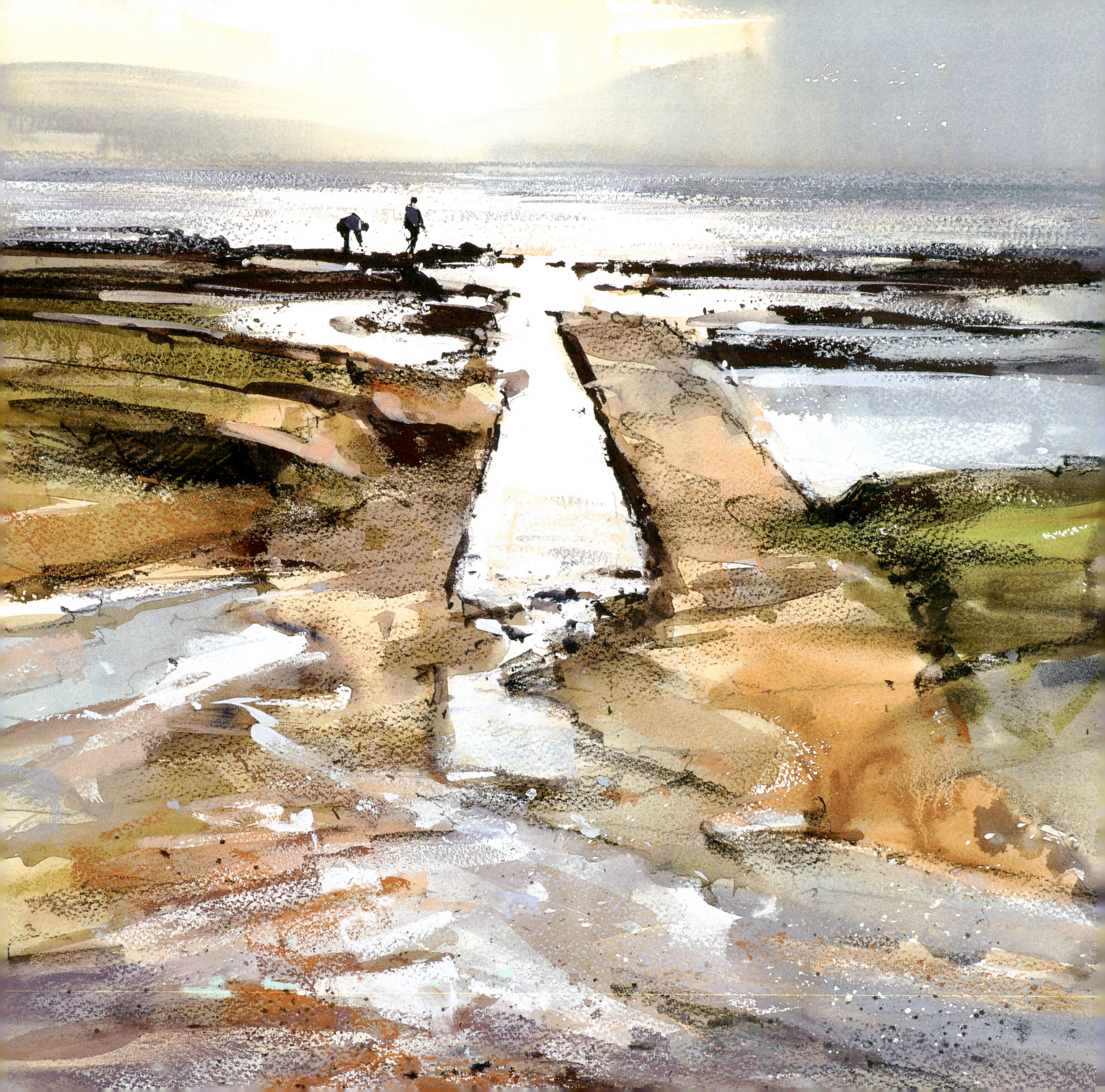

CHAPTER THREE

From wave-lashed cliffs to sheltered coves...

'For one whose heart draws him to the sea must, in the first place have a retentive memory, and be able to grasp in a few moments the effect of the ever-changing movements of the sea and sky; he must have a delicate and subtle sense of colour, and have the ability to place the main features of his impression of the subject on the canvas with few strokes of the brush, and beside this, he must be prepared to face a brave fight with the elements, which will be frequently against him.'

This is how Julius Olsson (1864–1942), in my opinion one of Britain's finest sea painters, once described his feelings. His words not only describe my own sentiments on the subject, but it also rings true for many other painters too. Whether it is the sparkle of sunlight on sea, thundering windswept waves crashing on rugged rocks, or fishing boats rolling gently at their moorings in a tranquil harbour; it is easy to understand the creative need to capture these emotional moments in paint.

The sea has always been important to Devon with its two long and contrasting coastlines. For the past two thousand years the coast has been the lifeblood of Devon's prosperity, with trading, shipbuilding and fishing all playing major roles in its importance. Today, that has all changed and now tourism, recreation and conservation have replaced the traditional skills. Pounded by gale-lashed Atlantic seas, rugged and towering cliffs dominate the north, whereas sheltered estuaries and sandy coves punctuate the much gentler south coast. In Charles Kingsley's books the whole panorama of the North Devon coastline is unrolled in evocative descriptions: 'What a sea wall they are those Exmoor hills! Sheer upward from the sea a thousand feet rise the downs; and as we slide through the deep water which never leaves the cliff, the eye ranges, almost dizzy, up some five hundred feet of rock dappled with every hue.'

Ray Balkwill. *Maer Rocks, Exmouth*
Mixed Media 17x17in (43x43cm)

Living by the sea at Exmouth, it is little wonder that the elemental forces in nature and the wide-open spaces of sea and sky have long been an inspiration in my own work. Certainly where the edge of the land meets the sea is where you truly understand your insignificance. As painting subjects go, the East Devon coast is as varied as you would find anywhere, with its red sandstone cliffs at Exmouth, giving way towards Beer, to chalk cliffs of a startling whiteness. The Jurassic Coast, as it has been called, is also England's first designated natural World Heritage site. Here one can see 185 million years of history unfolding before one's eyes. The shoreline is equally varied too, sandy beaches alternating with steep shingle and pebble banks.

Dotted along the coast are a variety of contrasting subjects that I have always found inspiring, from the quaint fishing village of Beer, to the elegant and genteel towns of Sidmouth and Budleigh Salterton. Each has provided me with a wealth of subjects over many years. It was at nearby East Budleigh, two miles inland, that Sir Walter Raleigh, one of Devon's most famous sea-faring sons, was born. Sir John Millais' painting of 'The Boyhood of Raleigh' was created at Budleigh Salterton in 1871, using his two sons and a ferryman for his models. The sea wall, which featured in the picture, and the Octagon, the house where Millais lived, still stand as a reminder. The painting is in the Tate Gallery in London, but occasionally returns home on loan, to be displayed in the fascinating Fairlynch Museum, next to the where the eminent artist once resided. The museum owns a small, but important collection of works by Devon artists including John White Abbott, F. J. Widgery and Joyce Dennys and original topographical prints from 1810 onwards. Around the next headland in Exmouth another notable painter once lived. This was Francis Danby ARA and he settled there in 1846, remaining to his death in 1861. It was the changing aspects of sea and sky that inspired him, particularly the magnificent sunsets for which Exmouth is famous.

One painter whose name is synonymous with the rugged North Devon coastline in particular, is **Alan Cotton, Hon.D.Litt, FRSA, SWAc,** one of Britain's most distinguished contemporary landscape painters and his sumptuously rich oil paintings are internationally known. Born in Redditch, Worcestershire he moved to Devon in 1970 to be a Senior Lecturer in Painting and Art History at Rolle College, Exmouth. A post he held until 1982, when he resigned in order to devote more time to painting.

Firstly, he painted extensively in the landscape around his home in the Otter Valley, in East Devon. His early images were of the River Sid and River Otter and it was the sheets of coloured light reflected in the water that excited him. The subject led to a large series of paintings made in different lights at different times of day, but then he discovered Hartland. 'My love affair with Hartland began in the mid 1970s, not long after my arrival in the Westcountry, when a chance visit to North Devon revealed an area of landscape which was to become the inspiration for me to produce some of my most vigorous paintings. I remember with great clarity that first mind-blowing experience of coming down the hill to Hartland Quay, standing on the cliff edge and looking along the coast. It was a stormy day and as I watched that great solid mass of water constantly hitting the coastline, with such power, fragmenting on the rocks, I knew that what I was observing would provide the springboard for large dynamic paintings.' His associations with Hartland span twenty years and it is a motif he has recently returned to. 'Two things prompted me to go back. One was to do an exhibition in Devon on some local material and see how I responded to something I painted all those years ago and, two, the Royal Albert Memorial Museum in Exeter commissioned me to do a schools' project, so I did a project on Hartland.'

Alan is an artist who loves the act of drawing for its own sake, as well as the sensual physicality of applying rich oil paint on to canvas with a knife.

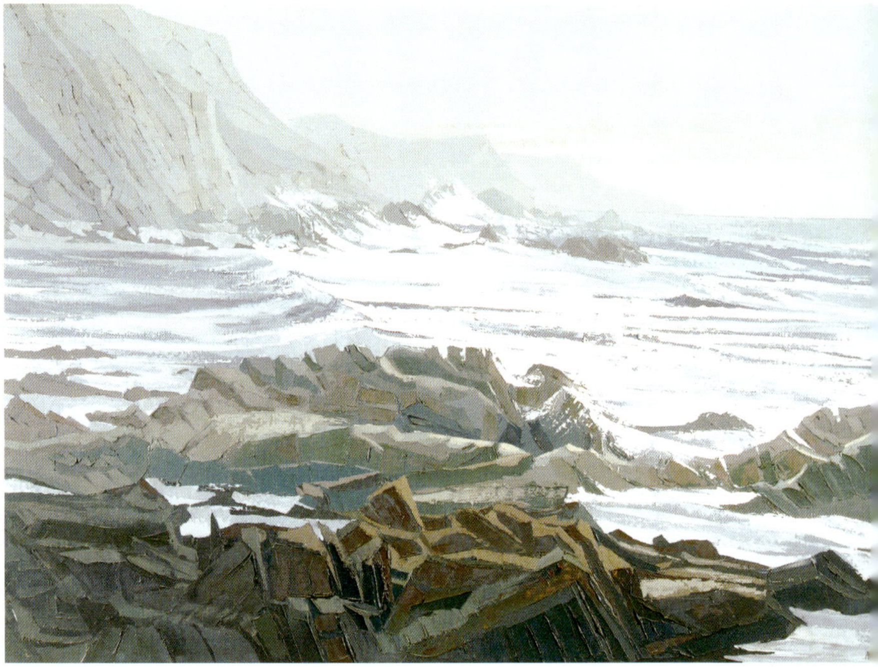

Alan Cotton. *Hartland Quay*
Oil 40x60in (102x152cm) Collection Royal Albert Memorial Museum, Exeter

'When I was a student I use to take everything out on location with me, bags of various things, pastels, watercolours, oil paints, as I lumbered through the landscape. But by the time I got there I was absolutely shattered. I soon realised I was taking too much. The point about painting is spontaneity in a sense; you find images that inspire and you just have to get on with the work. What I began to do was to take less and less with me and I travel light now. I travel with drawing books, watercolours perhaps, lots of things to make marks with. A lot of painting is what you see, what you feel, what inspires you, so I didn't feel that I needed to do everything on the spot. What I do on the spot is to draw; essentially I draw, I look, I take in and absorb what is there and then use these images as an aide-memoire back in the studio.' Alan's many trips throughout Europe and further afield have provided a rich repertoire of ideas for his paintings. For the past twenty years he has held annual exhibitions at Messum's in Cork Street, London, many of which have been sell-outs. In 2005 he was honoured to accompany His Royal

Highness, The Prince of Wales to Australia, New Zealand and Fiji as his Tour Artist. This resulted in his work now being held in the Royal Collection.

However, despite these demands, Alan has never lost touch with his roots in Devon and has always found time to support and promote the arts here. For many years he was a Director of the Exeter Phoenix Arts Centre and is also Patron and President of a number of art societies. He has also worked with children, students and disabled painters, along with raising funds for local charities. He was a founder member and, until recently, the President, of the much-acclaimed South West Academy of Fine and Applied Arts, founded in 2000 in Exeter. His efforts towards the appreciation of the arts here has been immense and in honour of his many achievements Alan was awarded an Honorary Doctorate (D.Litt) in 2006 by the University of Exeter for his 'outstanding contribution to the arts'.

Paul Lewin is another painter who has also gained a particular connection to this coastline. He is perhaps best known for his dramatic portrayals of the westernmost tip of Cornwall, where he now lives. But for seven years he lived at Abbotsham, near Bideford, making the coast and countryside around him, subjects of his paintings. Born in Manchester he studied fine art at Stockport and Bristol before eventually moving to the South West. He says of his working methods: 'Most of my work is painted directly from the subject, that's my real passion, being out in the landscape and experiencing it, and getting it into the painting. It gives urgency to the painting that you don't get in the studio; you are up against the tides, the weather, the position of the sun, and it is generally quite uncomfortable. You put a lot of energy into it to get the painting working, but the energy brings the painting to life'. He uses watercolour and gouache as a base for his mixed media paintings, and then works pastels, both oil and soft, into this as well as much scraping and scratching of the surface.

He told me that rock climbers particularly like his work because they can recognise the climbs in the cliffs, and this has resulted in a number of commissions. 'I have been painting on the cliff when a climber has pulled himself up. I've been working away when suddenly two hands have appeared – quite off-putting for both parties.' His relationship with the landscape is intense and for one project, 'The Abbotsham Oak,' he painted the same tree over a five-year period. 'It was in a wild meadow near our home and I probably did thirty, or forty paintings of it in all seasons. It was a very Devon subject.' His consuming interest in the landscape has even extended to the use in his paintings of a pigment made from the Devon soil itself. This is known as 'Bideford Black' and it was mined in the Bideford area until the 1960s. It had a number of uses, including painting ships' hulls and making mascara. Paul told me: 'At Abbotsham cliffs you can actually see where the seams start and where they mined it. And when the fields were ploughed, you could see a black line across the fields which went directly beneath my studio.' By collecting the raw material, processing it into paints and pastels, and then returning to the landscape to work with it, he was able to achieve a deep level of connection with the local landscape. The Burton Art Gallery and Museum has purchased one of these paintings for their permanent collection.

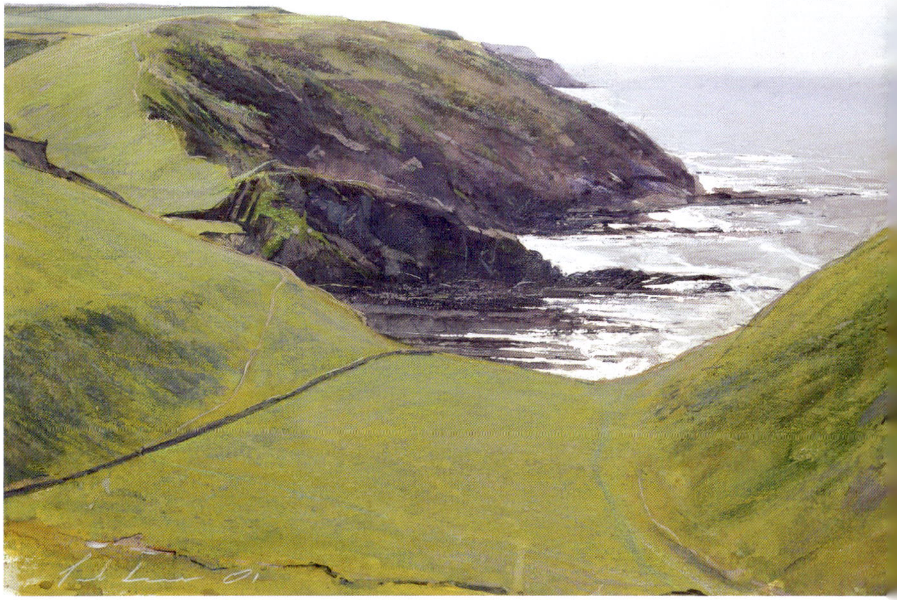

Paul Lewin. *South Across Spekesmill Mouth*
Mixed Media 21.5x29in (55x74cm)

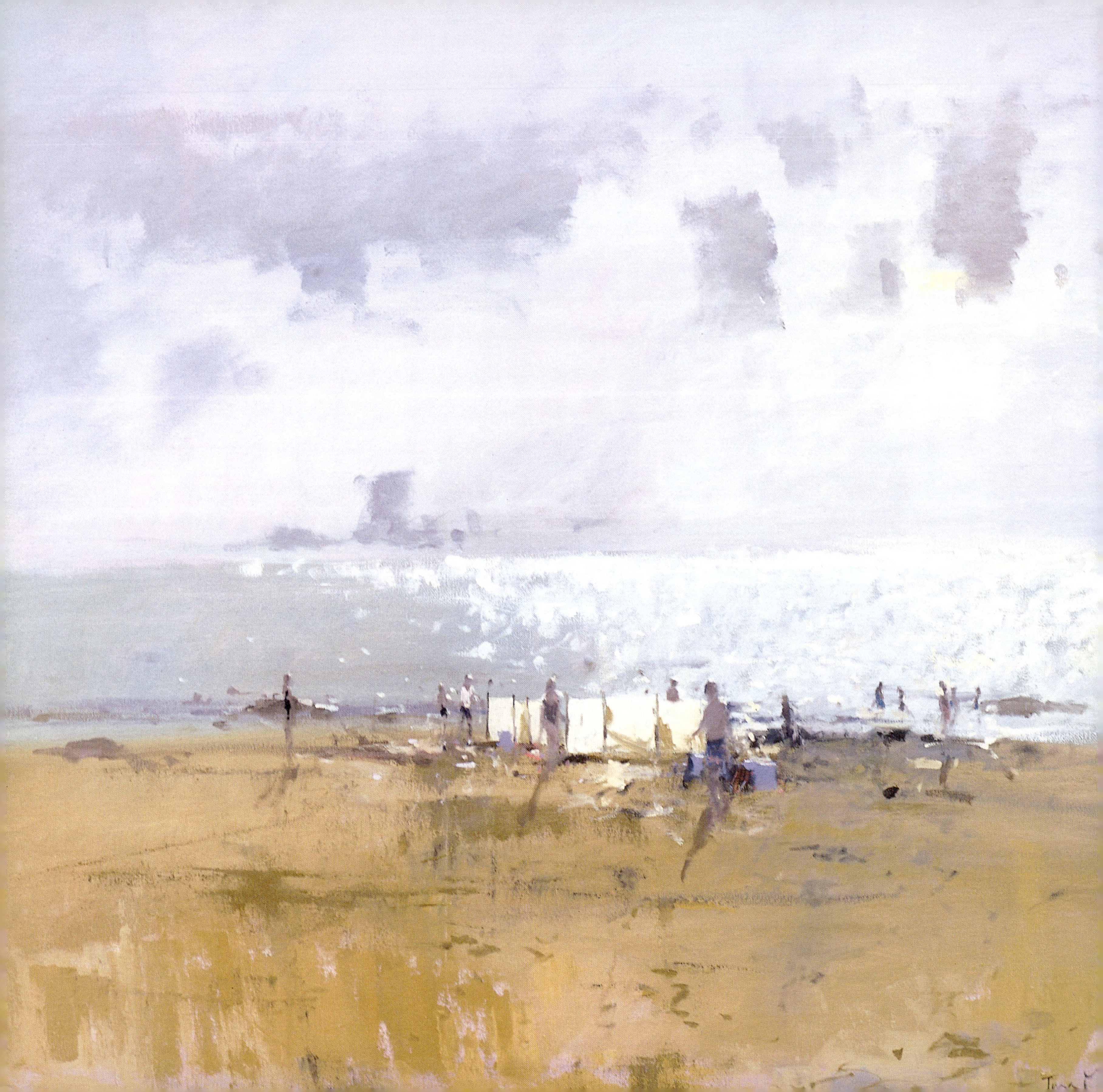

Another painter also inspired by light is **Tina Morgan, SWA, SWAc**. Looking at her oils one is immediately struck that colour and people are also of great interest to her. Whether it is the heat of a summer's day on the beach, sun glistening on the water, or bustling quaysides, her paintings capture the atmosphere perfectly. 'I lived on a North Devon farm until the age of eight and remember going into the fields with my father before breakfast to pick mushrooms. There was a wonderful Devon lane near the farmyard with tall overgrown hedges on either side that I used to wander down on sunny days. It was here that I first became aware of the colour of the foliage and flowers and how the sunlight and shade enhanced everything around.' The rest of her childhood was spent in a house on the Lizard Peninsula in Cornwall that overlooked the sea and 'waking up to the sound of the gulls and seeing the sun glistening on the water' has left a lasting impression on her. It was here at the age of twelve that she first started to paint in oils. 'Next to our house was a village hall and one year an artist hired it for the summer. I was fascinated by the vibrancy and colours of all the paintings and spent many hours in there.'

Before becoming a professional artist, she had a highly successful career working as an Art Director in London. In 1986 she decided to return to Devon to live in the countryside, yet close to the sea. Tina says 'I like to work mostly from memory, as it gives me the flexibility for creating a more interesting painting, and one that gives a greater feeling of mood than reality. I tend to experiment with colour and tone until I'm happy with the overall feel of the painting.' Although she also travels extensively for subjects, it is the diverse beaches and countryside of the Westcountry that she always returns to.

Richard Thorn is another painter who is mesmerised by the sea, perhaps not surprisingly as he was born in Torquay. Many of the places he now paints, he also frequented when he was a small boy. 'In my youth I use to explore the caves and go fishing in the rock pools, seemingly endless days of fun in the sun. They were places of excitement and wonder and now they are places of peace and meditation.' He is also a member and supporter of the Campaign to Protect Rural England and

Tina Morgan. *Blue Lunch Box*
Oil 32x40in (981x102cm)

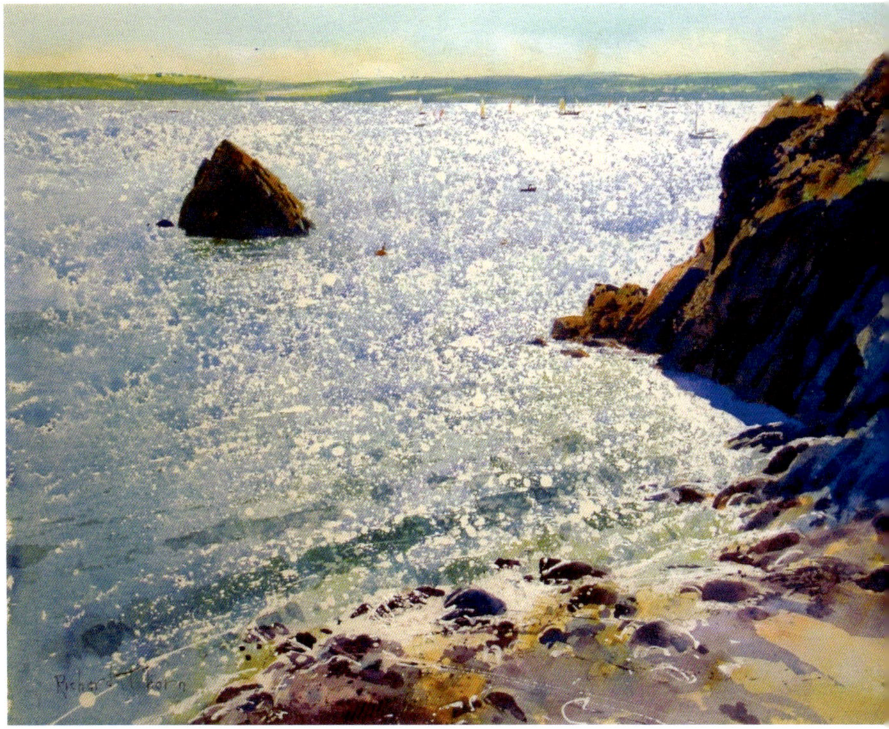

Richard Thorn. *In the Faltering Light*
Watercolour 17x19in (43x48cm)

the rivers and countryside around his home have been a major influence on his work. He began drawing at an early age and then trained at Newton Abbot School of Art. Early influences soon emerged from studying the paintings of the American masters such as Andrew Wyeth, Winslow Homer and Philip Jameson. Richard's style owes much to these contemporary exponents of the watercolour medium. His penchant for rich colour and strong light, especially the play of sun-dappled light on water, has helped to make his work instantly recognisable. His paintings evoke a strong sense of atmosphere as well as a sensitivity for the subject that is equally endearing.

For **Michael Hill** it is Plymouth and its surrounding coastline that captivates him. This is probably not surprising, as he was born in the city and has lived and worked there all his life. He now lives near The Barbican, an area rich in character and maritime history. It is a place that

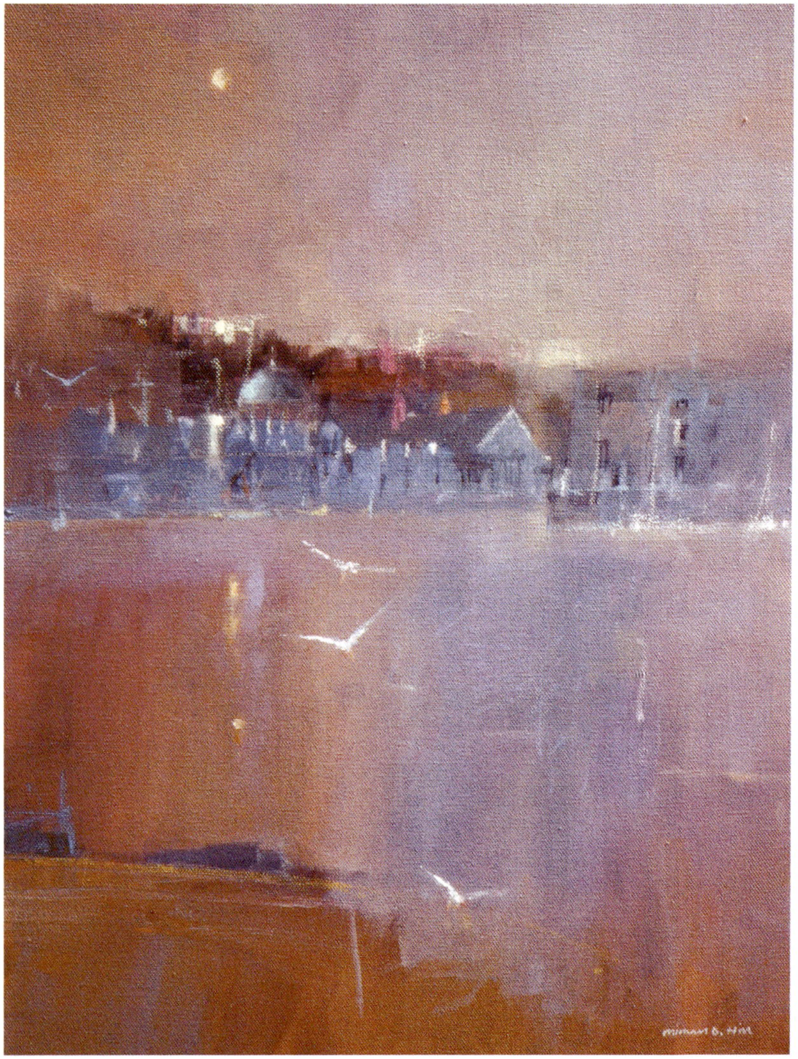

Michael Hill. *Reflections*
Acrylic 19.5x16in (50x41cm)

has fascinated him from the age of five. He says, 'My earliest memories of The Barbican are from an upstairs window in my grandparents house. They lived in the North Hill area of Plymouth, which rises steeply above Sutton Harbour. I remember a heavy old pair of binoculars, these I would hold as long as I could pressed against the window pane catching a glimpse of a new and exciting world, shimmering water, fishing boats, high masts and coloured flags. The house was pulled down many years ago, but I still carry the memory of the harbour like a painting in the window frame.' The fascination is as strong as ever and these colourful images manifest themselves in his paintings. Michael studied graphics at Plymouth College of Art and Design and then worked as a freelance illustrator. He says: 'On leaving college I decided to try watercolour as a medium and like most beginners I felt the need to describe every detail in the landscape. It's now my aim to give a simpler impression of the scene; less is more of course.'

Like many other artists, the greatest influence on him has been the work of J.M.W. Turner. 'Seeing an exhibition of Turner's paintings made during the tours of the South West in the City of Plymouth Art Gallery really confirmed this. His fearless approach to painting was truly breathtaking and he pioneered the way for the rest of us mere mortals to follow.' Michael works more now in acrylic and mixed media, but he still does some painting in watercolour. 'I find the medium invaluable for working outside and in planning out a bigger piece of work. But it is the sketches done on location that provide me with the excitement and inspiration.'

Although **John Hammond, SWAc** lives and works in Wiltshire he is a regular visitor to the county. He feels that he has adopted Devon as his second home and says: 'I hold fond memories of childhood family holidays on the North and South coast, and those long days playing on the sand and in the sea are recalled in many of my summer beach paintings.' He also has strong family ties in East Devon as well as having strong professional links, being an active member of the South West Academy since 2002.

John was born in Woodford Green and trained at Wimbledon Art College and Bath Academy of Art. His inspiration to paint comes from an emotional response to the visual world. Subject matters are not so much sought but found; landscapes, seascapes, cityscapes and interiors encountered on his travels are embraced with equal enthusiasm. These seemingly disparate themes are for him united by his desire to understand, distil and convey their unique quality of light and atmosphere, with the aim of creating for the viewer an environment as compelling and absorbing as his own first hand experience. John works almost exclusively in acrylics that allow him to paint quickly, building up layers of

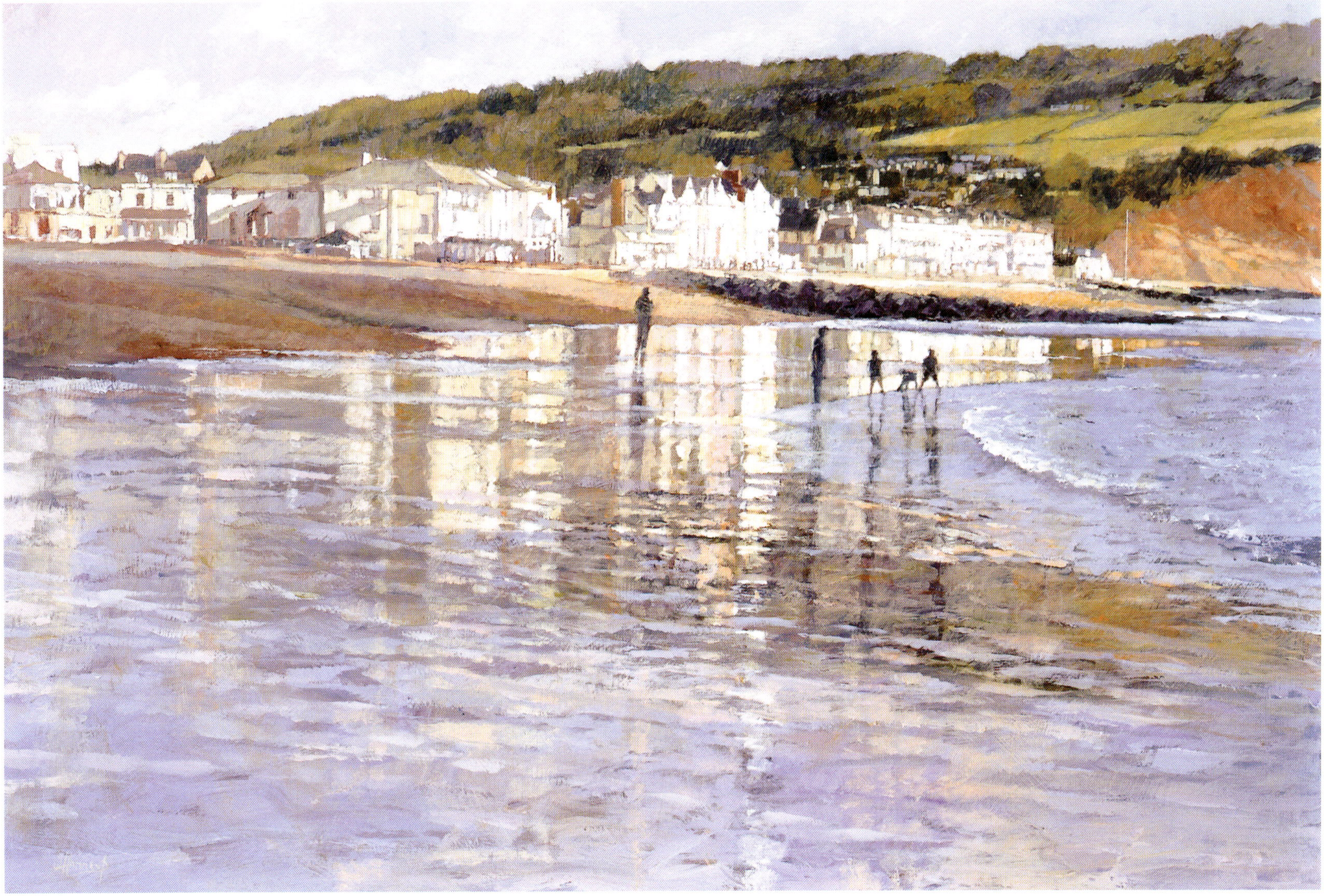

John Hammond. *Low Tide Walk*
Acrylic 24x36in (61x91cm)

the richest impasto work interlaced with the subtlest of glazes. Small works are often painted *en plein air*, while larger studio pieces are developed from sketches and written notes. He has always thought of himself as an impressionist at heart and although the painting methods differ in some ways from the true impressionist technique, he does share the love of mark making, desire for an immediate and personal response to a subject, and the wish to capture the atmosphere and physical ambiance of an environment. He says: I believe painting is about communication and if my work evokes the same excitement in the viewer as I felt at the outset then I know I have succeeded.'

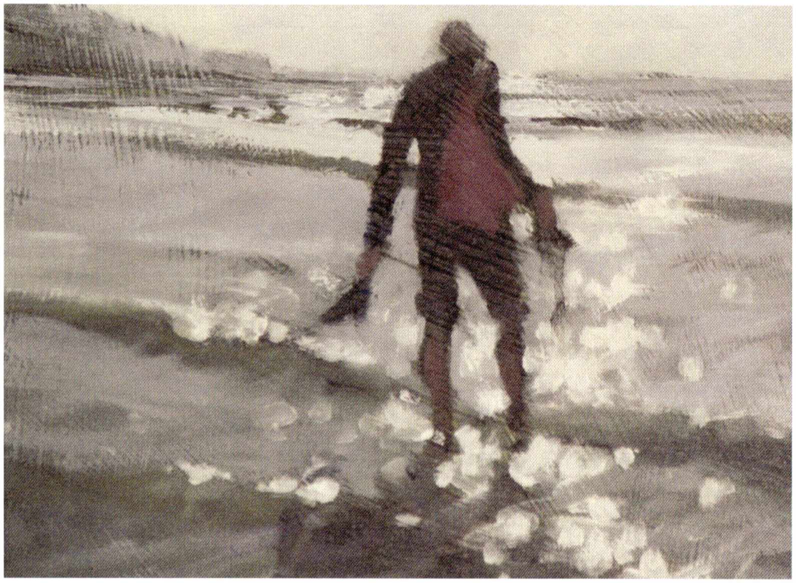

Tony Williams. *Paddling at Westward Ho!*
Oil 6x8in (15x20cm)

Below: Judy Hempstead. *From Prawle Point to Bolt Head*
Mixed Media 10.5x 38.5in (27x98cm)

Having spent my formative years only a stone's throw away from the red sandstone cliffs that lie between Dawlish and Dawlish Warren, it is perhaps not surprising that the coastline forms the inspiration for the majority of my work. These paintings typify my absorption with the way in which natural forces have shaped, coloured and textured cliff faces over thousands of years. The sea mists, which often swathe the coastline, add mystery and emphasise the flowing lines of the topography.

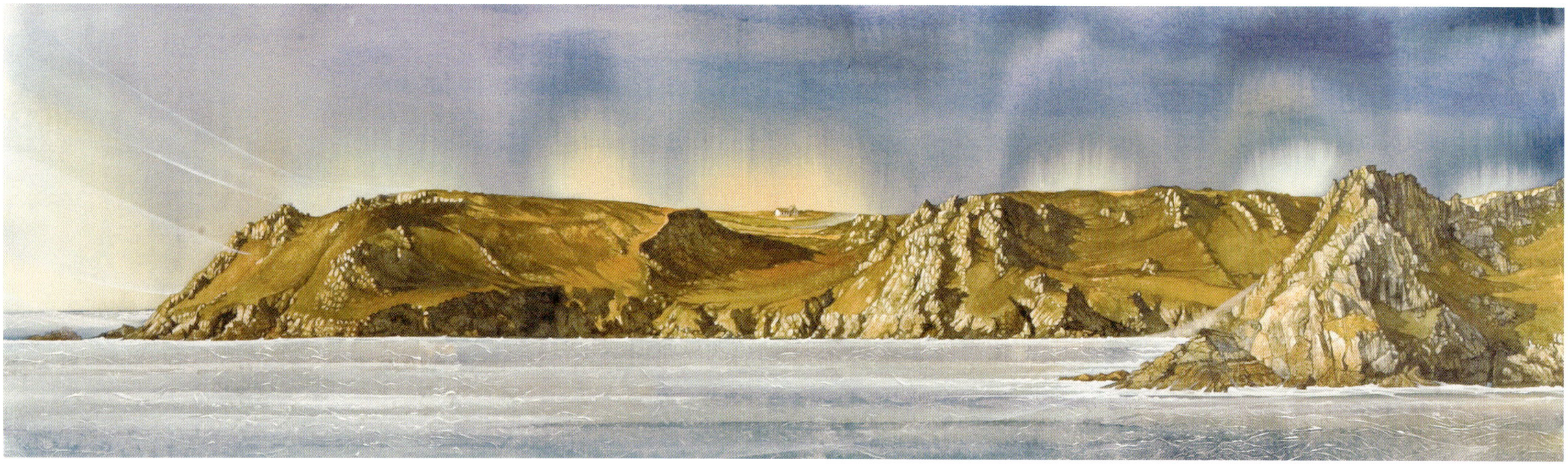

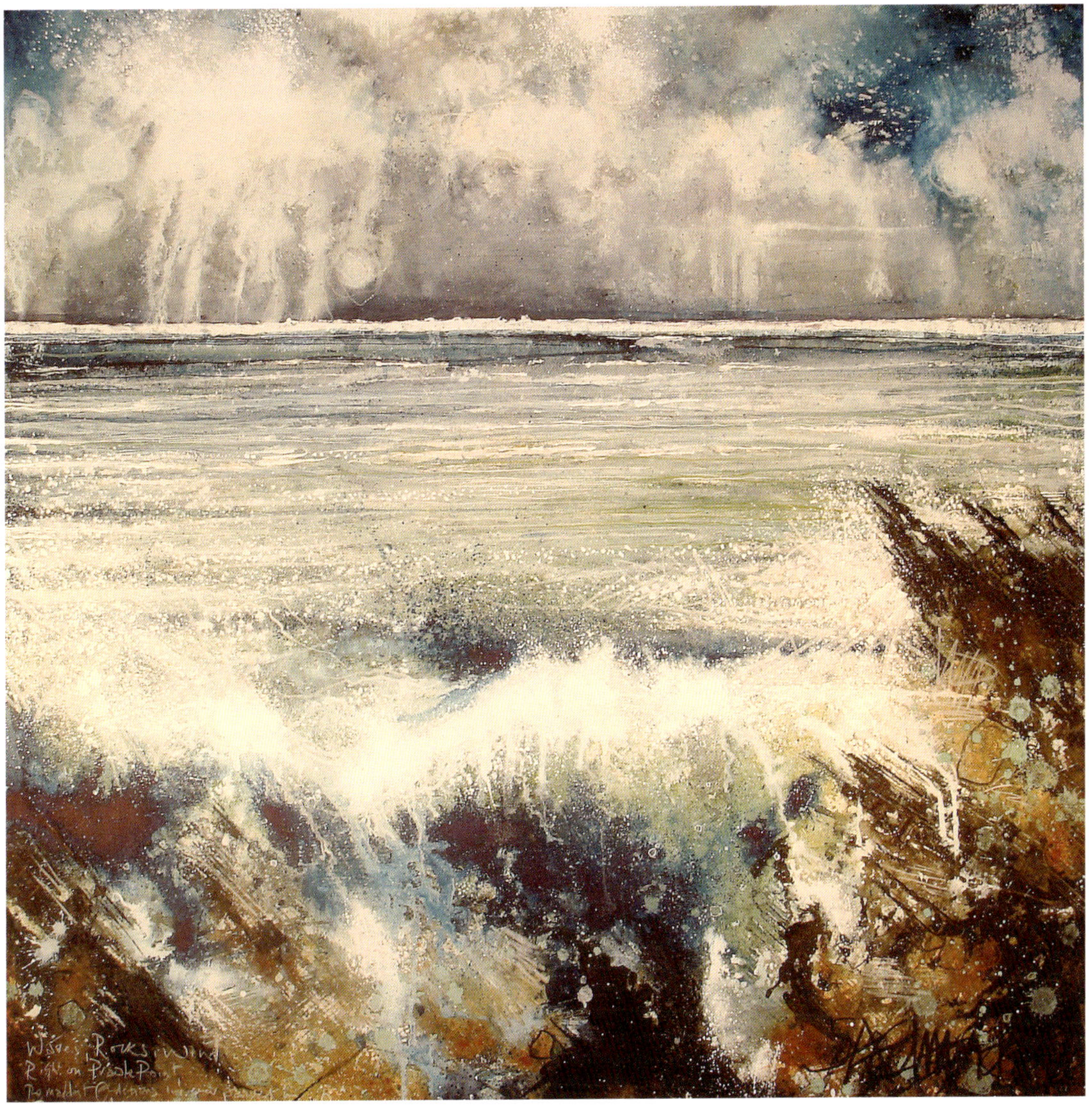

Stewart Edmondson. *Waves, Rocks, Strong Winds – East Prawle*
Mixed Media 31x31in (80x80cm)

This painting was done just before a fierce storm hit, the tide was coming in and large waves whipped up by the wind were crashing on to the rocks – it's just so exhilarating being down amongst the breaking waves. The wind ripped my painting board out of my hands and flung it across the rocks, spreading paint pots and brushes all over the place.

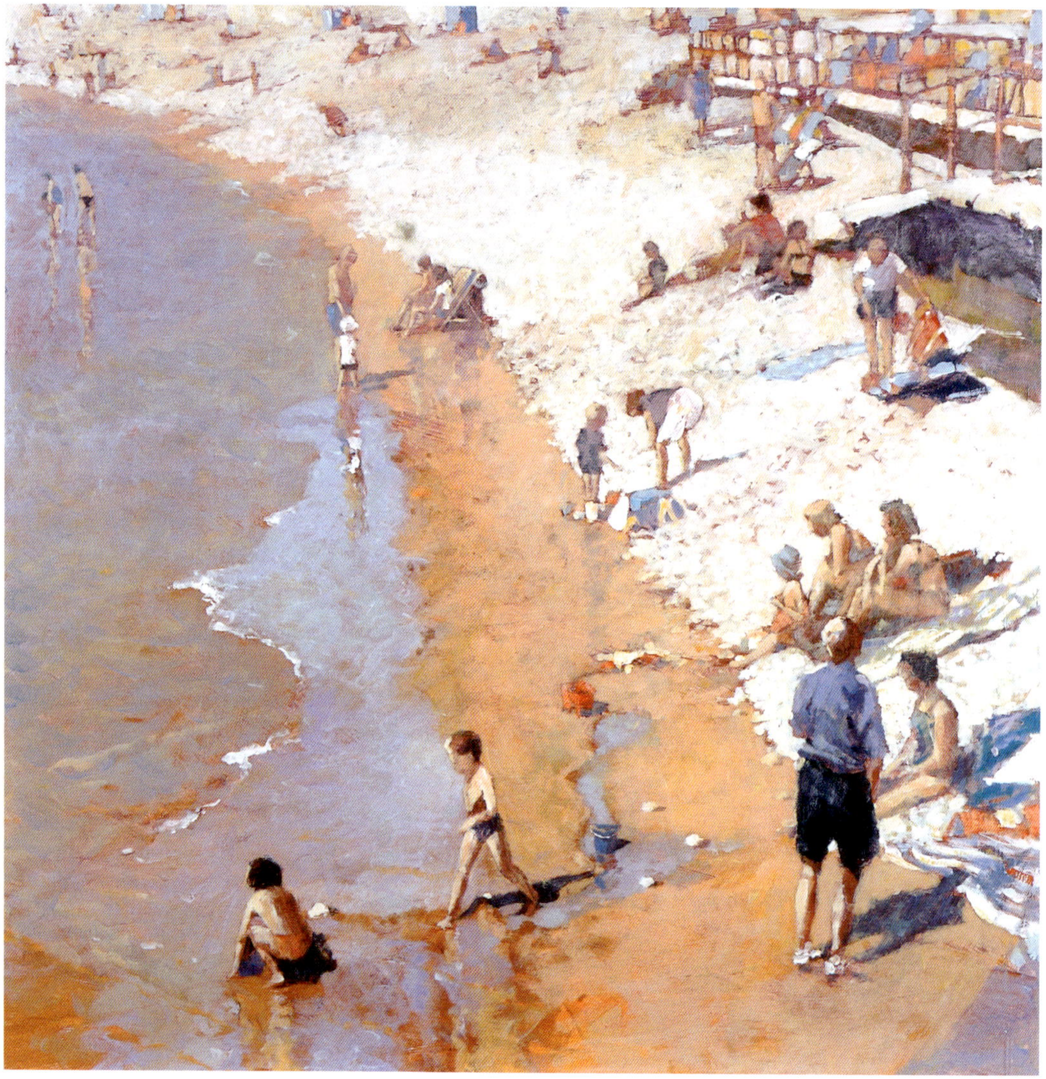

John Hammond. *Shoreline, Sidmouth*
Acrylic 24x24in (61x61cm)

This is definitely a painting that brings back strong memories of childhood holidays. I was fascinated by this vertical composition with its contrasting bands of stones, sand and water, punctuated by the staccato notes of figures at play.

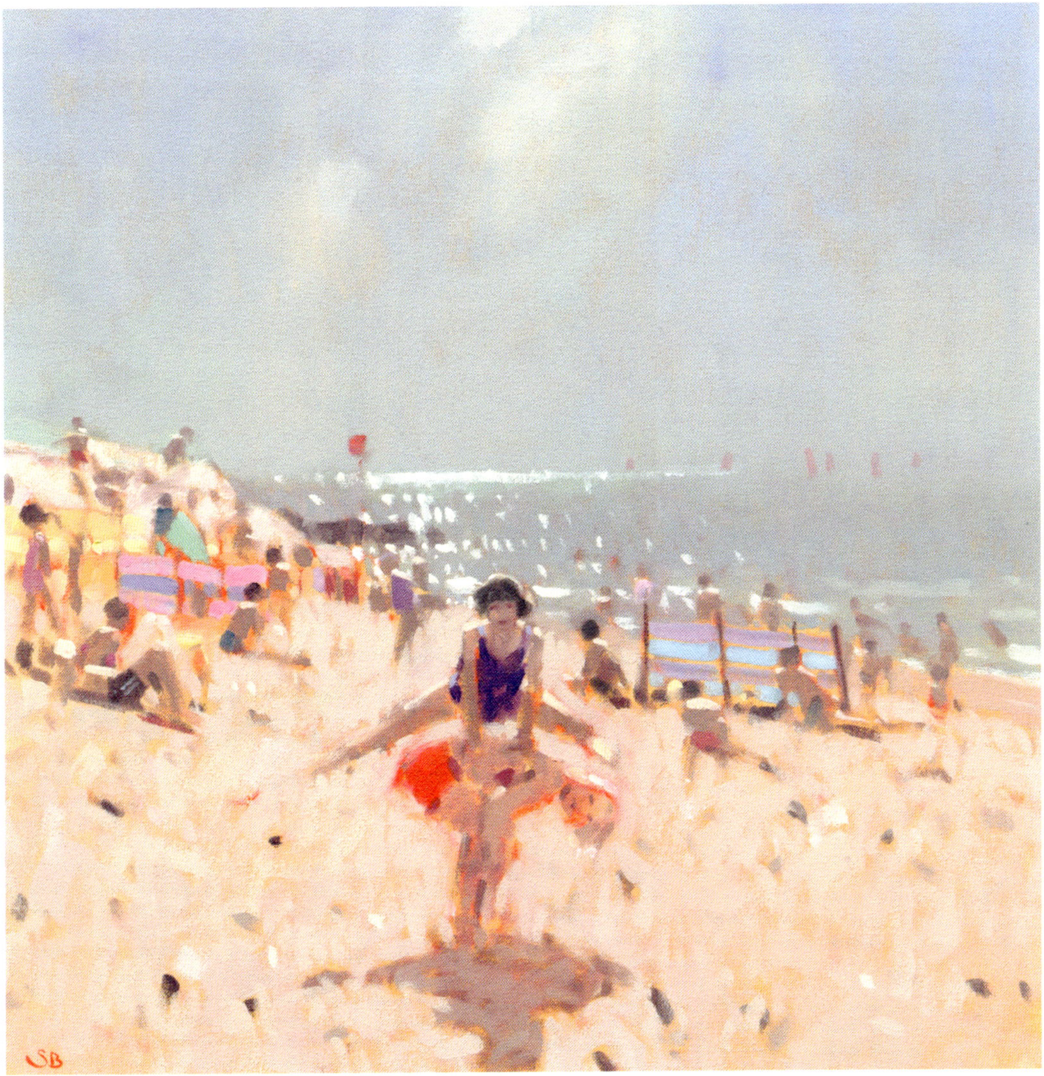

Stephen Brown. *Leapfrog, Sidmouth*
Oil 16x16in (40x40cm)

Sidmouth beach on a warm sunny day takes some beating! No camera this time, so a very quick sketch in pencil, with one or two colour notes, of these children playing leapfrog, gave me enough information to paint this canvas.

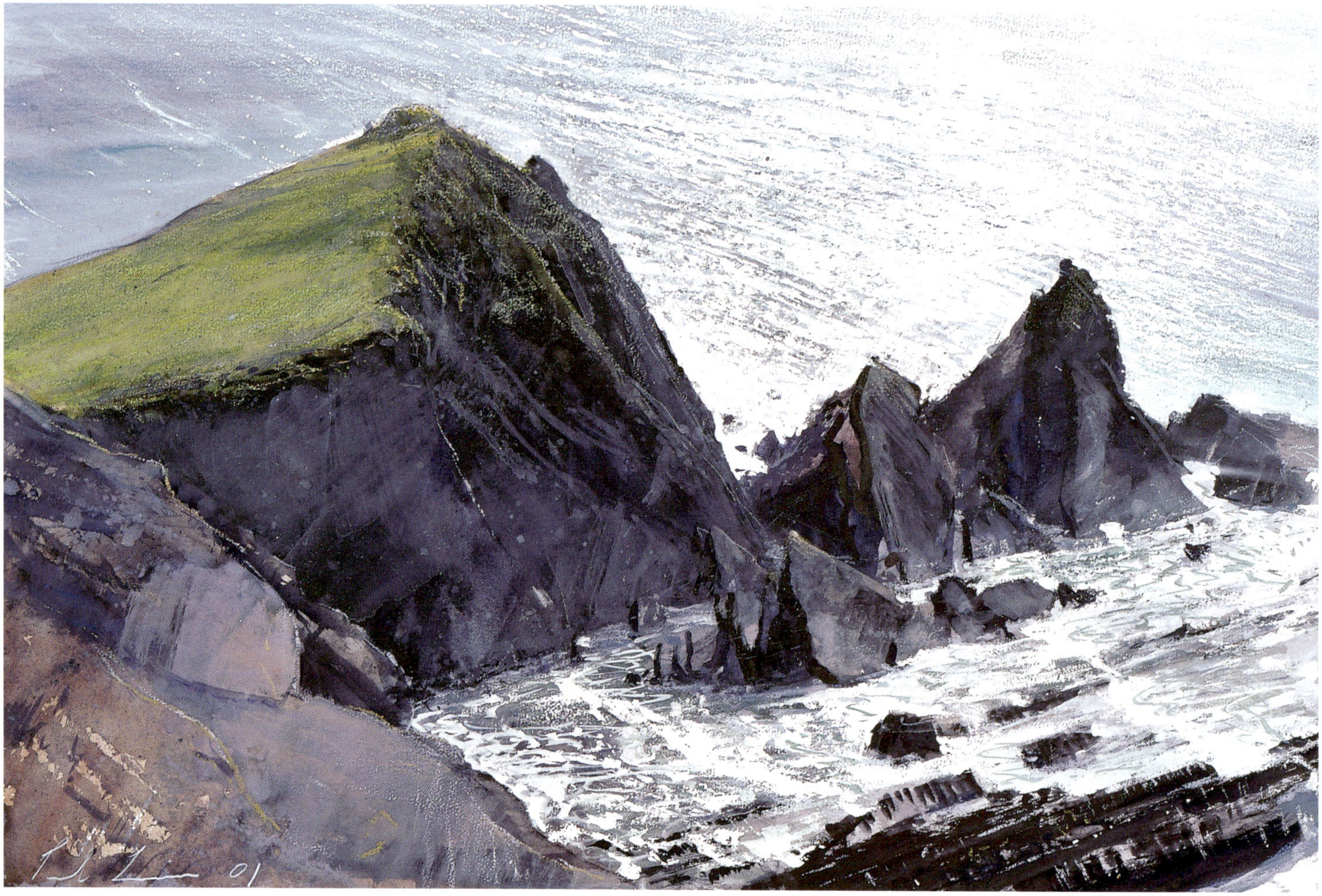

Paul Lewin. *Screda Point into the Sun*
Mixed Media 33.5x39in (85x99cm)

These rock formations are unmistakably North Devon and Screda Point near Hartland Point is perhaps the best example of this dramatic geological folding and erosion.

Opposite: John Hammond. *Silver Sand, Sidmouth*
Acrylic 24x28in (61x72cm)

There is a wonderful contradiction in the subject of this painting between the underlying permanence and stability of the rock formations and the transitory nature of the light catching the water, the wet sand highlighting the figure walking his dog among the gulls.

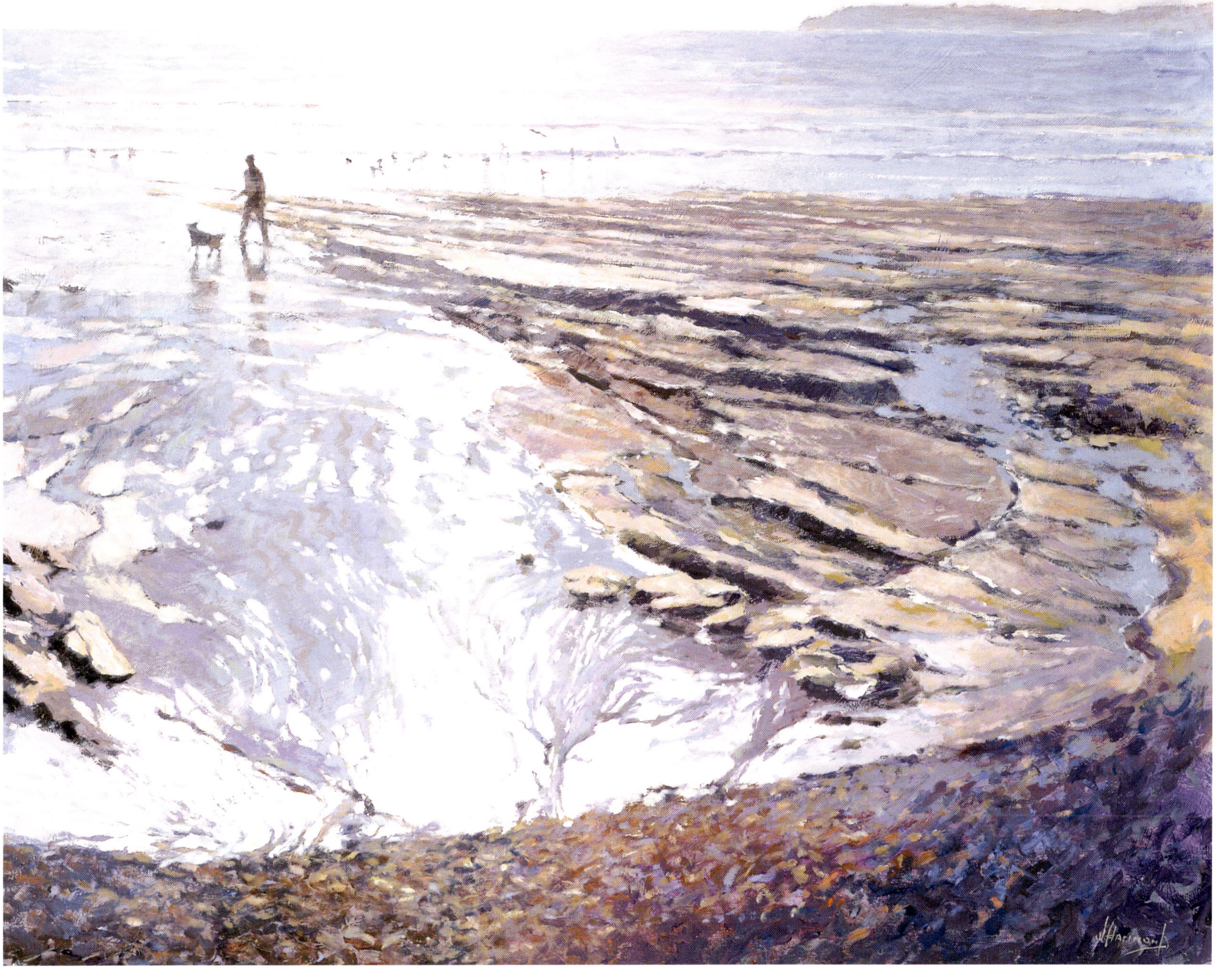

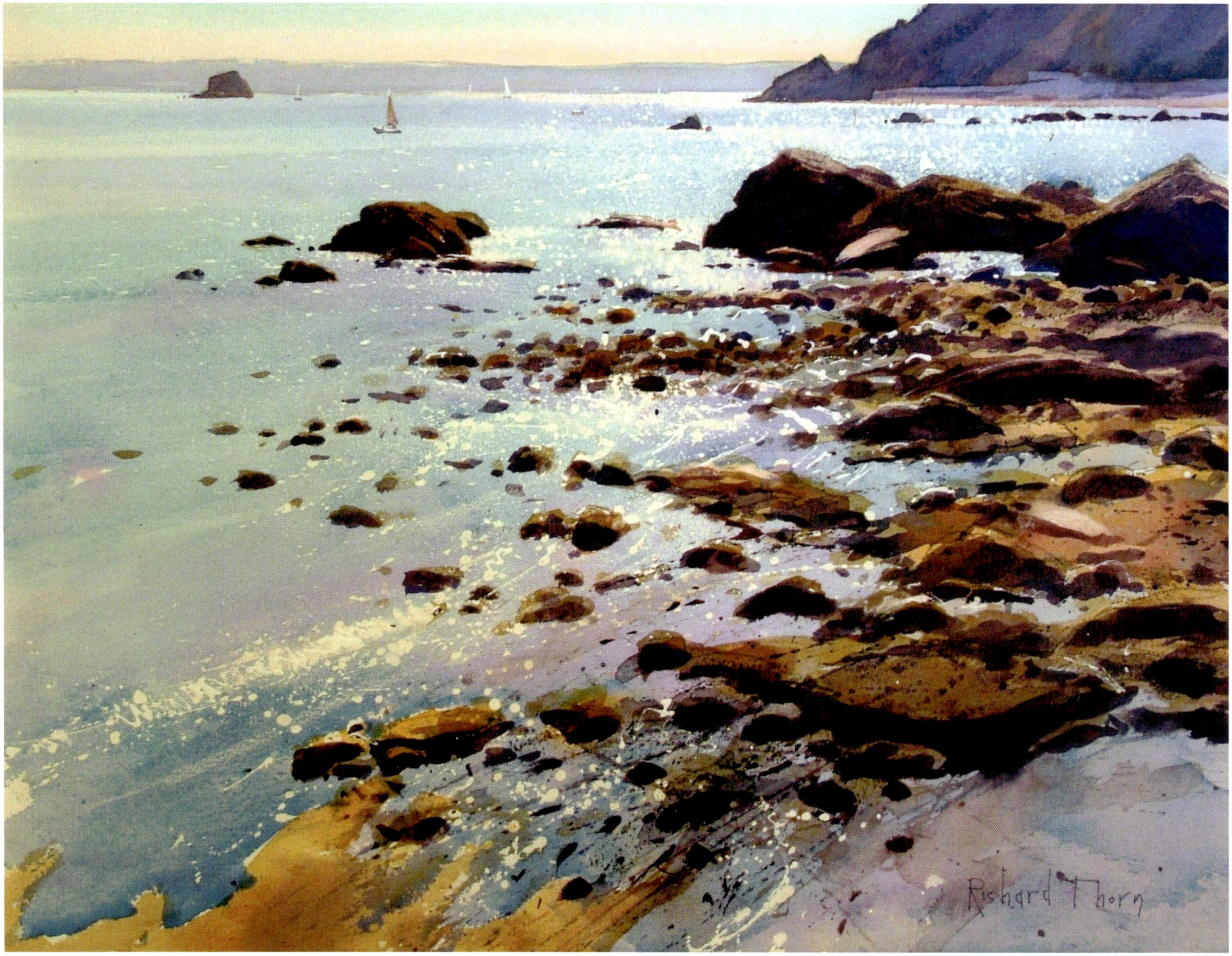

Richard Thorn. *The Sun Went Down, The Tide Went Out and The People Went Home*
Watercolour 20x23in (51x58cm)

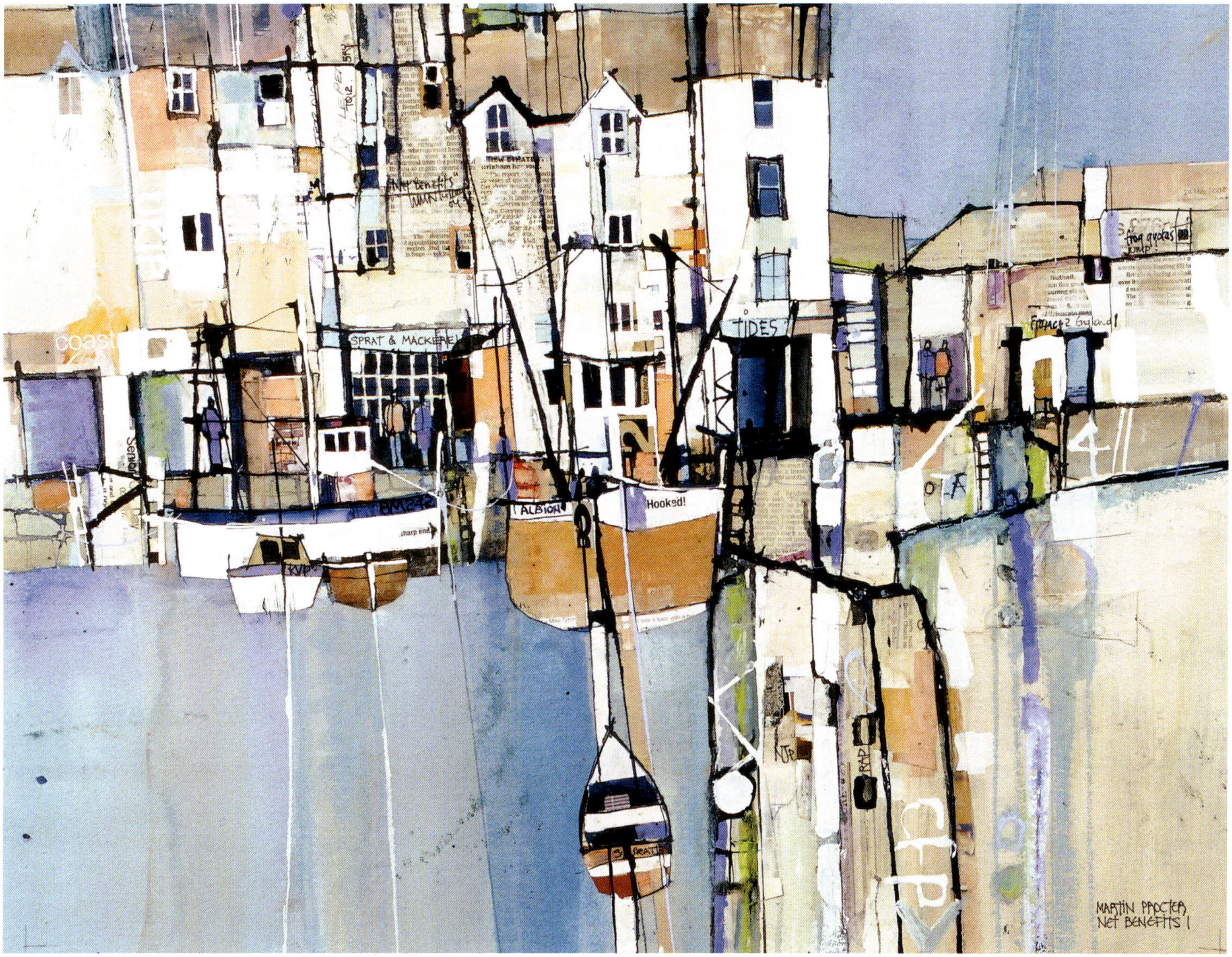

Martin Procter. *Net Benefits 1*
Mixed Media 20x24in (50x61cm)

Part of a set of paintings about the fishing industry, this is based on Brixham and there are some obvious references to establish the location of the issues. Fishing has become a political 'football' within Europe and I used collage cut-outs from newspaper articles to make some sardonic comments on the contradictions of the supposed benefits of quotas and tie-up days; amongst the bits of text.

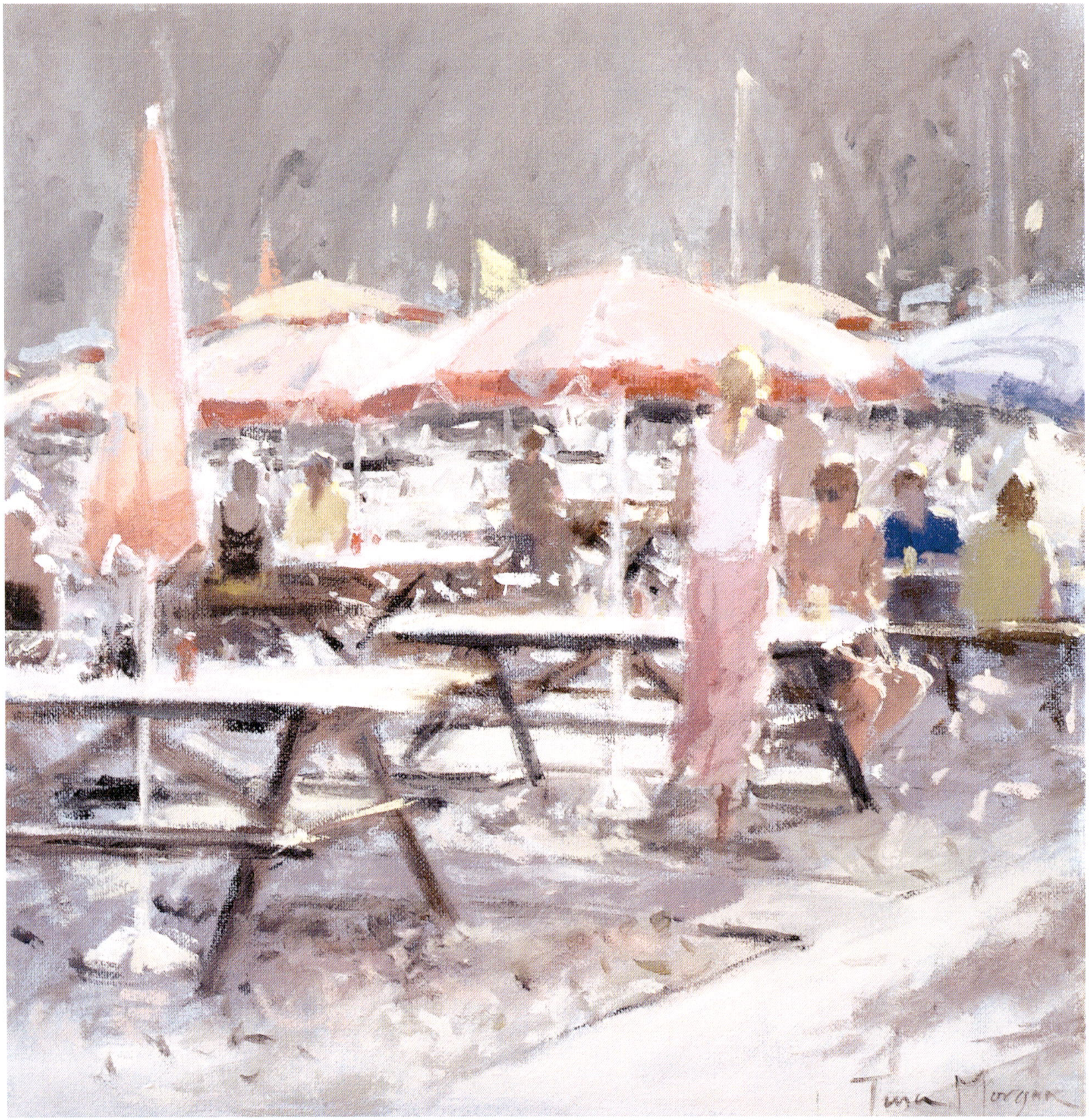

Tina Morgan. *Pink Skirt, Beer*
Oil 12x12in (30x30cm)

The beach at Beer has a very unique atmosphere with its walkways over the pebbles, cafes, benches and striped deckchairs. I could spend a lifetime painting it.

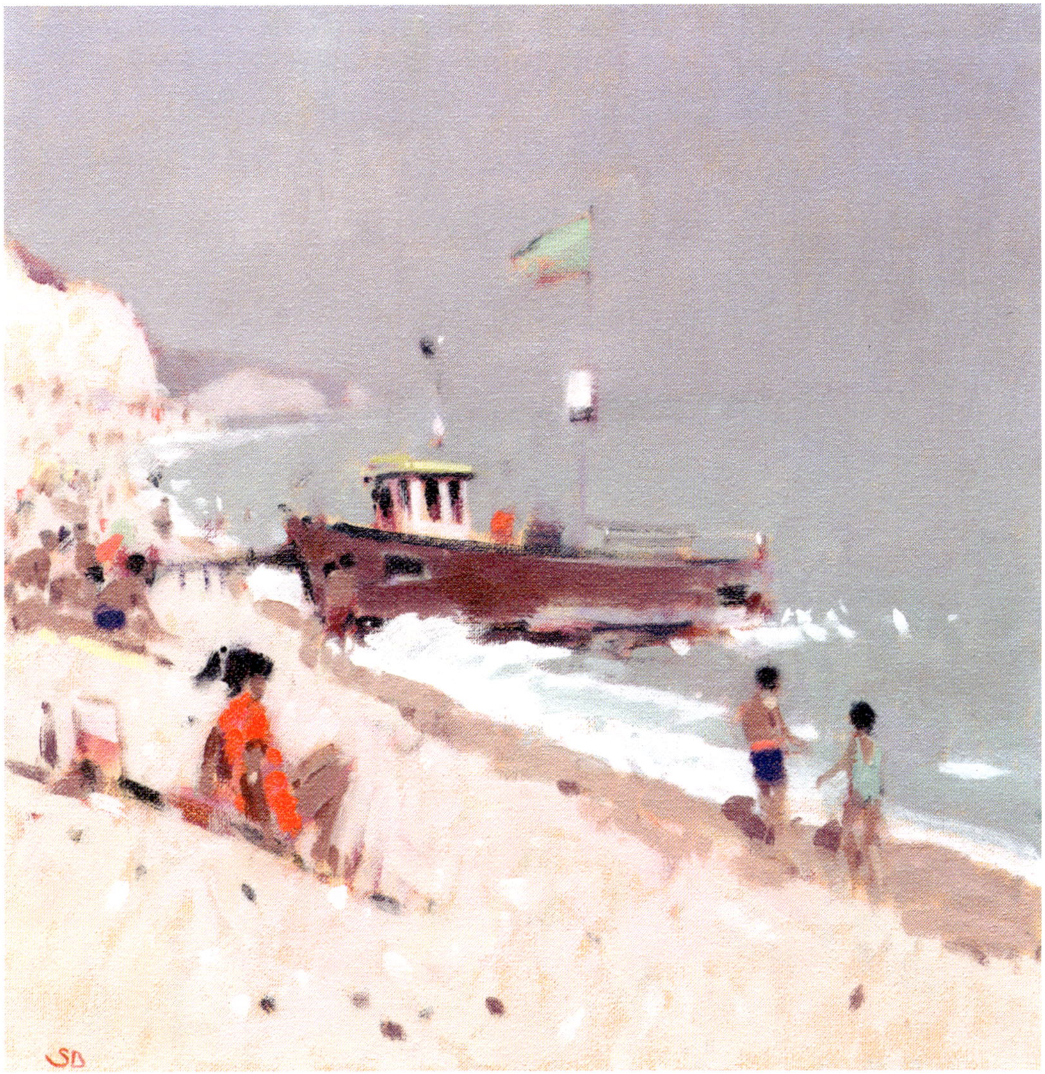

Stephen Brown. *The Mackerel Boat, Beer*
Oil 12x12in (30x30cm)

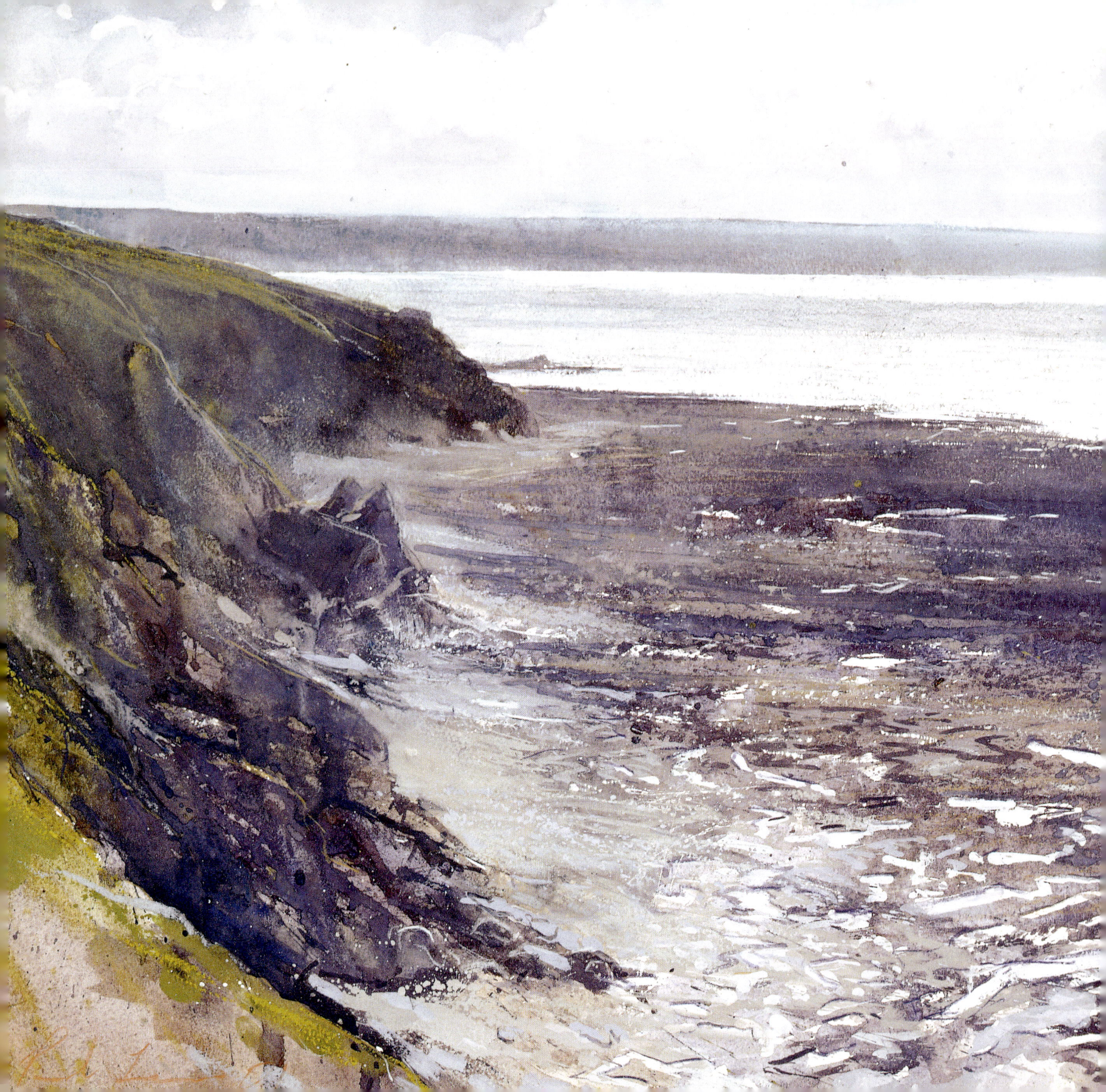

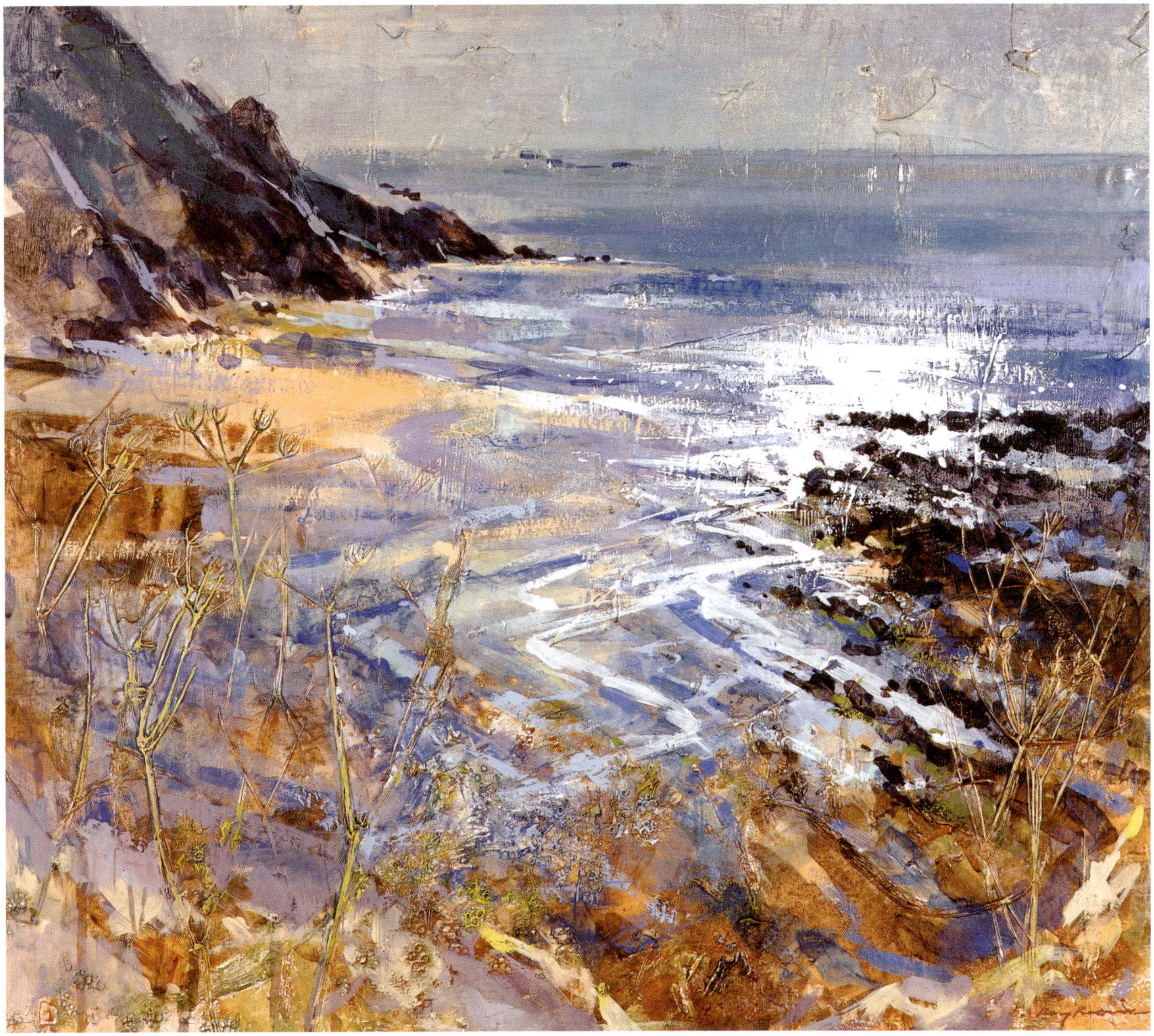

Ray Balkwill. *Silver Sea, Hope Cove*
Mixed Media 17.5x20in (44x51cm)

Paul Lewin. *Cornborough Cliffs Looking South*
Mixed Media 17.5x20.5in (45x52cm)

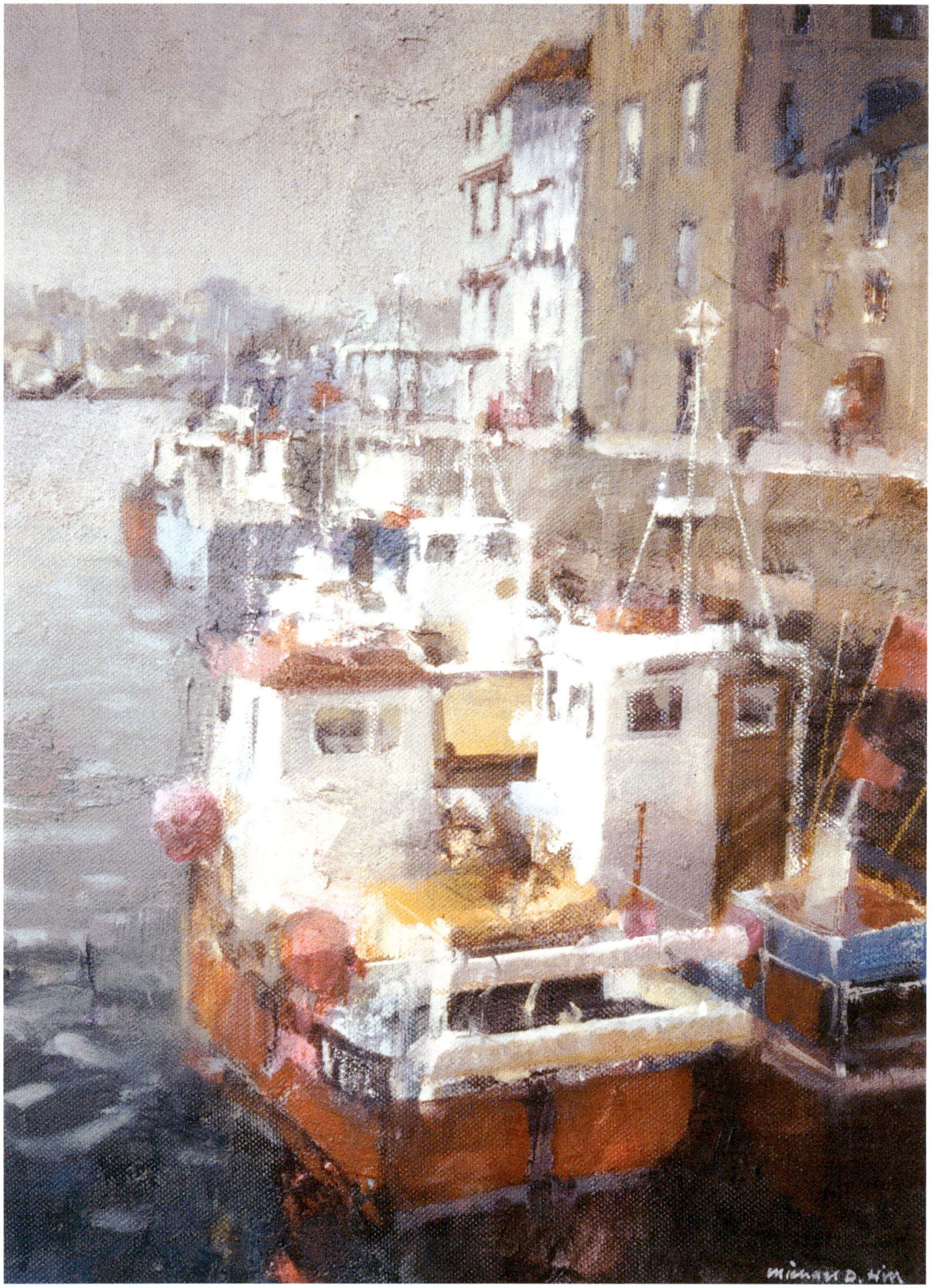

Michael Hill. *Quay Road, The Barbican, Plymouth*
Acrylic 15.5x12in (40x30cm)

Opposite page:
Alan Cotton. *Hartland – Dramatic Coastline in Silver Light*
Oil 28x36in (71x91cm)

I discovered something special in Hartland. The dramatic ruggedness of it for instance, its fingers of rock going out into the sea and its great cathedral-like structures. Looking into strong light, so dazzling that you can hardly see it. The shapes are so dark and rich and the tonal contrast is mind-blowingly dramatic.

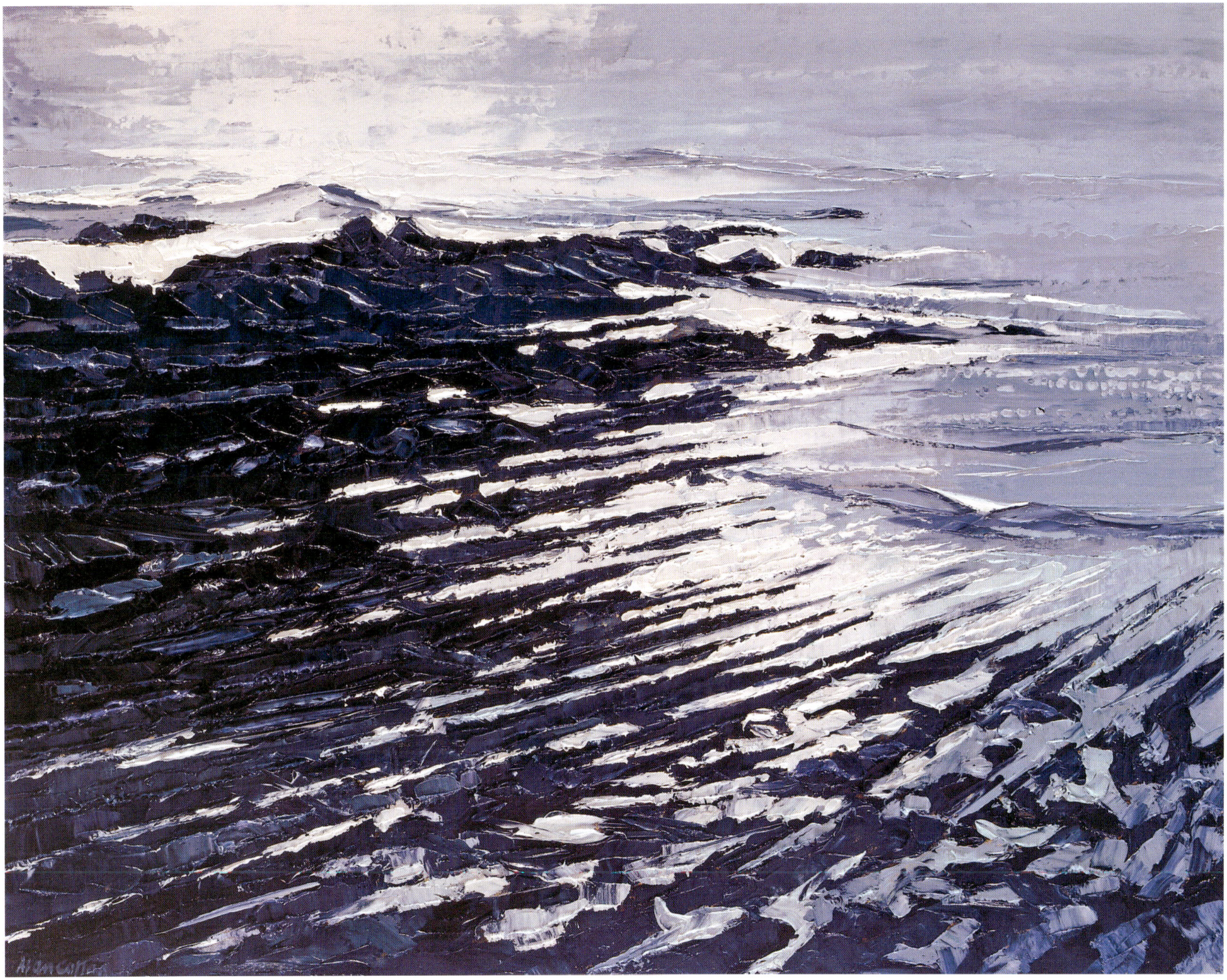

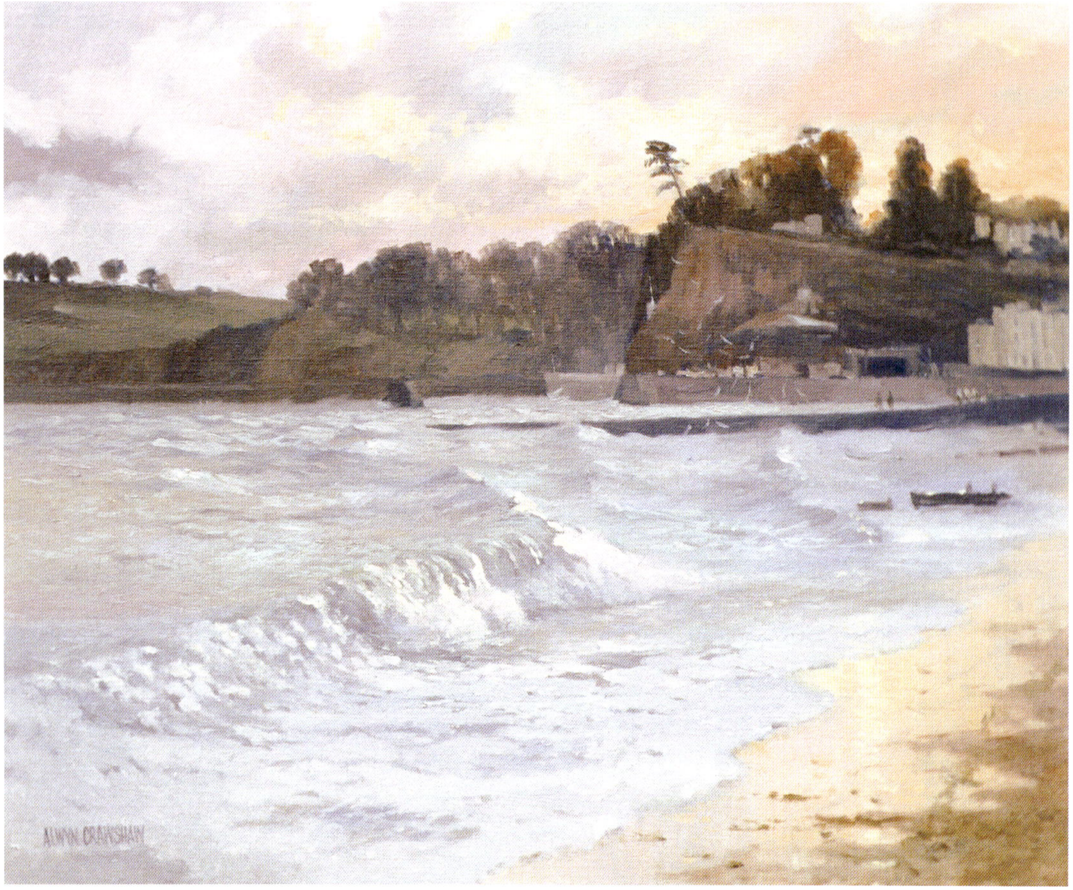

Alwyn Crawshaw. *Dawlish Beach*
Oil 16x20in (41x51cm)

Judy Hempstead. *After the Storm, Start Point*
Mixed Media 7.5x30in (19x76cm)

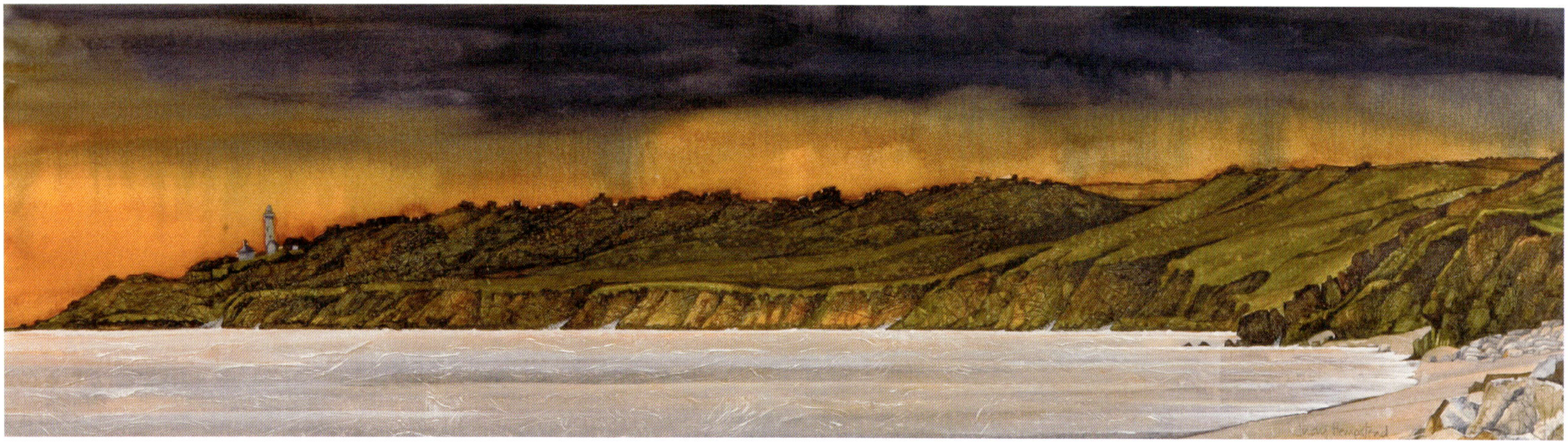

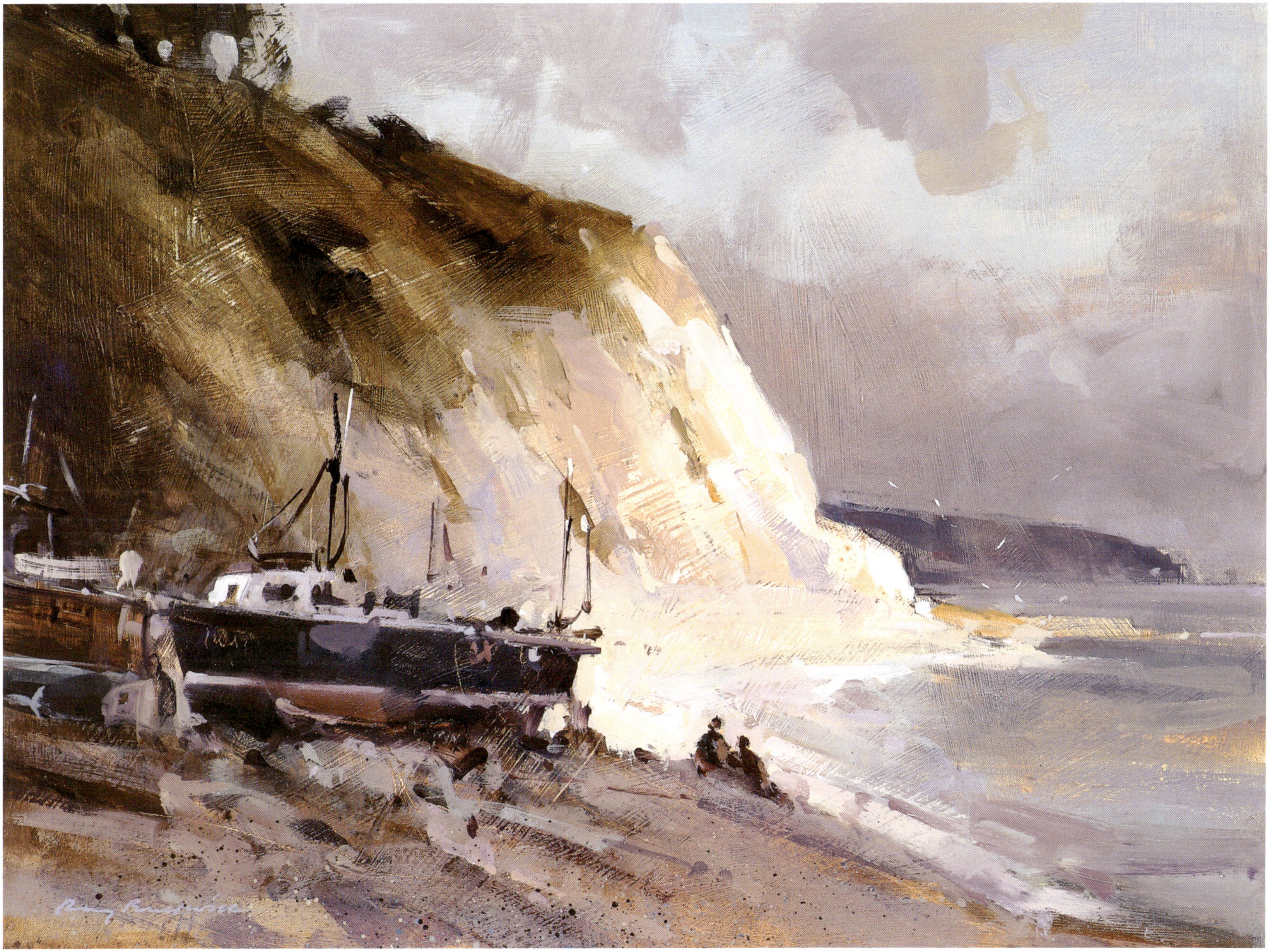

Ray Balkwill. *Sun and Shade, Beer*
Oil 10x14in (25x36cm)

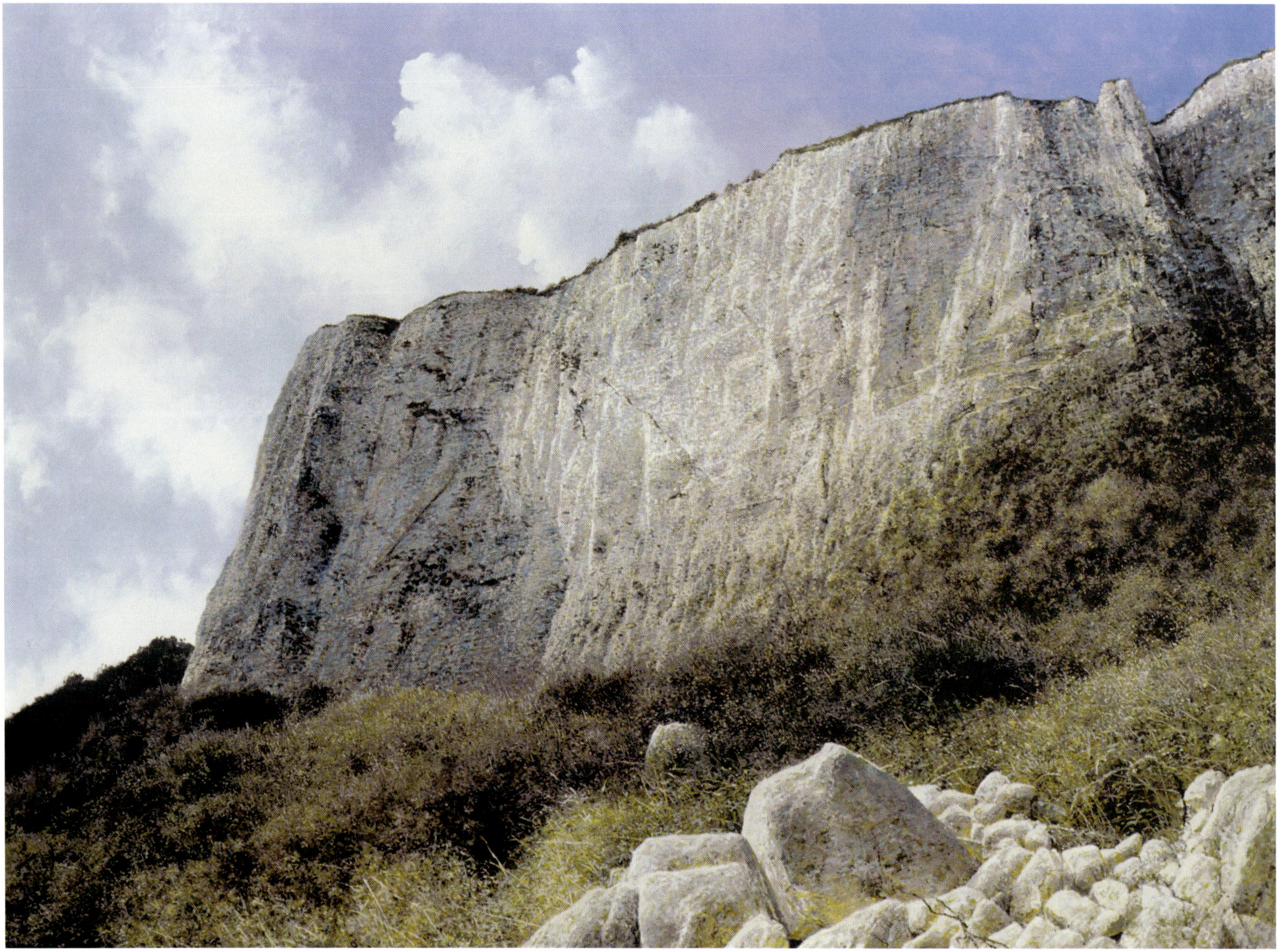

Andrew Coates. *Cliffs between Seaton and Beer*
Oil 26x36in (61x91cm)

I love our piece of Devon coastline. The colour and textures are like nothing else seen in the British Isles. There is a softness in colour and a vulnerability to our cliffs and coastline that makes it very special. The cliffs are constantly being eroded to reveal life forms from a distant past, as our tenure on this earth lies precariously perched high on that very thin layer that meets the sky.

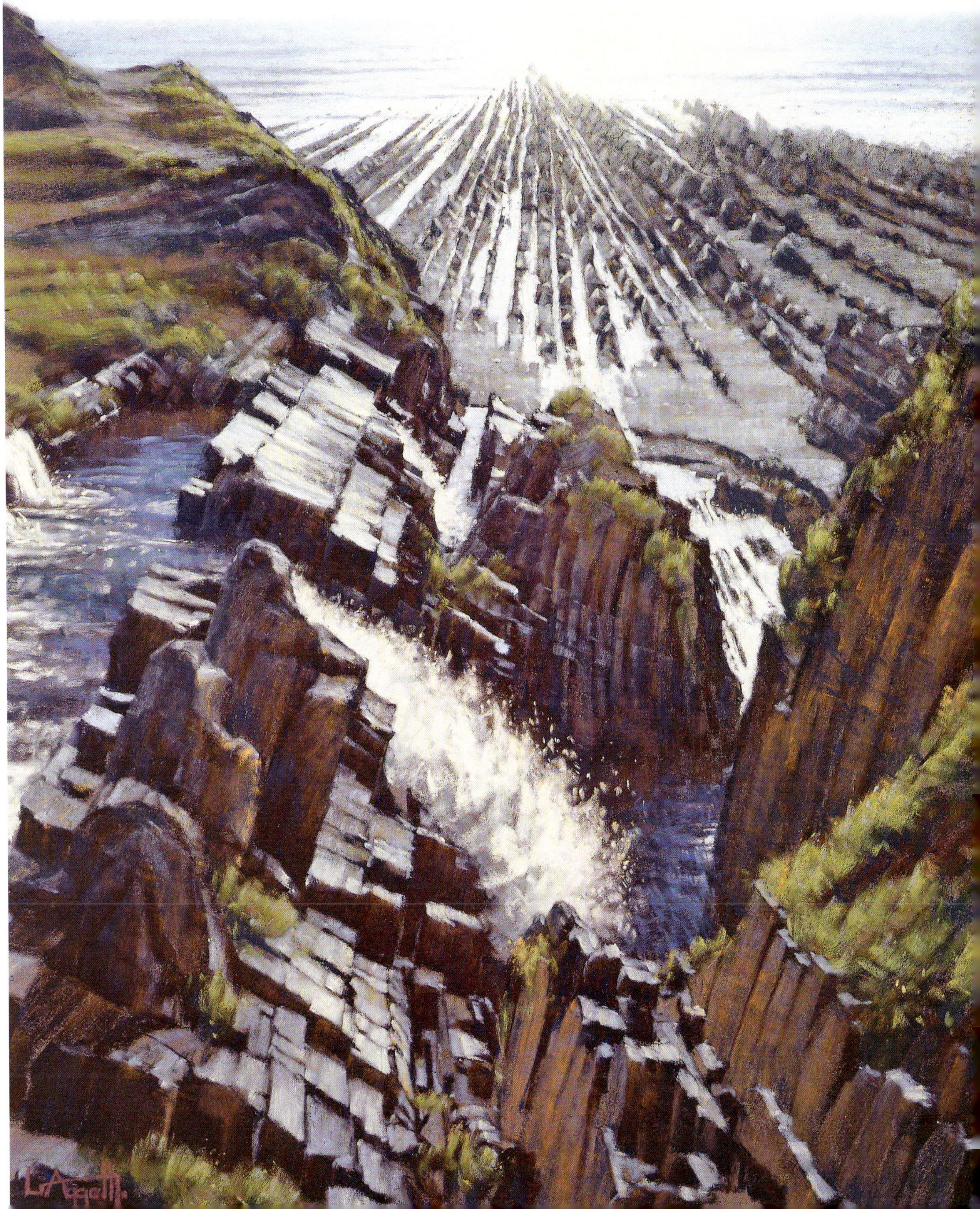

Lionel Aggett.
North Devon Coast, Nr Hartland
Pastel 26x20in (66x51cm)

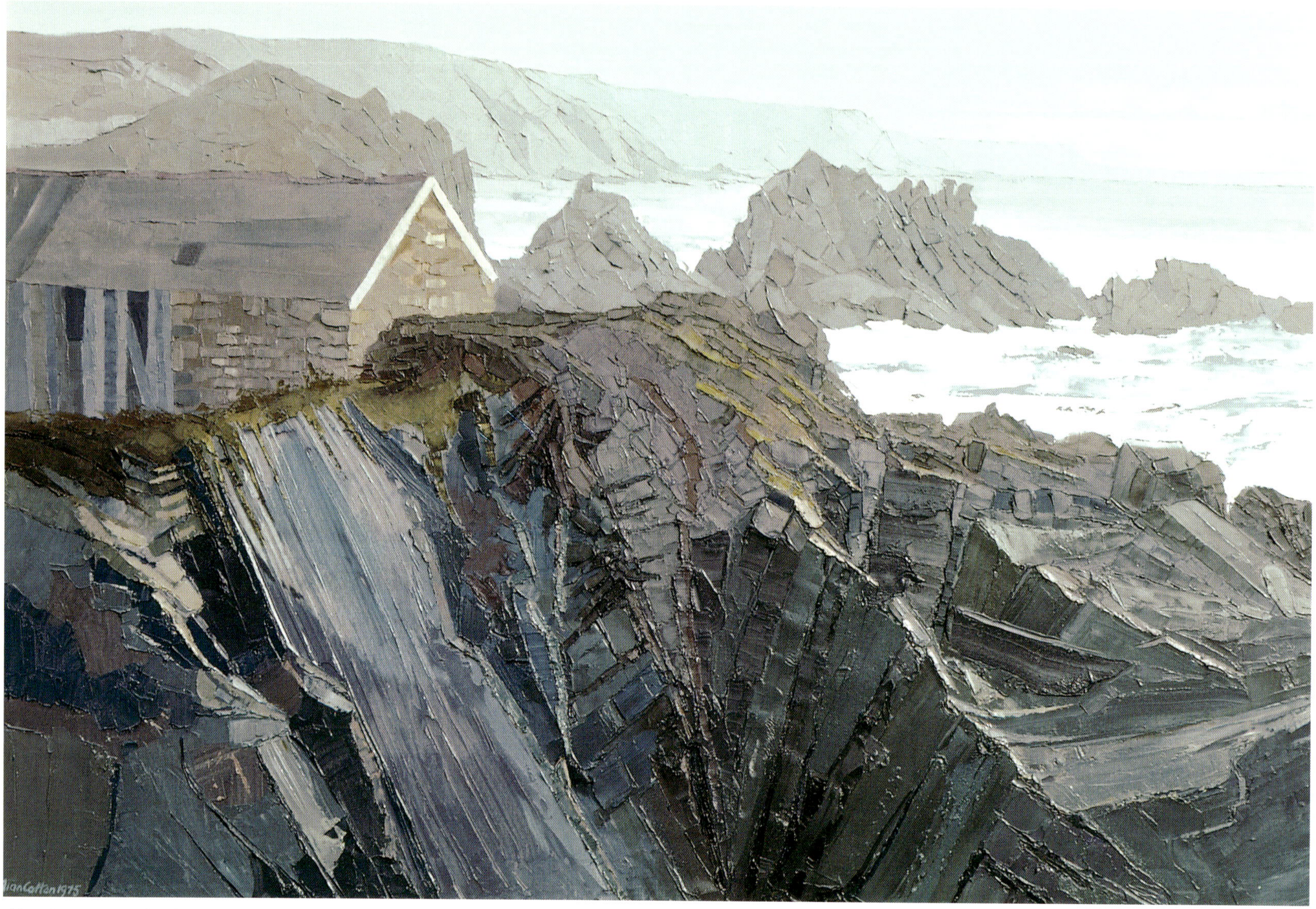

Alan Cotton. *Hartland Coastline*
Oil 40x60in (102x152cm)
Collection City of Plymouth Art Gallery

Somehow Hartland is so big, so powerful so dramatic. It demanded a huge kind of format, and I am at my best when I'm expanding, doing big physical paintings, where even the expression of using the paint is a physical act.

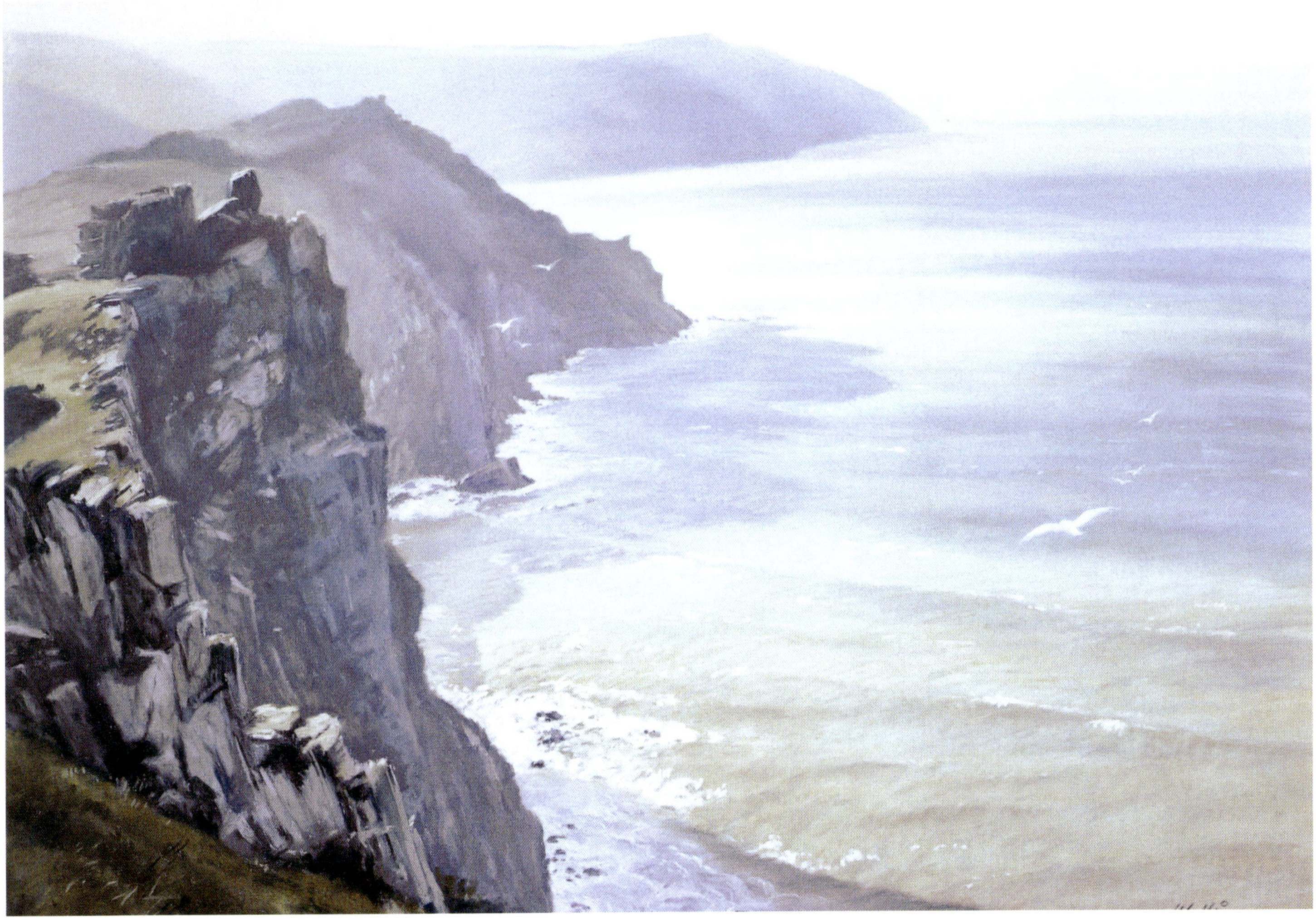

Barry Watkin. *Force 9, Valley of Rocks*
Pastel 25x30in (64x76cm)

Conditions were so frightening from my lofty (700ft) and precarious perch I was forced to retreat to safer ground. The painting was finally executed in the studio working from my shaky, sodden sketch and a photograph.

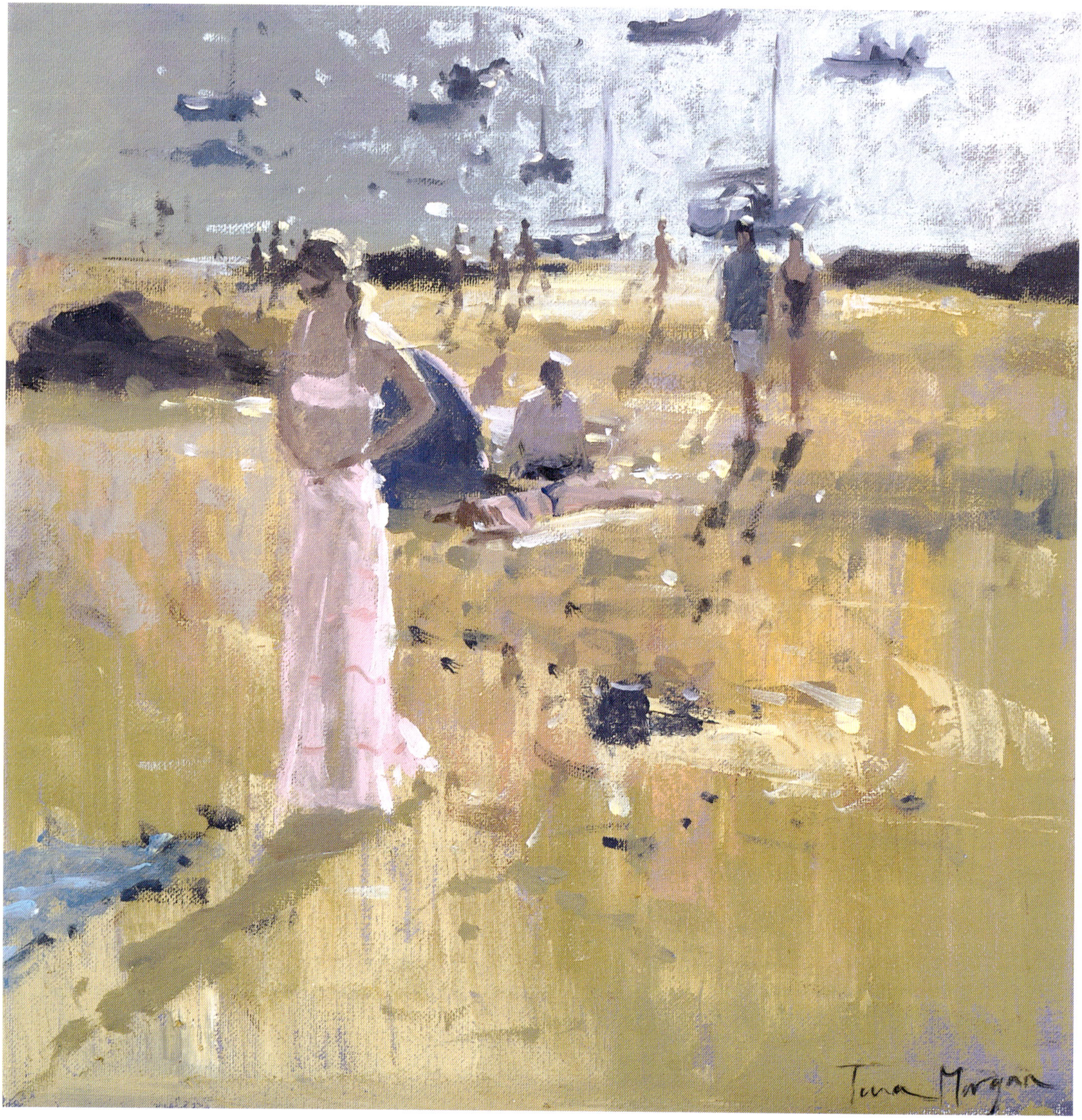

Tina Morgan.
Girl in a Sarong
Oil 12x12in (30x30cm)

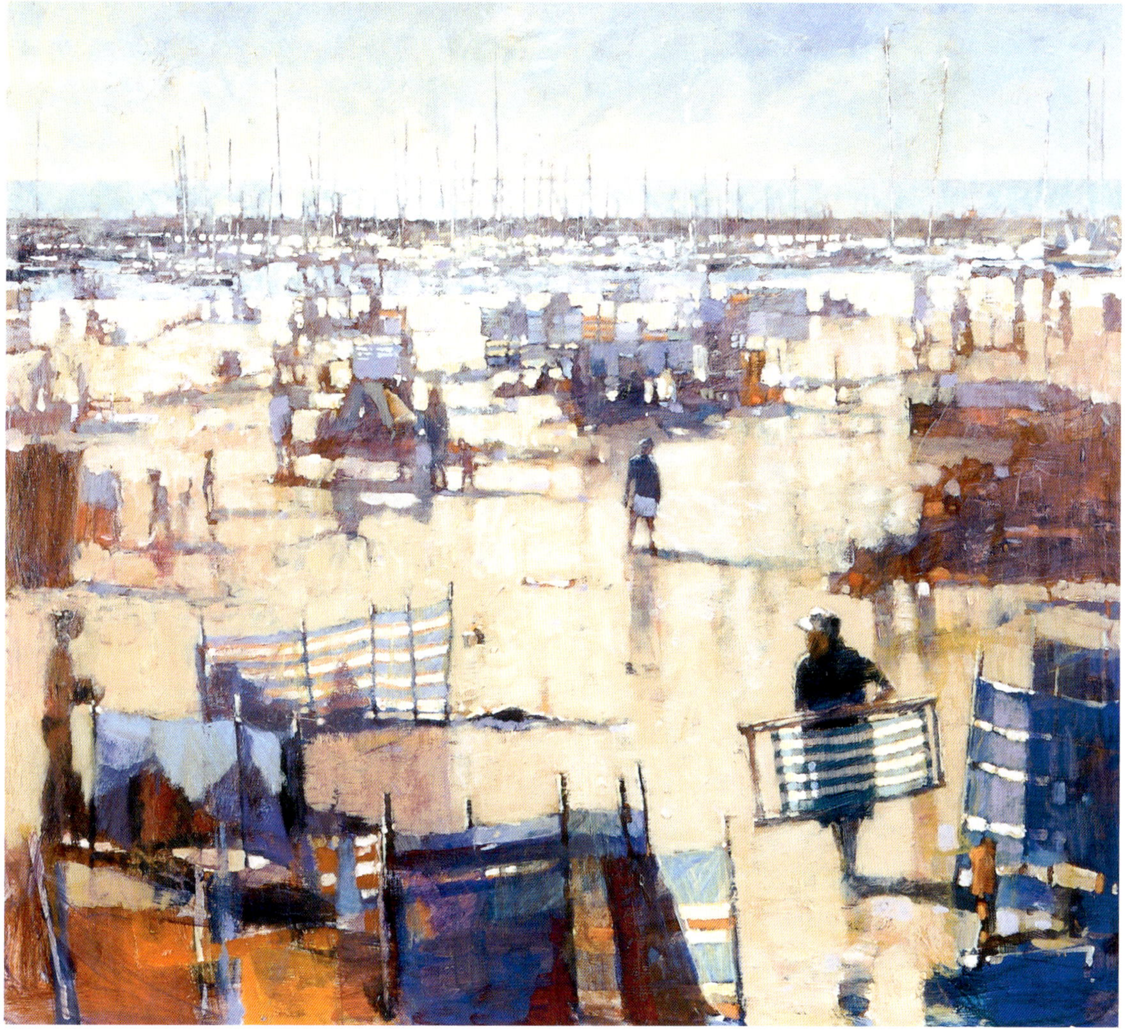

John Hammond. *Windbreaks*
Acrylic 36x31in (90x80cm)

Beach landscapes such as this offer such great opportunities to play with form, colour, light and shade. The sunlight shining through the deckchair being carried up the beach became the focal point for this painting.

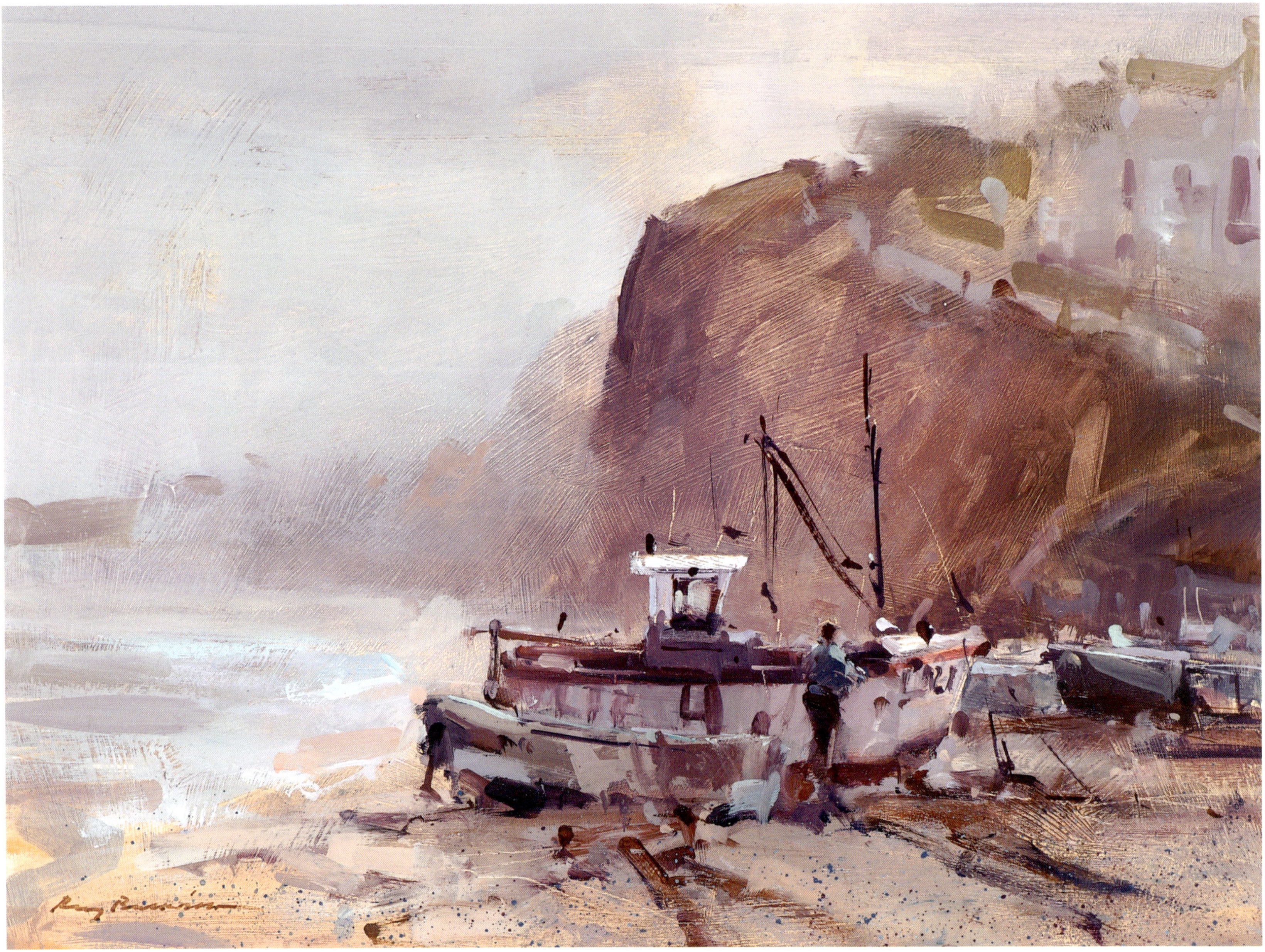

Ray Balkwill. *Rising Mist, Budleigh Salterton*
Oil 10x14in (25x36cm)

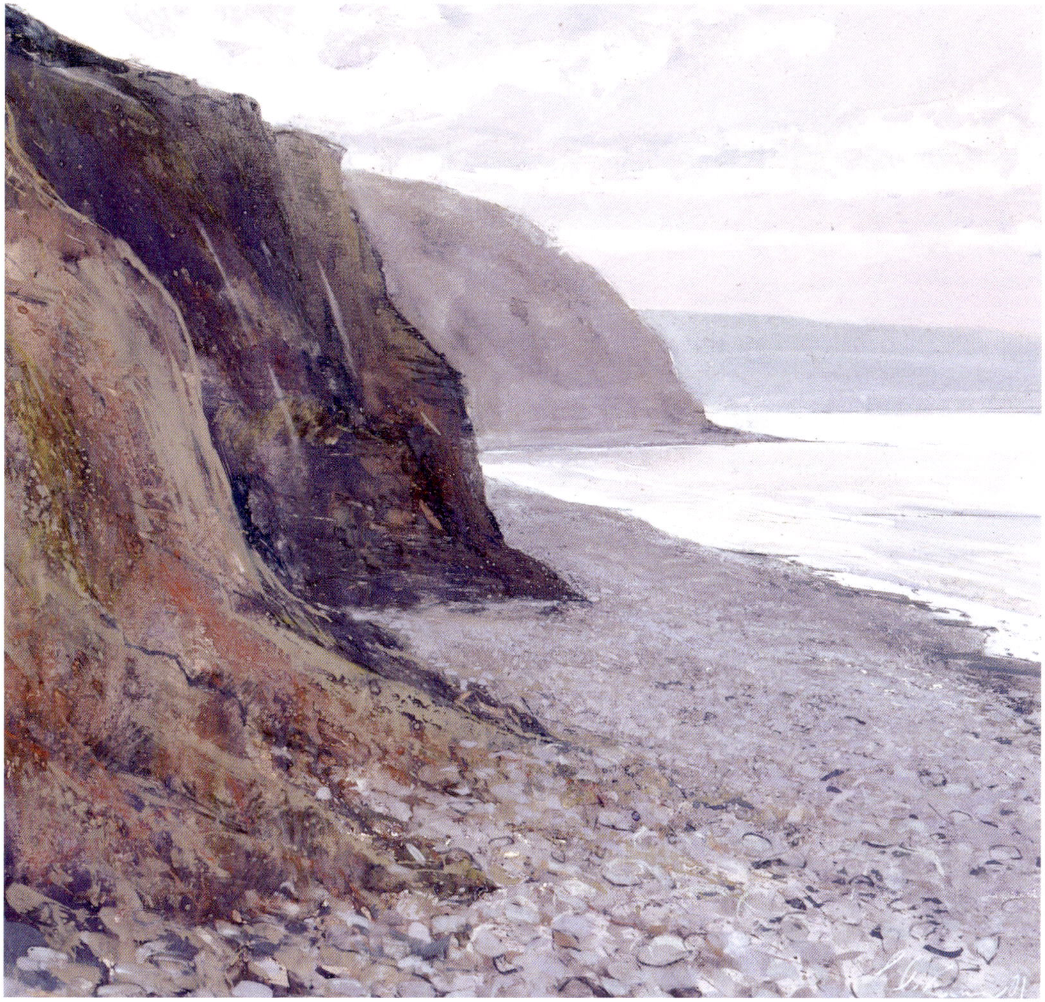

Paul Lewin. *Winter Cliffs, Devon, Late Sun*
Mixed Media 15.5x17in (39x43cm)

These cliffs at Greencliff, near Bideford, were the closest within walking distance to my studio in Abbotsham. They are also some of the most inaccessible and least visited of cliffs I have painted in England. It always felt very remote painting here, despite the fact that Bideford was only two miles away! This painting was done very close to where the seam of the pigment Bideford Black starts its journey inland to Bideford and East The Water.

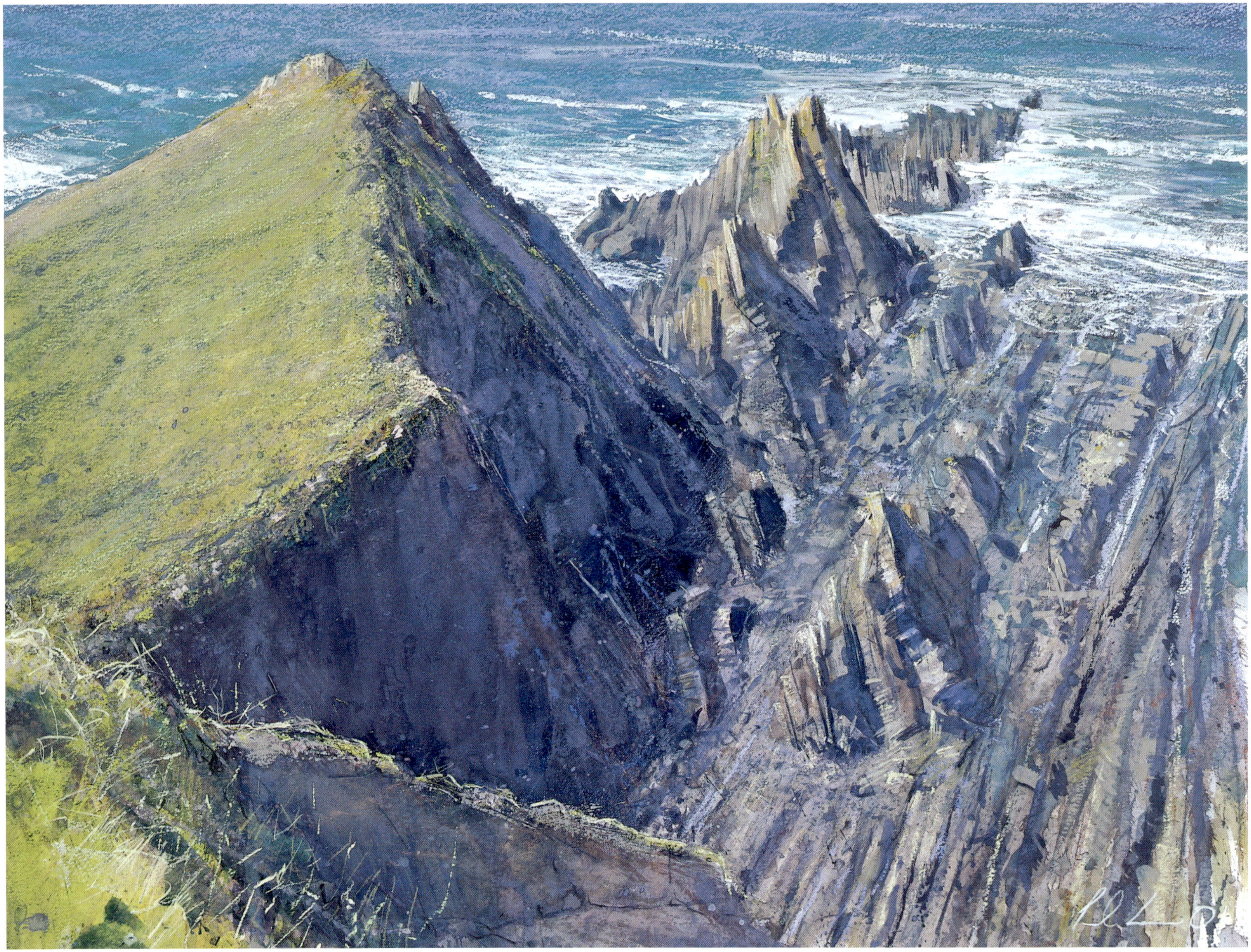

Paul Lewin. *Screda Point, Low Tide*
Mixed Media 21.5x29in (55x74cm)

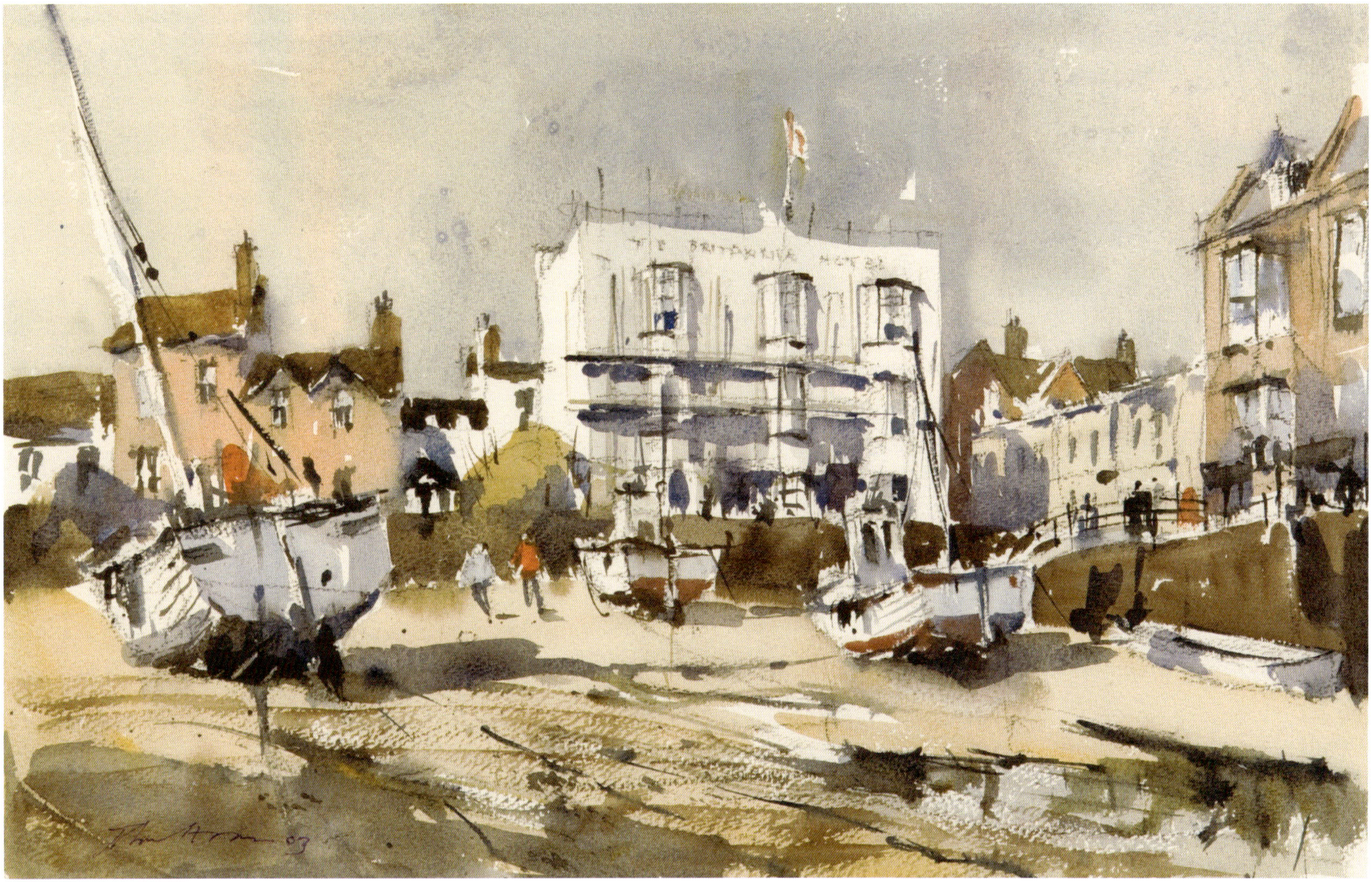

John Hoar. *Ilfracombe*
Watercolour 12x18in (30x46cm)

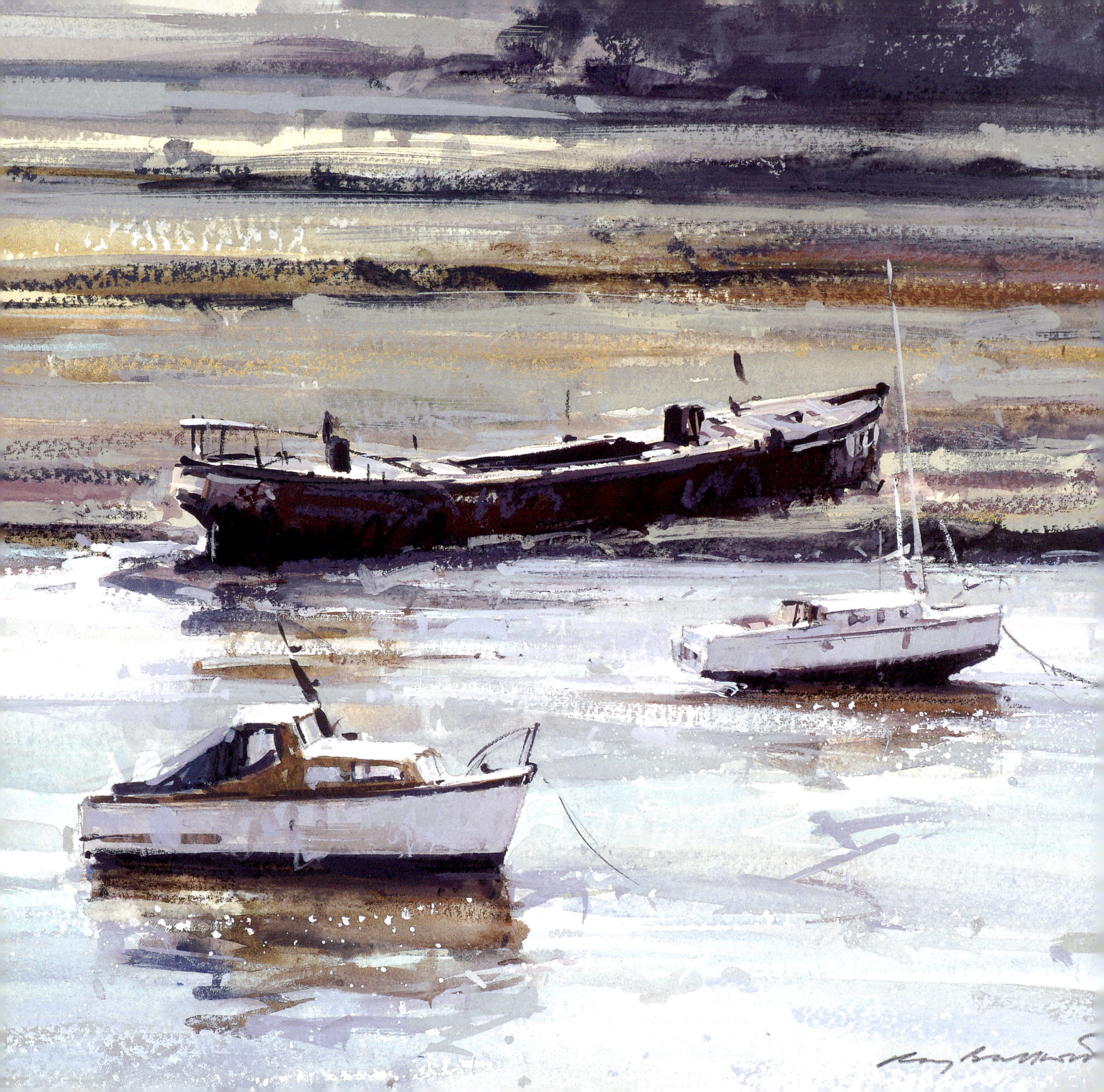

CHAPTER FOUR

From tumbling waterfalls to estuary mud flats...

Whether it is the sounds of a roaring river, or the gentle lapping water on a falling tide, there can be no more enchanting places for an artist to paint than on the banks of a river or estuary. Probably nowhere offers an artist such a variety of rivers, streams and estuaries than Devon. This is due to the fact that many of its great rivers are born in the spongy moorlands of Dartmoor and Exmoor, and from their hidden hearts bubbling streams spring forth to form the lifeblood of many of Devon's most majestic rivers. 'The spicy torrent that seems to be water which is spirit and blood' is how the poet Ted Hughes described it in his poem 'The West Dart'.

The Dart is one of eleven estuaries in Devon, including the Tamar, which it shares with Cornwall. In fact, it has more estuaries than any other county in England. Water in all its many forms, has been the mainspring of my work for the past three decades. In that time I have painted all of the estuaries, as well as many of its rivers. Each estuary is quite different in mood and character. Some are secret and sheltered places with steep banks, their creeks clothed in ancient woodland; whilst others are vast open places where the call of the curlew softly 'bubble' across the mudflats. The Exe estuary is a very special place to me and although I have travelled throughout the UK and abroad, it's an area that I never tire of painting. In fact, I can honestly say that there is nowhere I would rather paint. I feel at home here and the 'spirit' of the place is very real to me. My experiences of painting on the estuary over the past two decades resulted in a book also published by Halsgrove, as well as an art instruction film made by APV Films.

Ray Balkwill. *Across the Exe, Topsham*
Mixed Media 9x10in (23x25.5cm)

Dominated by the tide as it sweeps into the estuary to meet the river, the riverine landscape constantly changes. As each season proceeds, so does the mood. Whether it is in the calm, balmy evenings of summer, when the gently flowing waters blaze with sunset reflections, or in the autumn or winter months, when the Exe is shrouded in mist or storm clouds, the subject has much to offer the painter.

The area has attracted many fine painters including J.M.W. Turner, Thomas Girtin and Francis Danby. It is no surprise that writers have also found the Exe conducive to creative thought. Charles Dickens called the area 'the most beautiful in this most beautiful of English counties' and based the unusual character of Mr Pecksniff on a resident of Topsham. It was here also that Thomas Hardy once described the river, as 'It is where the Exe scents the sea.'

When I took up painting again back in the early 1980s, one artist whose work I found inspiring was that of **Hubert Coop R.B.A.** (1872-1953). I first came upon his work in the Burton Art Gallery whilst on a family holiday to North Devon and it has left a lasting impression on me to this day. He was born in Olney, Buckinghamshire, but came to live in Bideford in 1920. He chose Bideford because he enjoyed the subjects he found on the estuary, the river valleys and the neighbourhood, and his paintings inevitably captured the clear beauty and colour he saw there. He painted in both watercolour and oil, working mainly *en plein air* with his paintings

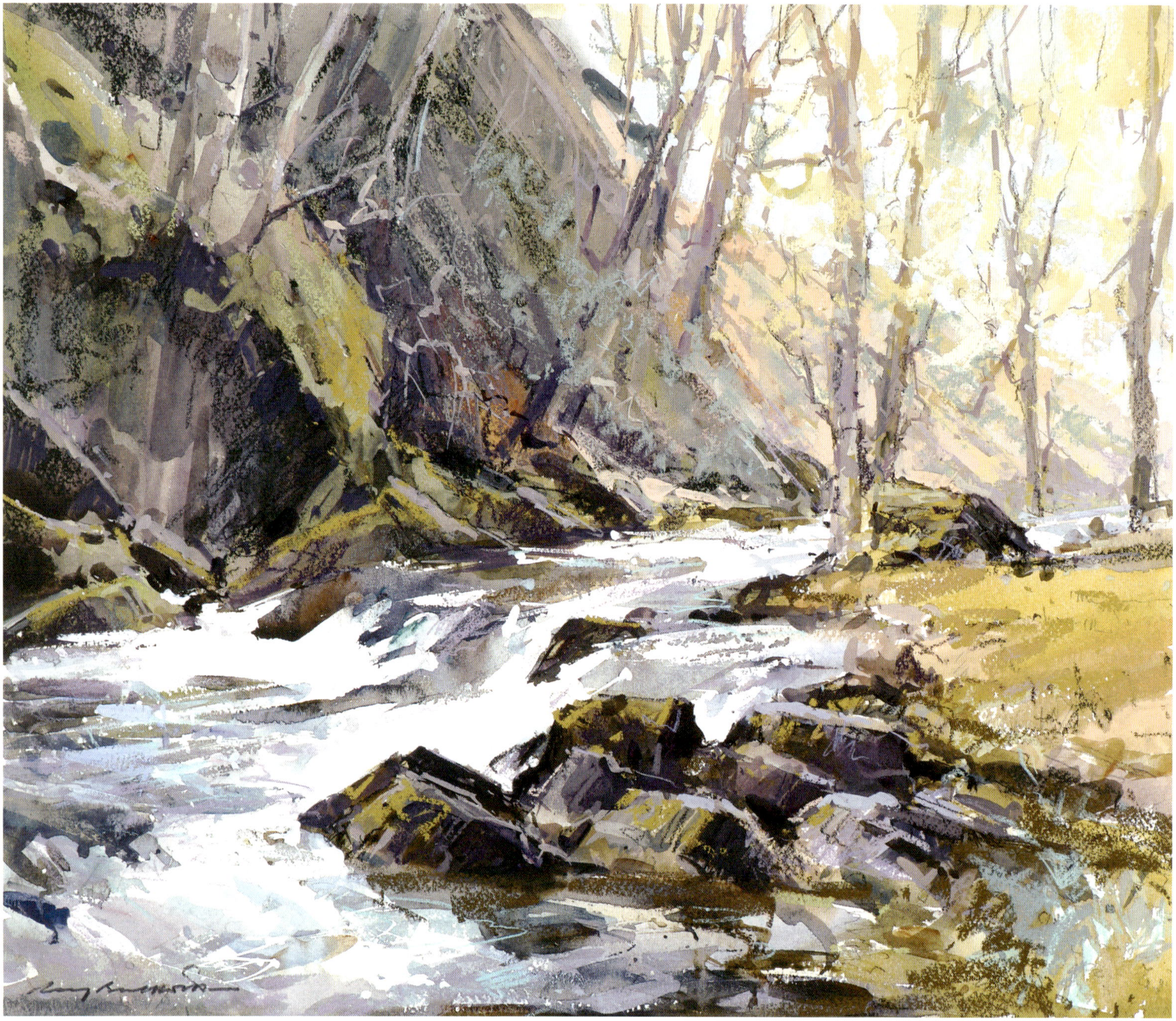

Ray Balkwill. *East Okement River*
Mixed Media 14x17in (36x43cm)

imparting a masterly skill and a sincerity of approach. Despite very little art training he was elected a Royal Academician at the age of 22 and exhibited at the Royal Academy, Liverpool, Glasgow and Manchester. In Bideford he helped to promote the development of the visual arts, and became Vice President of what is now the Westward Ho! and Bideford Art Society.

Throughout his life he amassed a fine collection of paintings, porcelain and antiques, and because he felt that there was a special appreciation of the arts in Bideford, he left his collection to the town, including his own sketchbooks and paintings, provided it would be 'properly housed'. He was eventually instrumental in assisting Thomas Burton, Mayor, Alderman, Freeman of the Borough, and philanthropist to build the Burton Art Gallery in memory of his daughter Mary, who was also a talented local artist. The Burton Art Gallery was finally opened in 1951, just two years before Coop died. In Coop's obituary in the *Bideford Gazette*, January 1953, it was said: 'His generosity in connection with the starting of the Burton Gallery will be a lasting reminder...'

When I am not painting on the banks of an estuary, I find that the rivers tumbling off the edges of Dartmoor equally inspiring. In particular the East Okement River and its greater neighbour and cradle companion, the River Taw. These are the only two Dartmoor rivers that flow north to the Bristol Channel – or the 'Severn Sea' as Charles Kingsley preferred to call it. Driving on the busy A30 as it skirts Okehampton, one is oblivious to there being a bridge crossing a river here. The only clue perhaps is the mere glimpse of an older railway viaduct directly alongside, as one drives over it. Yet, hidden deep below, at Fatherford, runs the fast flowing Okement and one of the most enchanting spots that I know.

As a young boy, long before this controversial road was even built, these ancient woods and boulder-strewn rivers were one of my favourite haunts. I have recently returned to paint here, scenes that have been implanted on my memory for so long. It was always going to be a nostalgic journey and although the scars on the landscape have healed, the noise created by such roads cannot fail to be intrusive. But the river was there long before man and is impervious to all of this, so she still flows on unconcerned. A few minutes' walk upstream and the tumultuous sounds of the river soon reclaims what is so rightly hers, as she tumbles and cascades down the wooded gorge in a succession of falls and pools. The Okement derives its name from two ancient words meaning 'swift and noisy' and here it certainly lives up to its name.

It's a place that truly touches all the senses and a retreat for the mind as well as the creative spirit. In spring, the sweet smell of wild garlic fills the air. Beneath a canopy of fresh greenery, dappled sunlight plays on the woodland floor amidst its carpet of bluebells and lush ferns. Whenever I am painting by these 'chattering' waters, I am reminded of the words of a well-known poem. 'Lines Written in Early Spring' by William Wordsworth penned as he sat by a brook over the border at Alford, in Somerset. The poem rejoices in the simple beauty of nature and yet laments on injustices and sadness. The first two verses read:

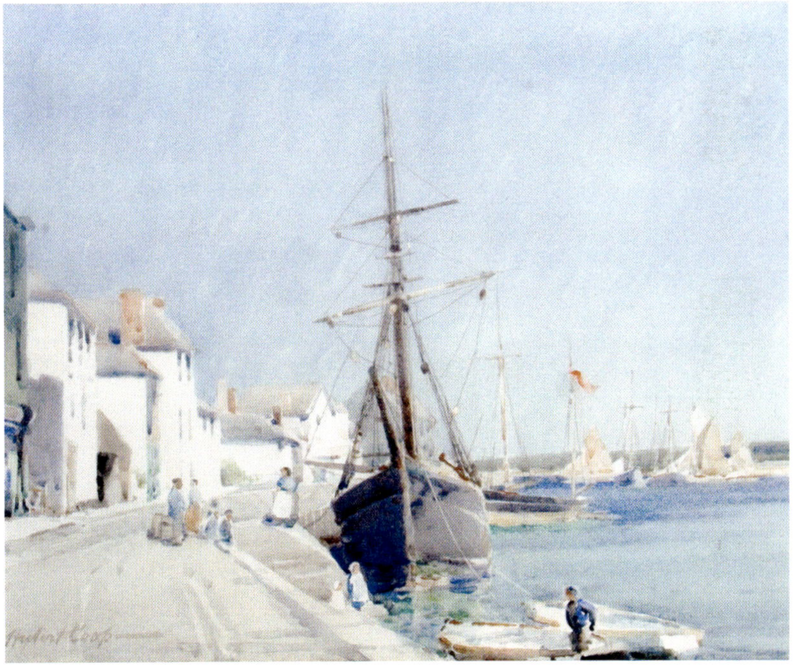

Hubert Coop,RBA. *Waiting for the Ferry, Appledore Quay*
Watercolour 14.5x19.5in (37x50cm)
Courtesy of the Burton Art Gallery and Museum, Bideford

The scene shows the slipway at the bottom of Bude Street, circa 1895-1900, with Dudley Johns the ferryman in the foreground.

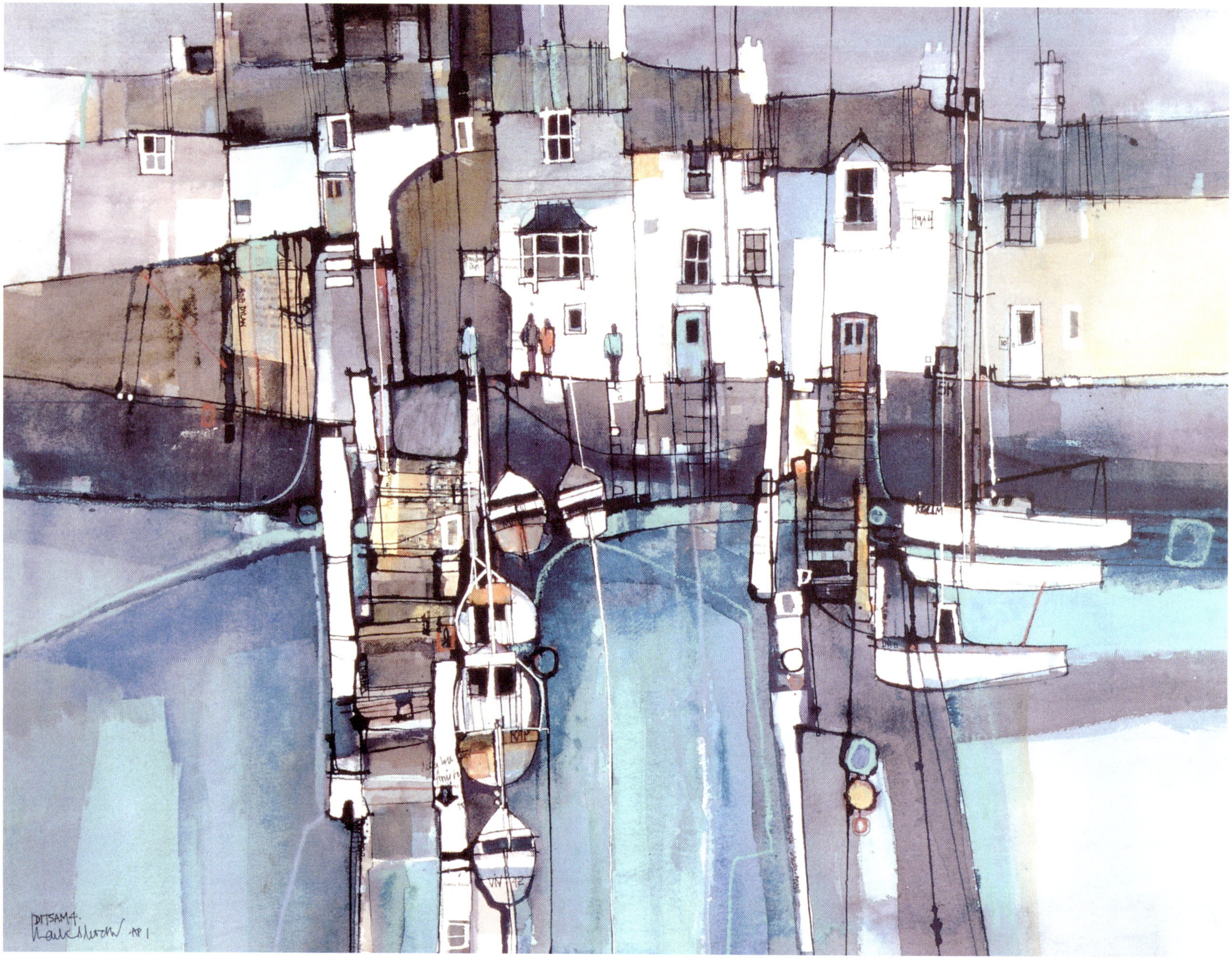

Martin Procter. *Ditsam 4*
Mixed Media 22x29in (55x72cm)

'I heard a thousand blended notes,
While in a grove I sate reclined,
In that sweet mood when pleasant thoughts,
Bring sad thoughts to the mind.

To her fair works did Nature link,
The human soul that through me ran;
And much it grieved my heart to think,
What man has made of man.'

Suffice it to say that these words still resonate two hundred years after they were first written.

The primitive spirit of the moor also flowed out through the River Taw into the veins of Henry Williamson, one of the country's most popular writers. It was in Belstone Cleave that Tarka the Otter ventured in Williamson's classic novel, to return and then follow the meandering river on its journey back to the sea in North Devon. A path through the gorge leads to a wooden footbridge over the river, on which a quotation from the book is carved on the handrails. One scene was set near the spot and it reads: 'By pools and waterfalls and rillets the River Taw grew, flowing under steep hills that towered high above. The river hurried round the base of the cleave on whose slopes stunted trees grew amid rocks, and scree that in falling had smashed the trunks and torn out the roots of willow, thorns, and hollies. It wandered away from the moor, a proper river, with bridges, brooks, islands and mills.'

For painter **Martin Procter** it is the River Dart, the river that Dartmoor takes its name from, to which he is draw, particularly its lower reaches. A Yorkshire man by birth, he has lived in the heart of South Devon since 1956. As with Michael Morgan, he was greatly inspired and encouraged by the Cotswold artist John Blockley. Living in South Devon, the 'back-country' as he calls it, twixt moor and sea, it is not surprising that both land and water inspire him. Much of his work is based on busy harbours, using the boats and buildings stacking up the hills behind to develop composition. He said 'I have spent a lot of time around the Dart, living within walking distance for many years and I return to all the places from Dartmouth and Kingswear up to Totnes. I once kept a small boat in Galmpton Creek messing about on the river, Stoke Gabriel, Tuckenhay and Dittisham – 'Ditsam' to the locals. The river Dart has everything, from its source on the moor down to the mouth, it offers a painter endless material, and it has been my good fortune to know it well.'

His architectural background shows clearly in his work, where a strong design element is the starting point. Martin loves the fundamental images that make up a scene and in Dartmoor it leads him to paint towards greater abstraction, looking to find the essence of the place. All his work is based on his sketches done in situ and then the composition development and the painting is done in the studio. Paintings are either acrylic on canvas, or watercolour and mixed media on paper. He often uses collage, canvas pieces and gesso for extra texture, and is not concerned with representational painting. He says: 'I am striving to pick the bones out a subject to crystallize a sense of the place, the atmosphere. Quite unconsciously, I have always painted in a way which denies perspective, simplifying everything into one-dimensional shapes.'

Andrew Coates is another painter who is fascinated with water in all its many guises. His finely executed oils depicting gently flowing rivers with their dappled light and shade evoke a feeling of calm and tranquillity to the viewer. However, for this internationally acclaimed artist their creation is quite the opposite. Andrew is a compulsive artist with each painting taking weeks of meticulous work in his soul-bearing search for perfection. His goal, using this technique, has been to capture the subtlety of light unique to a place at a specific moment in time. This light is at its most romantic and evocative along rivers, reflecting off the sea or in dramatic skies.

Andrew has found little need to travel far in his search for inspiration, the countryside and coast near his home provides vast treasures in its landscape to enjoy and transform into paintings. He constantly revisits and reinterprets his favourite locations such as the Rivers Dart, Axe and Otter, or the sweeping vista across Lyme Bay. As he says: 'Devon is not just one county but so many all rolling together as one. There is a diversity to this landscape unlike any other English county, with a geology that underpins some of the most beautiful and unique natural environments you will ever see.'

Born in Surrey, he moved to New Zealand with his parents when he was a child. It was here where he honed and refined his skills, rejecting the strictures of art school in favour of personal self-discipline to evolve his unique style. His paintings were critically acclaimed and, in search of a wider audience, he returned to Britain, living in London, before eventually moving with his family to Beer in the late 80s. They put in an offer for their large neglected turreted Victorian house high on the hill above the village, before they had even seen inside. 'I remember so clearly those first months of living here in Beer; the days and evenings working hard on the house or in the garden, and having to take a deep breath as I looked out across the village to listen to all the natural sounds that seemed to be captured both sides of the valley. Rooks flew in from the fields of an evening, vying for any limited airspace not occupied by gulls, and any number of other birds that had the freedom to fly at all other times of the day. As night time approached you had the expectation of seeing small Pipistrelle bats or the odd Horseshoe bat; and then through the silence came the hoot of a Tawny Owl which would draw a response from another across the valley.' Andrew's deep understanding and obvious love of his adopted Devon is evident both in his words, as well as in his paintings.

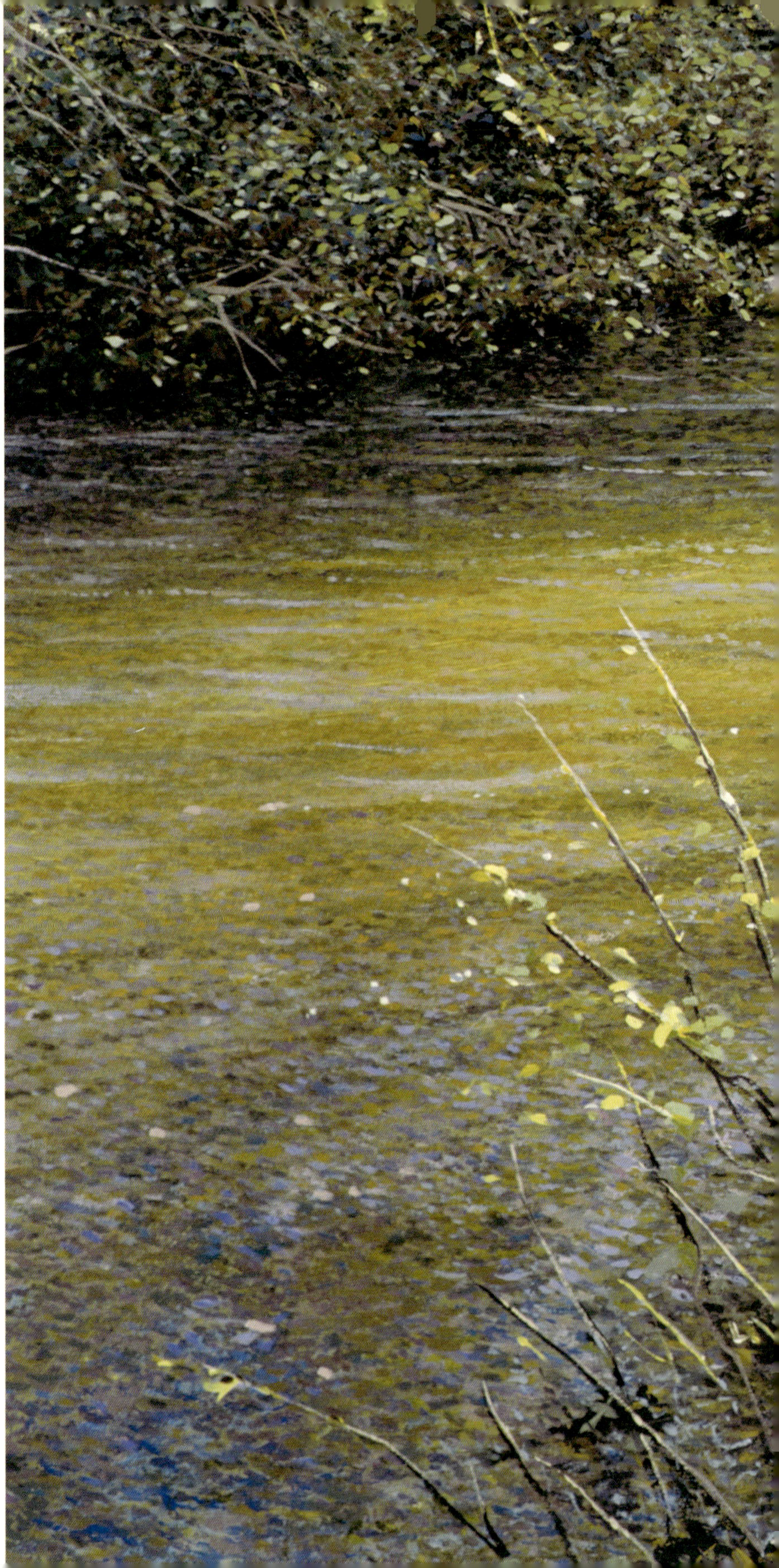

Andrew Coates. *Receding Waters, River Sid*
Oil 14x19in (36x48cm)

Rivers are constantly changing, rising and falling, while all around the landscape changes with every passing season. I hope in this painting I have been able to capture a moment in the life of a river as the low spring sun filters through the trees and the waters begin to fall. Often you have to push your way through the undergrowth to find a spot like this, but the reward is a painting that feels as if you have it all to yourself. I get completely absorbed in bringing a painting to life. The secret for me is to create restless shimmering effects through the application of tiny daubs of paint. This bounces light and colour throughout the painting never allowing the eye to settle comfortably in one place.

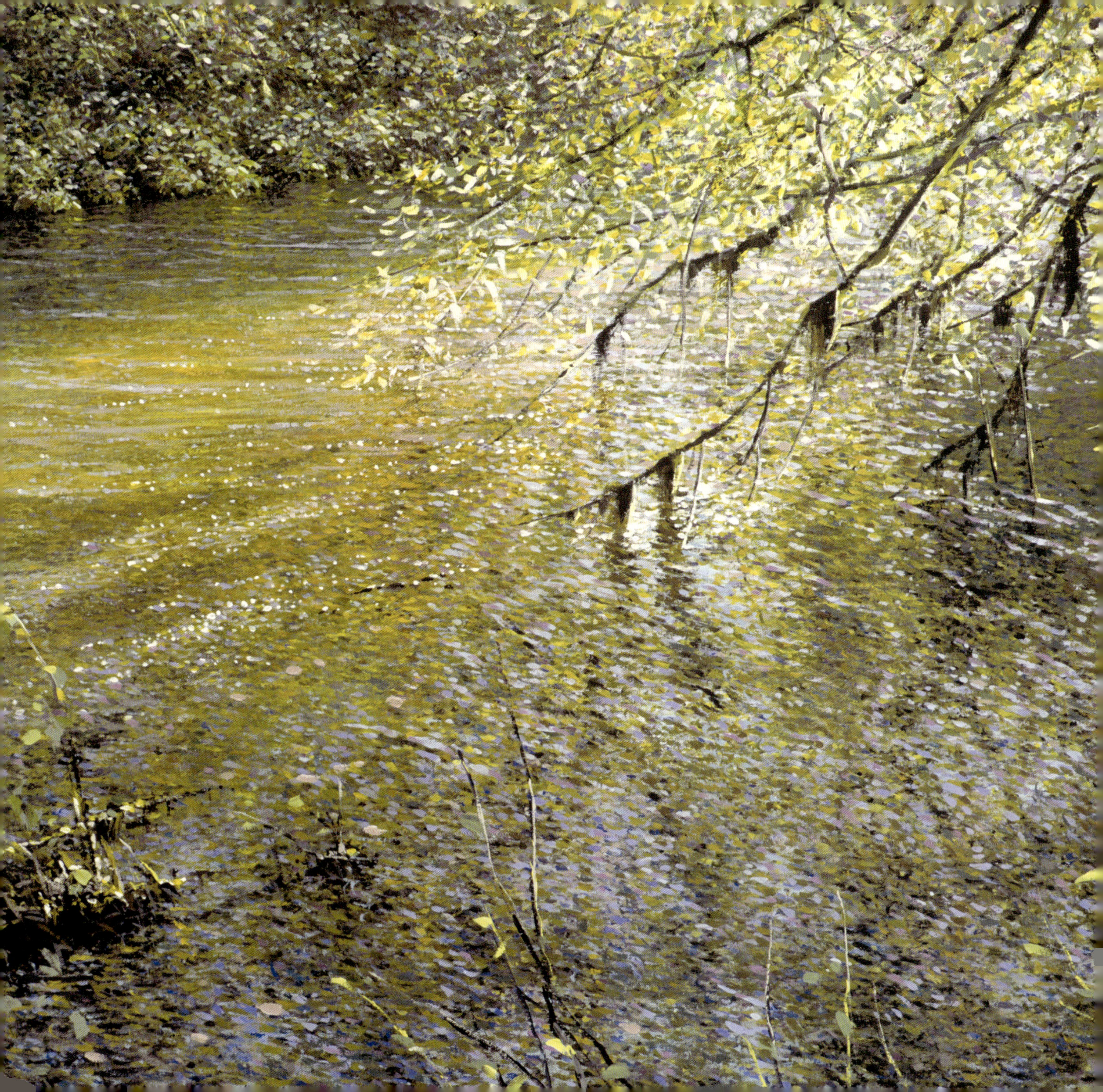

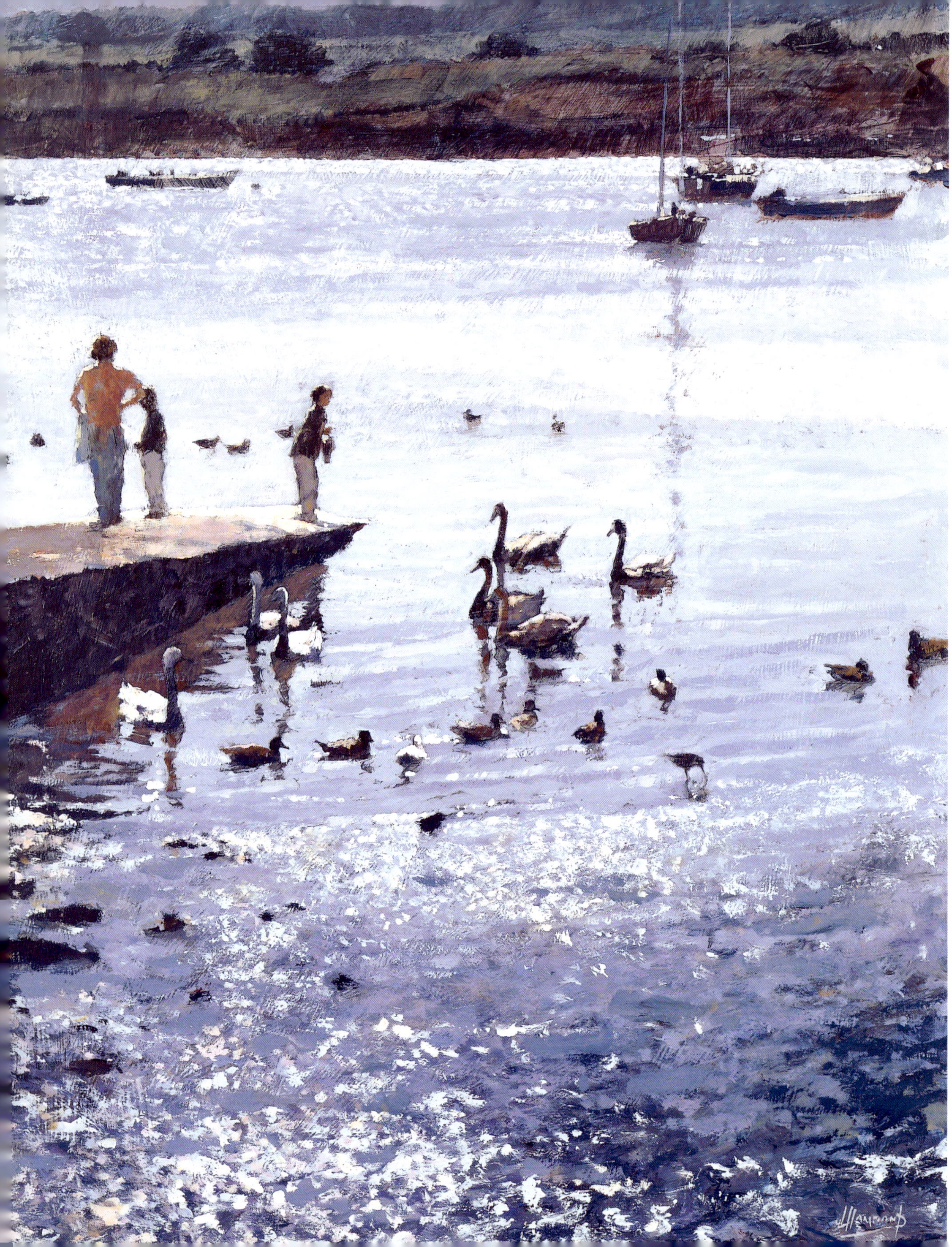

John Hammond.
Swan Watching, Topsham
Acrylic 23x18in (58x46cm)

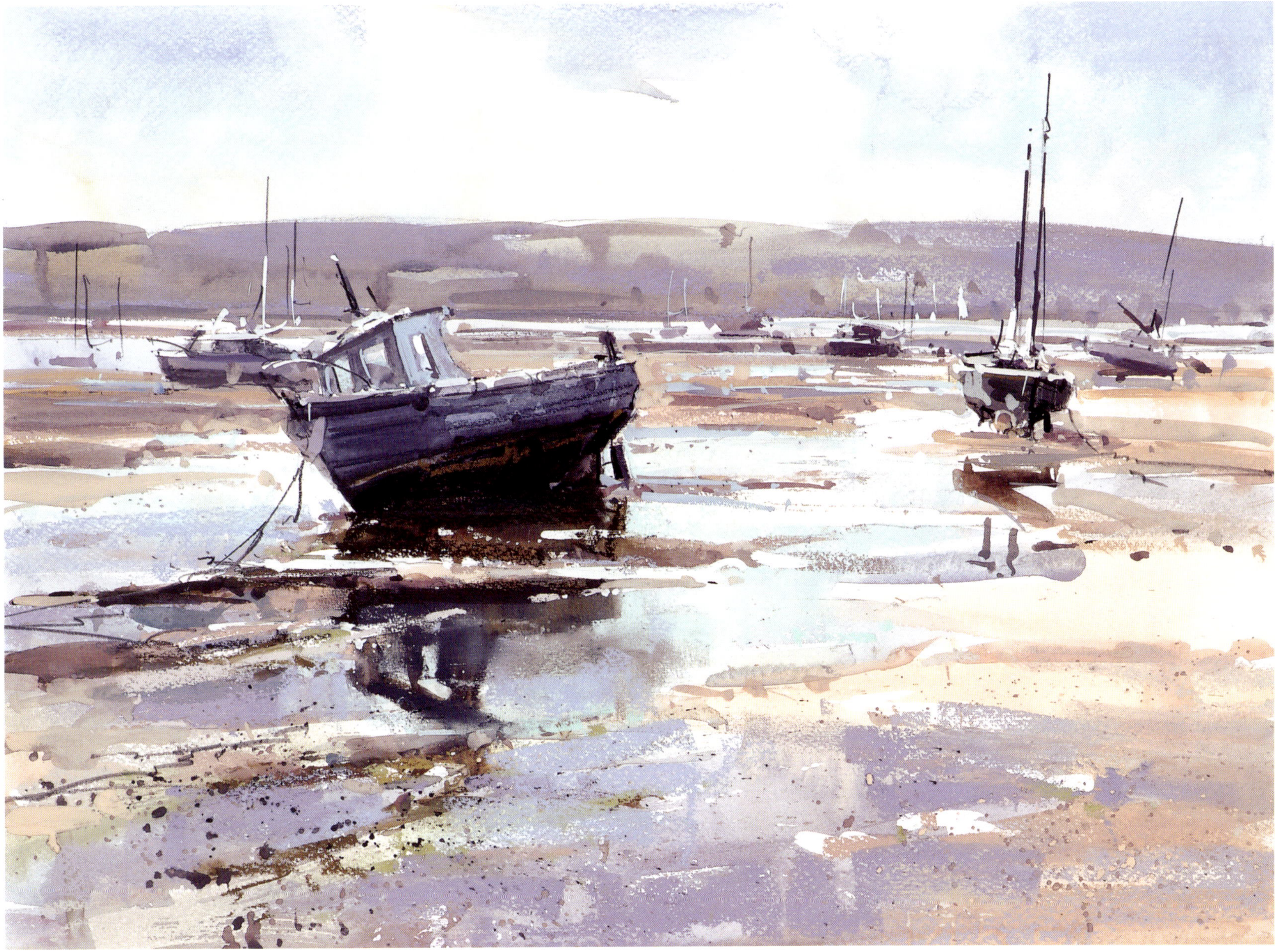

Ray Balkwill. *Tide Pools, Exe Estuary at Exmouth*
Mixed Media 12x17in (30x43cm)

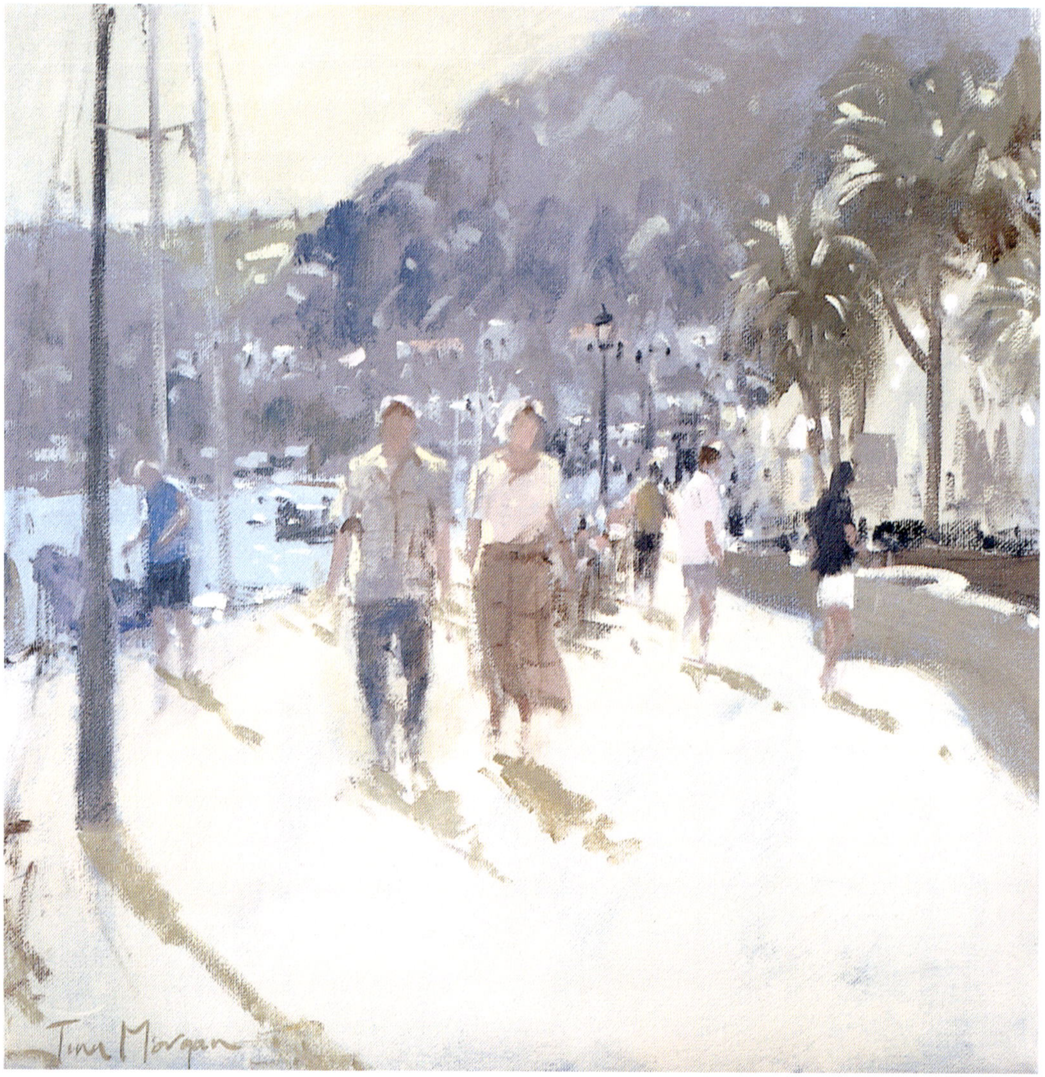

Tina Morgan. *Walking in the Sunshine, Dartmouth*
Oil 12x12in (30x30cm)

The promenade at Dartmouth is always busy with people walking past the many palm trees; yachtsmen coming ashore and those that just want to sit and watch the sea. On a sunny day you could be in the South of France.

Ray Balkwill.
Crabshell Quay, Kingsbridge
Mixed Media
11x12in (28x30cm)

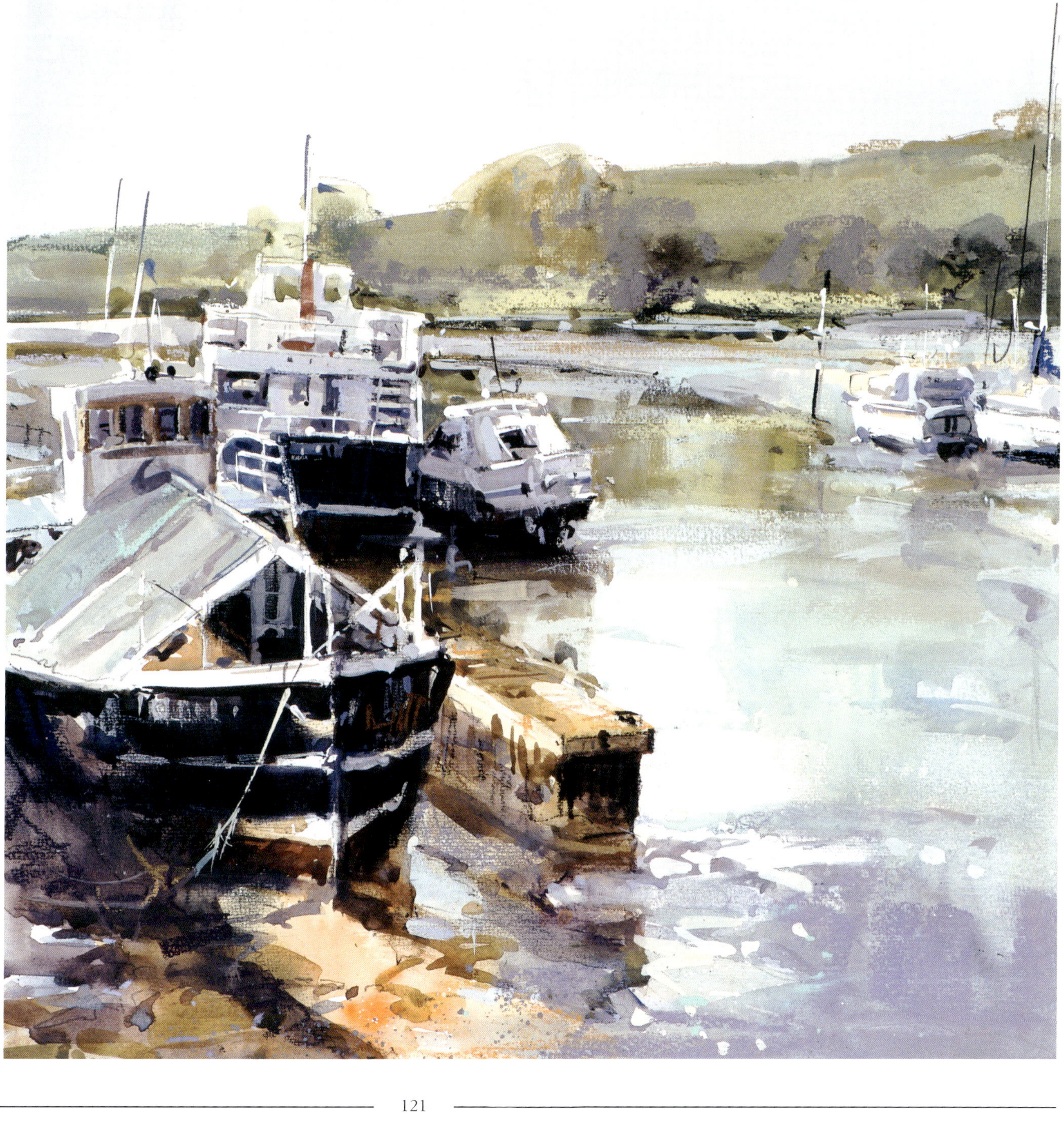

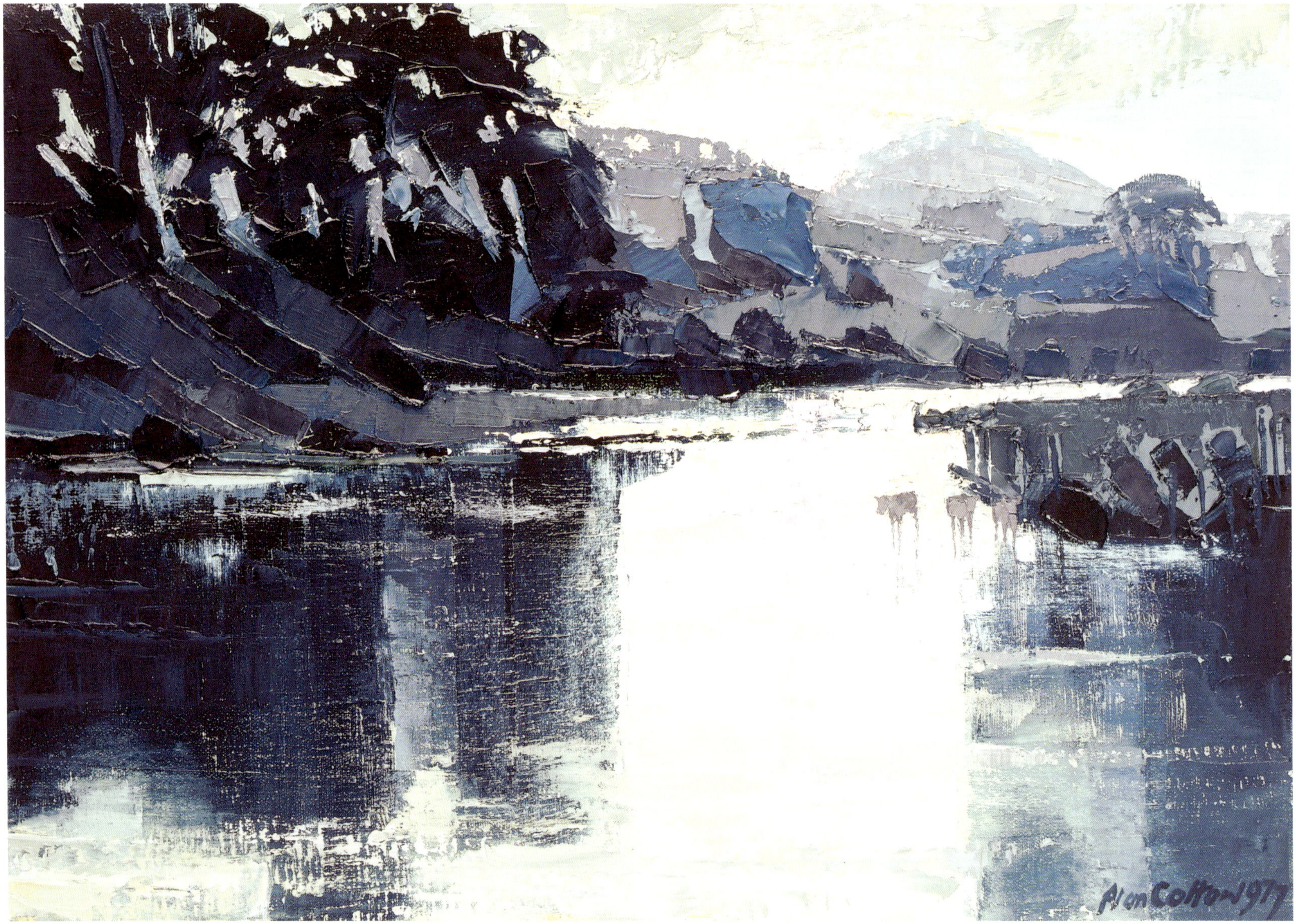

Alan Cotton. *Otter Valley, Morning Light*
Oil 14x20in (36x51cm)

Andrew Coates.
Shadows and Reflections, River Coly
Oil 32x34in (81x86cm)

In this painting the landscape is seen, or eluded to as reflections on the surface water, or as shadows over the diluted image of the gravelled riverbed. I love the warmth and enigmatic nature of this picture with just a few twigs reminding us where we are. Is there anything more revealing than time spent just gazing into a shallow stream?

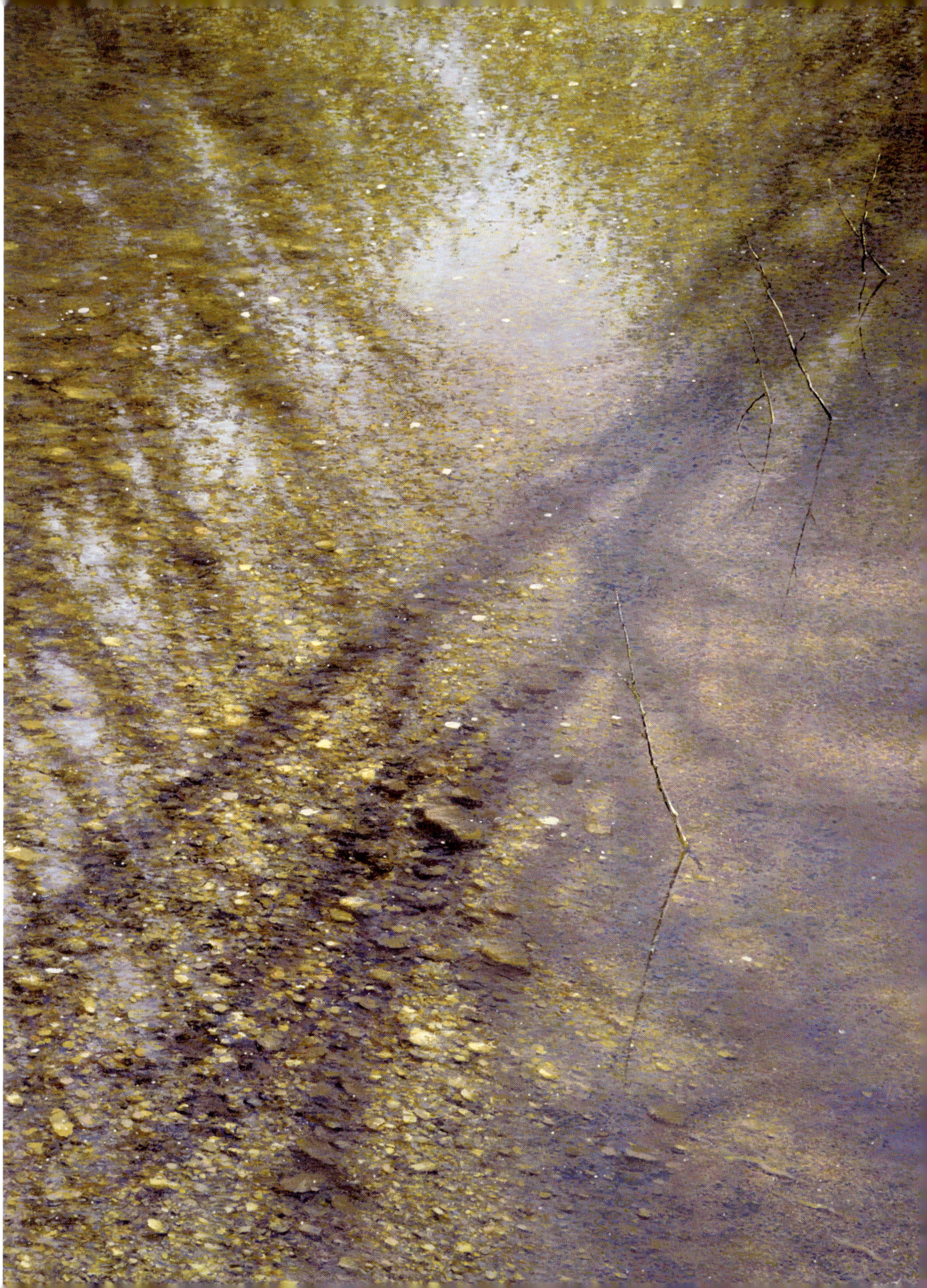

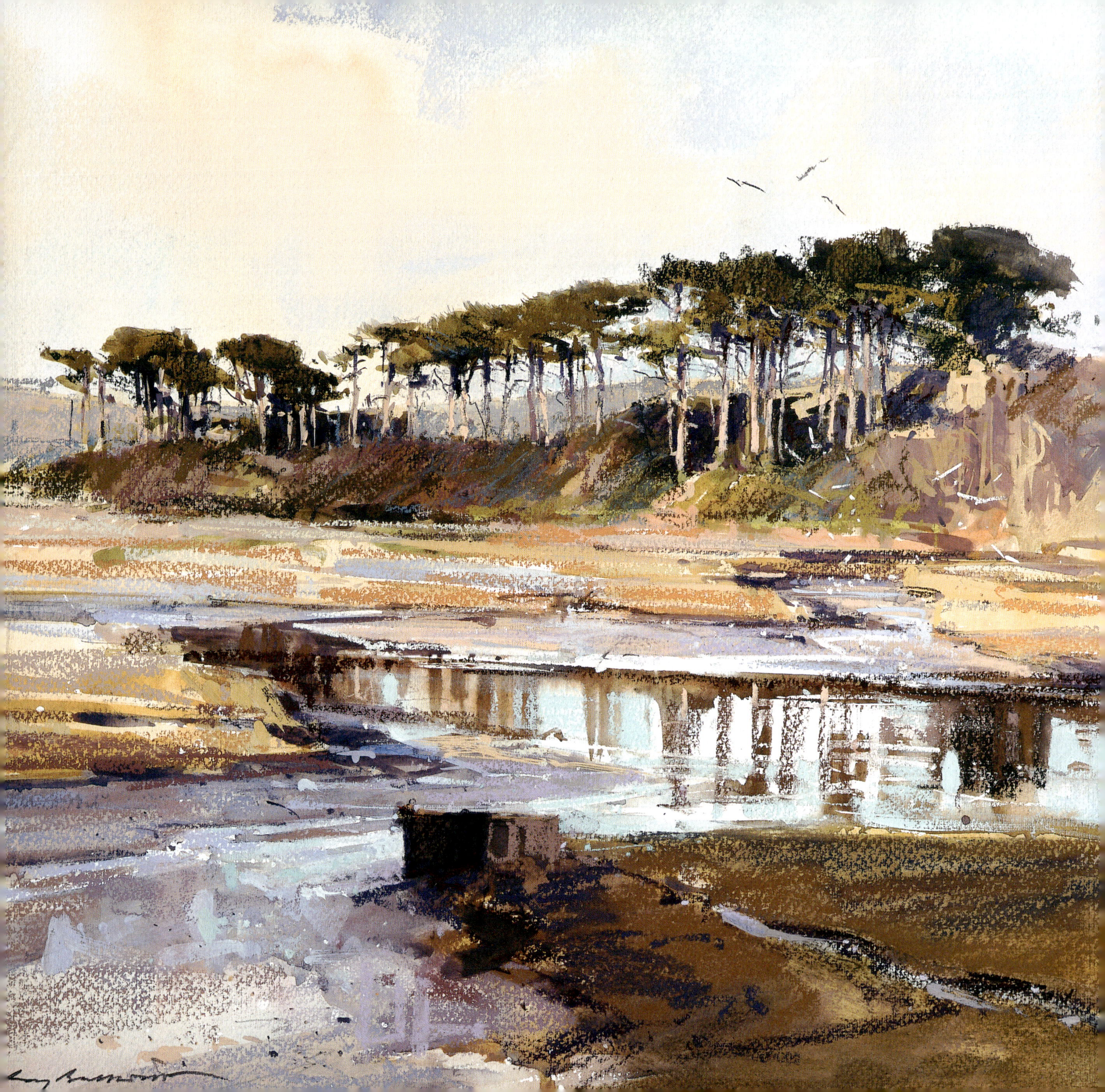

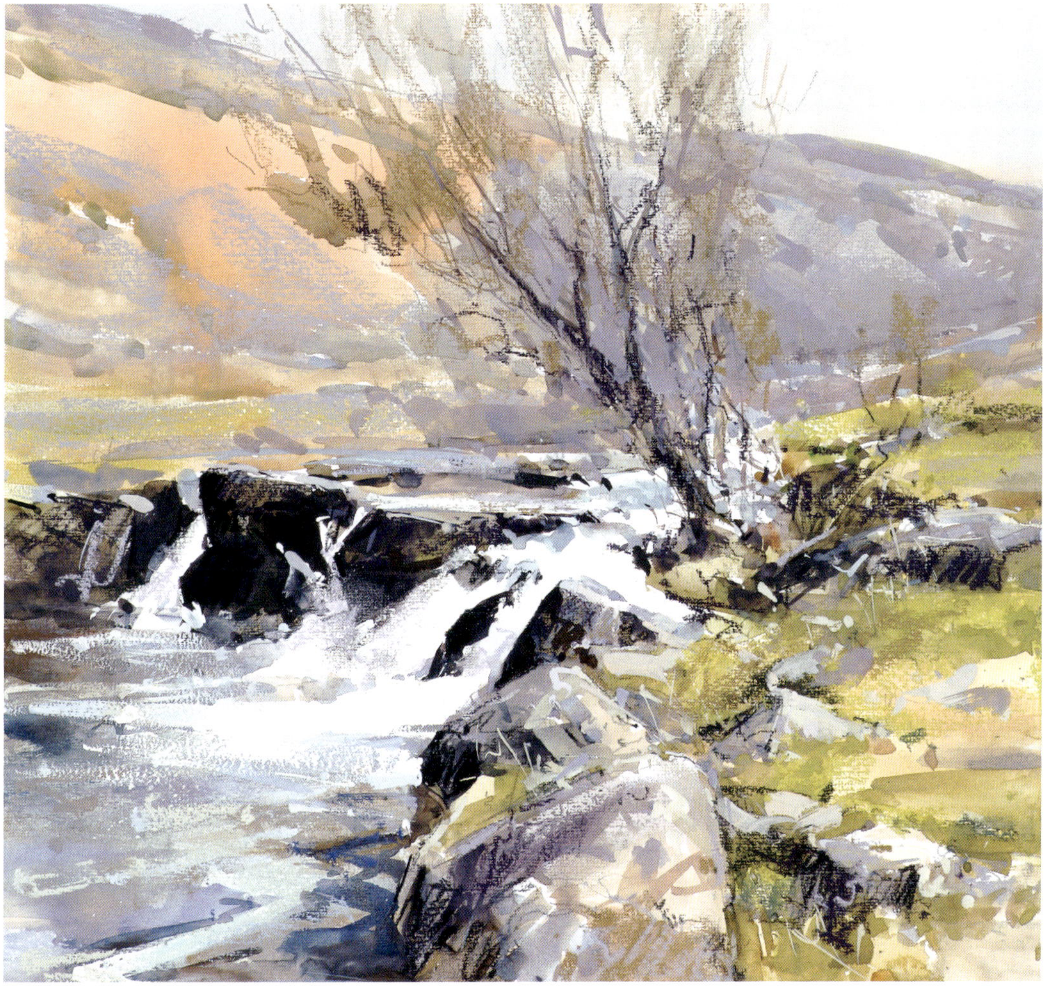

Ray Balkwill. *River Taw, Belstone Cleave*
Mixed Media 11x12in (28x30cm)

Ray Balkwill. *Evening Light, Otter Head*
Mixed Media 17x17in (43x43cm)

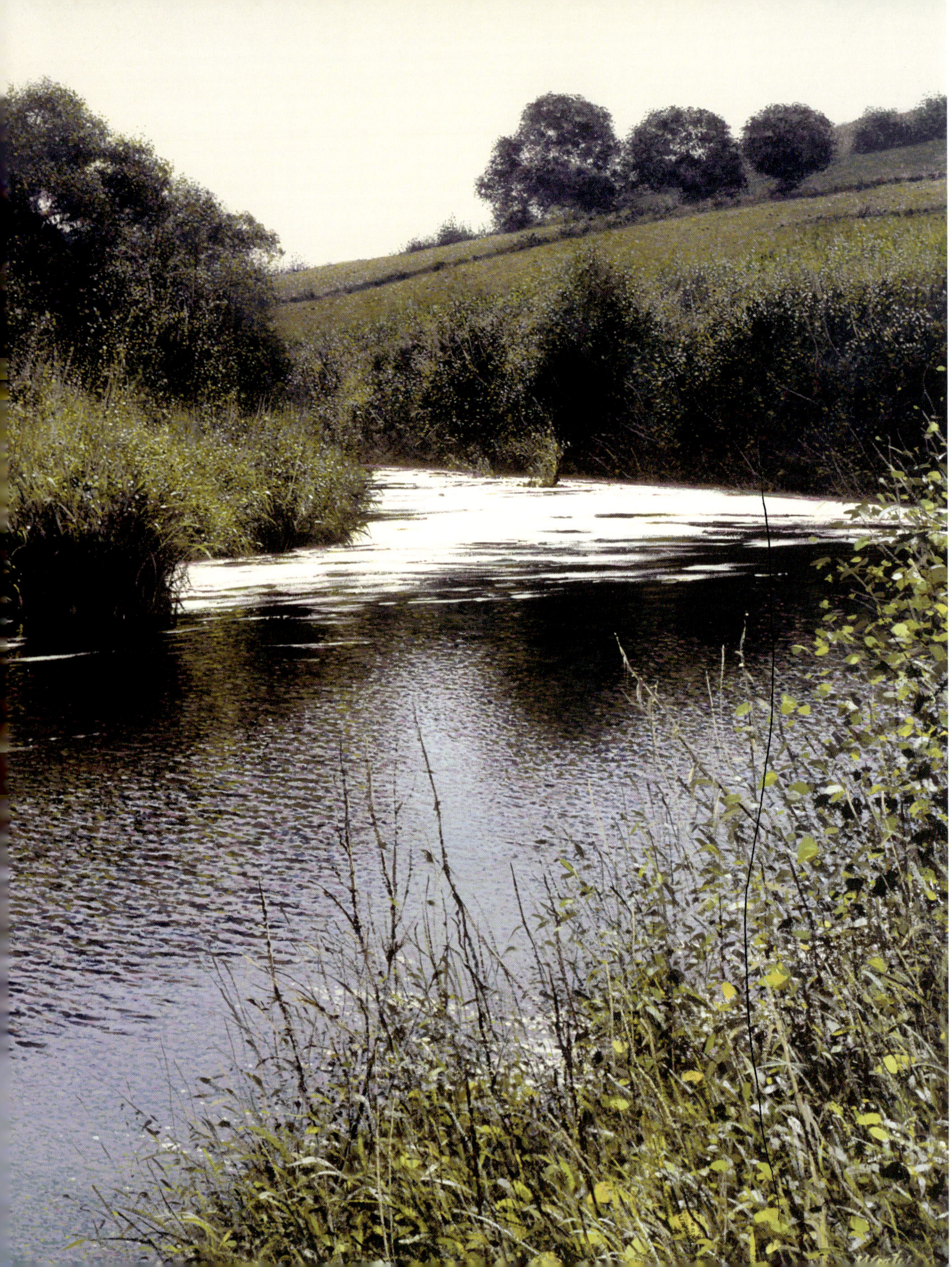

Andrew Coates.
River Coly Reflections
Oil 24x18in (61x46cm)

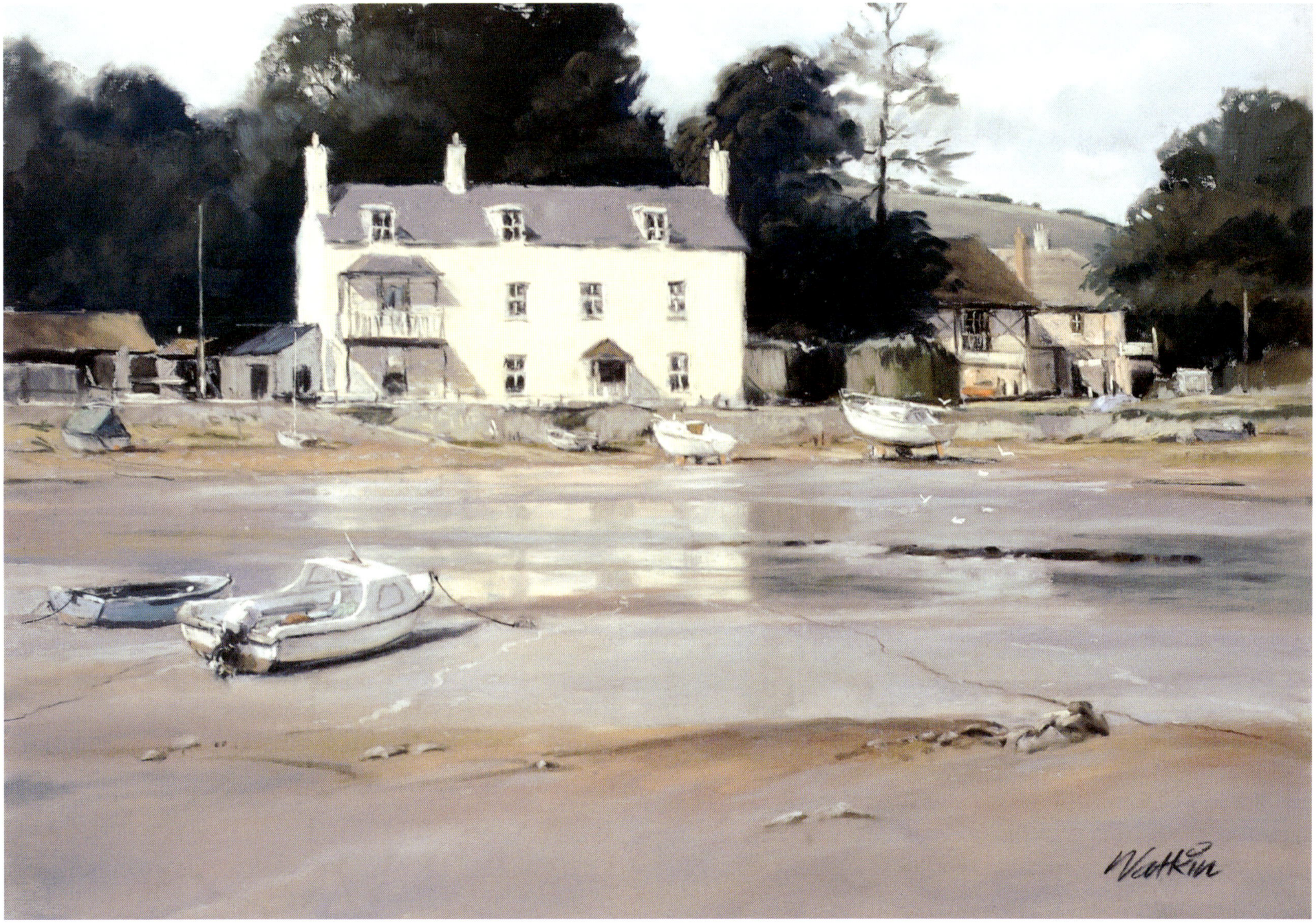

Barry Watkin. *Cockwood Harbour*
Pastel 15x22in (38x56cm)

The contrast of the grand house against the dark trees reflected in the water and wet mud caught my eye as I walked around the harbour looking for the best angle. Low tide is always much more interesting to paint than high tide.

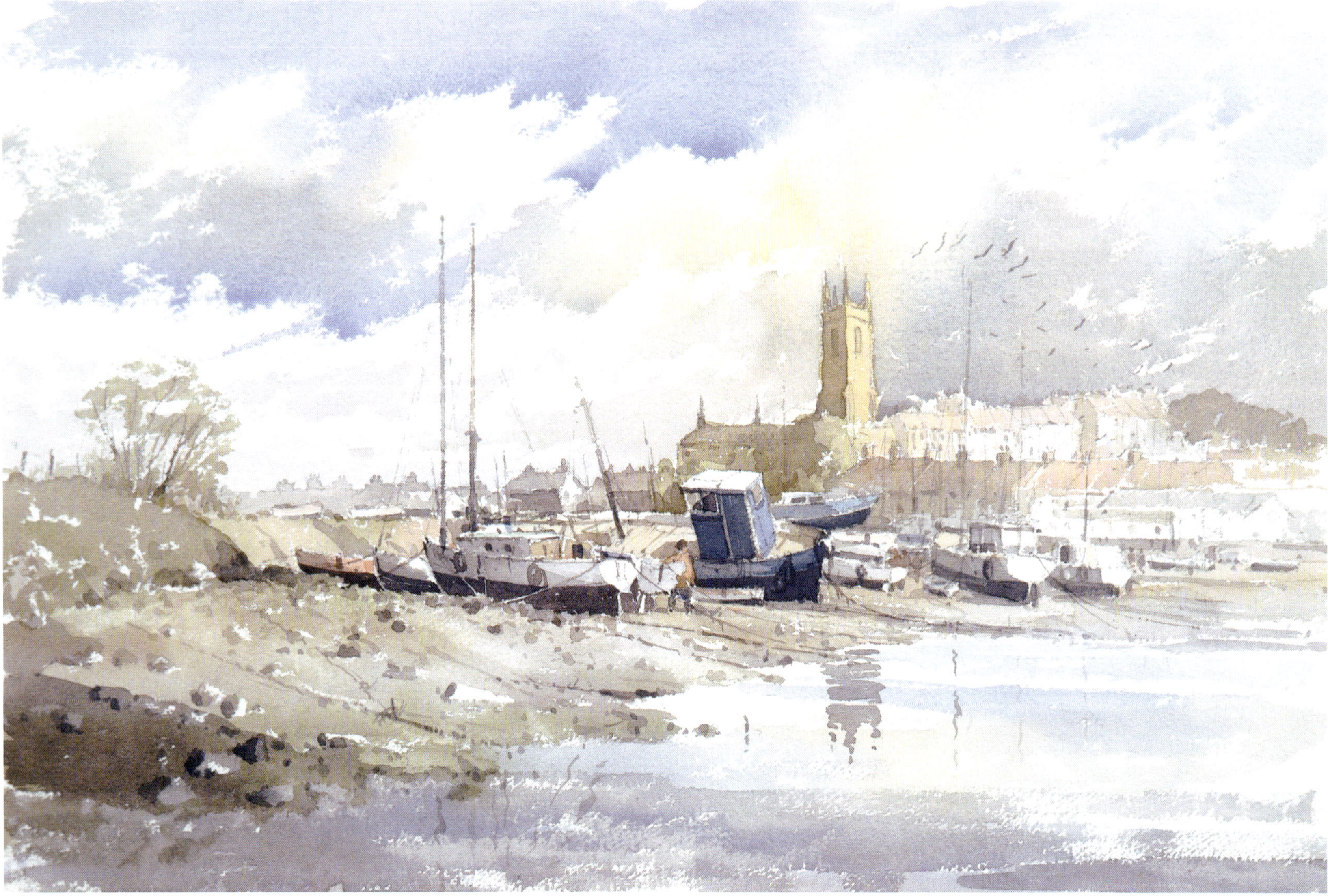

Alwyn Crawshaw. *Shelly Gut, Exmouth*
Watercolour 15x20in 938x51cm)

The inspiration here was the gorgeous tidal mud, the water and of course, the boats. The blue fishing boat became a must in all my Exmouth paintings, until one day I went there with some students and found it was gone – burnt to the ground!

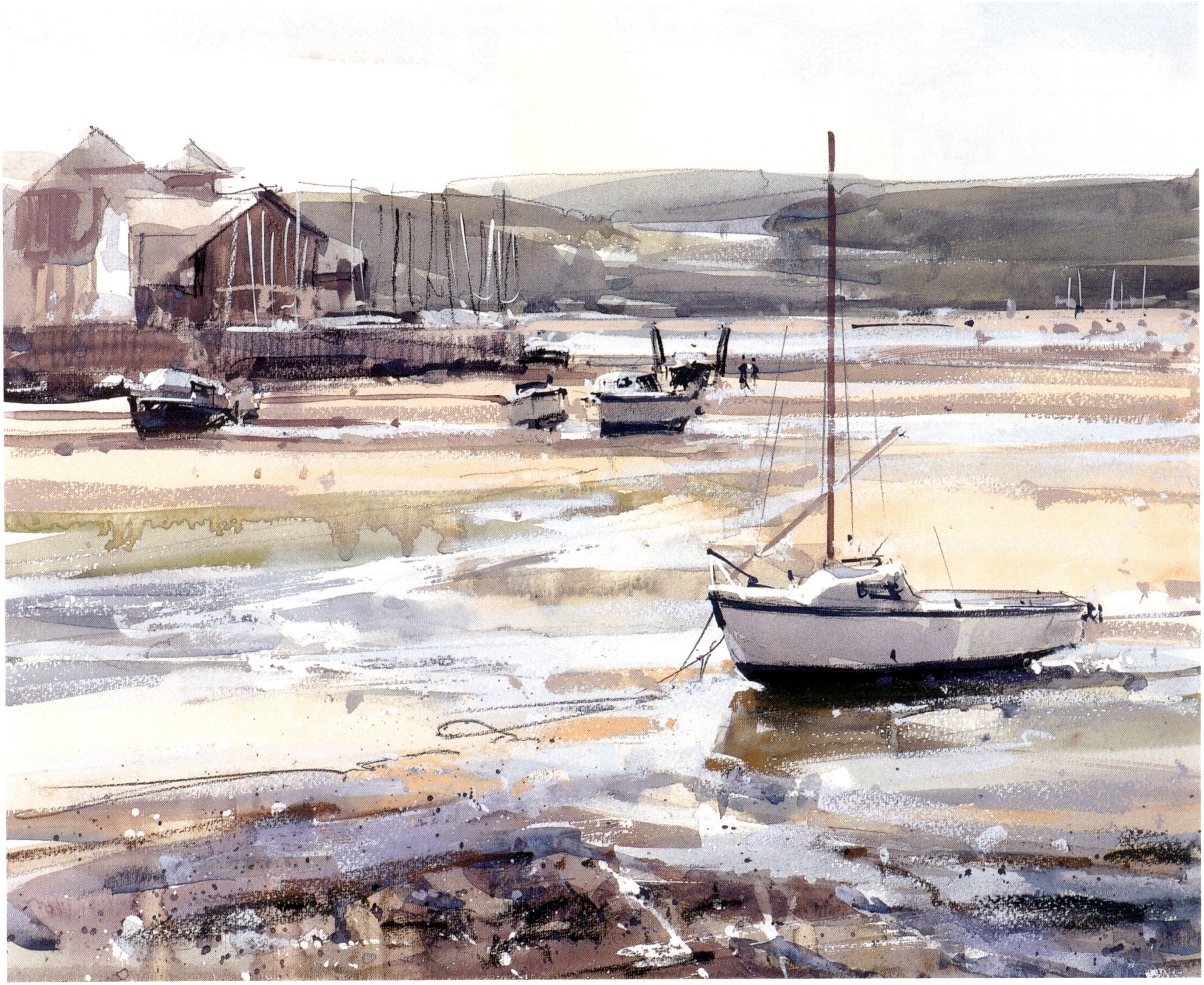

Ray Balkwill. *Across the Mud Flats, Exmouth*
Mixed Media 14x17in (36x43cm)

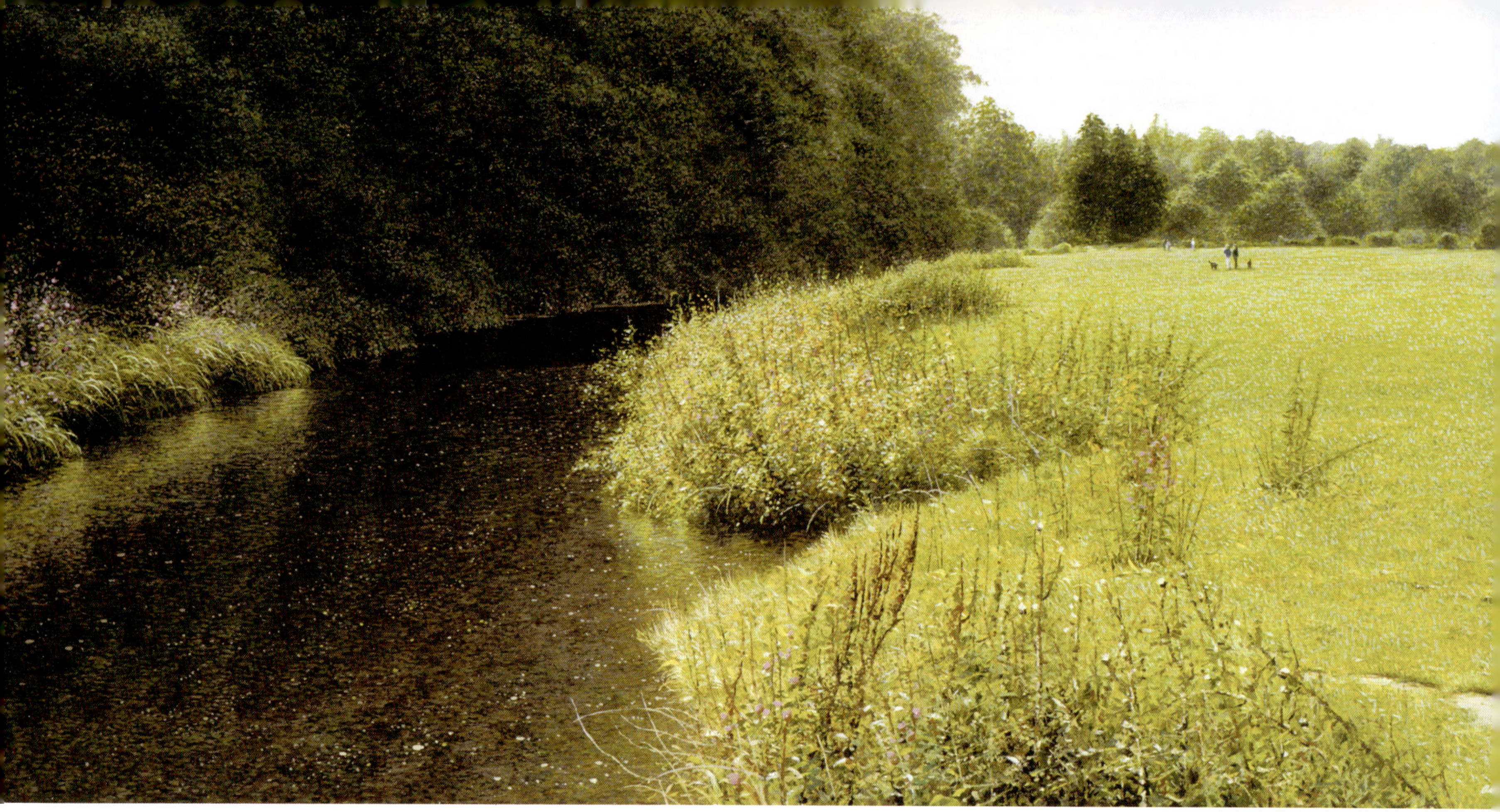

Andrew Coates. *A Summer's Day beside the River Otter*
Oil 12x24in (30x61cm)

The River Otter has not only inspired painters, but also poet and philosopher Samuel Taylor Coleridge, who was born in Ottery St Mary in 1772. It is easy to imagine him as a small boy playing in its placid, rippling waters, as the scene as changed very little. His first accomplished poem of his youth was a sonnet 'To the River Otter' which he wrote at the age of twenty-one, while still at university.

'Dear native brook! Wild streamlet of the West!
How many various-fated years have past,
What happy, and what mournful hours, since last
I skimmed the smooth thin stone along thy breast,
Numbering its light leaps! yet so deep imprest
Sink the sweet scenes of childhood, that mine eyes
I never shut amid the sunny ray,

But straight with all their tints thy waters rise,
Thy crossing plank, thy marge with willows grey,
And bedded sand that, veined with various dyes,
Gleamed through thy bright transparence! On my way,
Visions of childhood! oft have ye beguil'd
Lone manhood's cares, yet waking fondest sighs:
Ah! that once more I were a careless child.

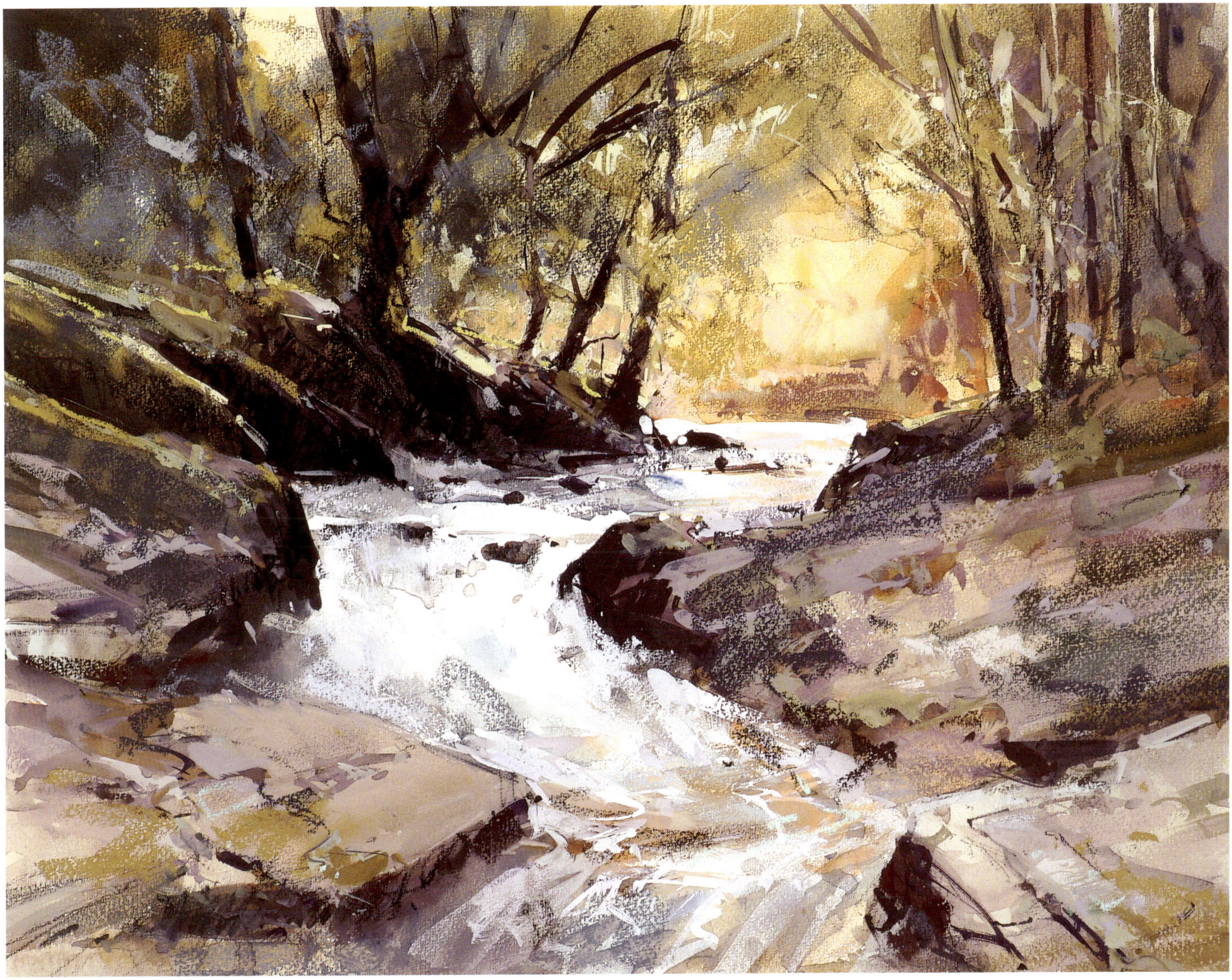

Ray Balkwill. *Waters Glide, East Okement River*
Mixed Media 13x17in (33x43cm)

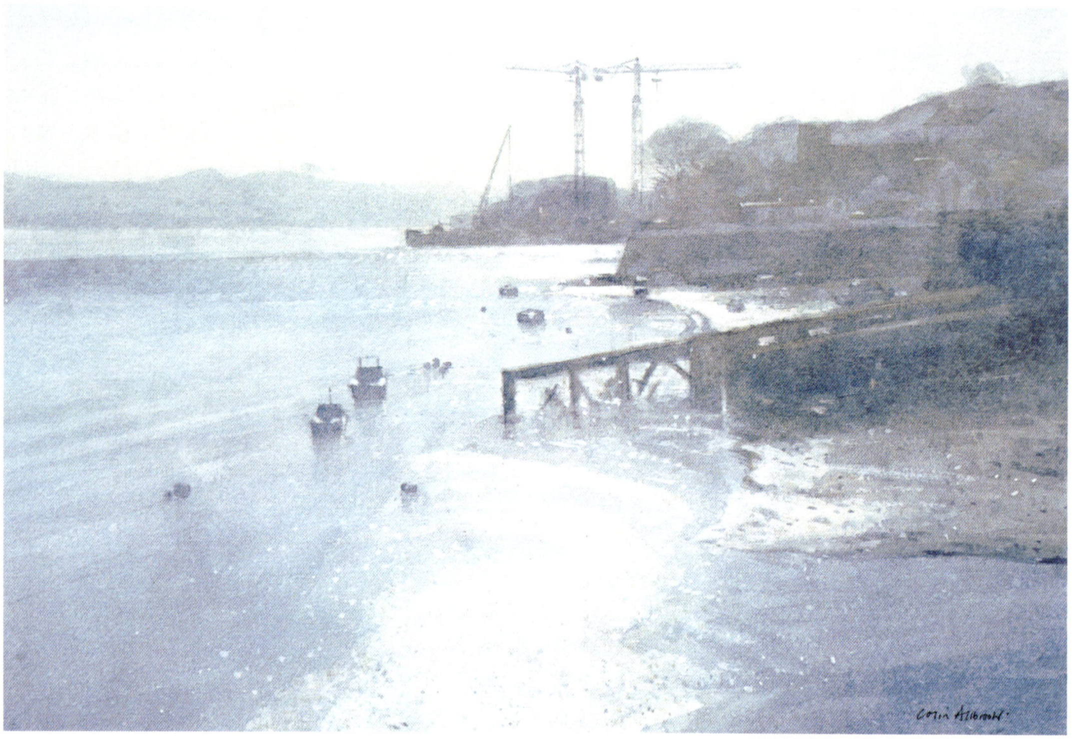

Colin Allbrook. *Appledore Sunlight*
Watercolour 14x20in (36x51cm)

Ray Balkwill. *Low Water, Appledore*
Watercolour 5x14in (13x36cm)

Described by Charles Kingsley as that 'little white fishing village' its maze of narrow lanes are an attractive jumble of closely packed, brightly painted cottages. Near the quay stand tiny whitewashed cottages, former homes of fishermen and shipwrights, employed to build the schooners, ketches and barques that Appledore was once famous for.

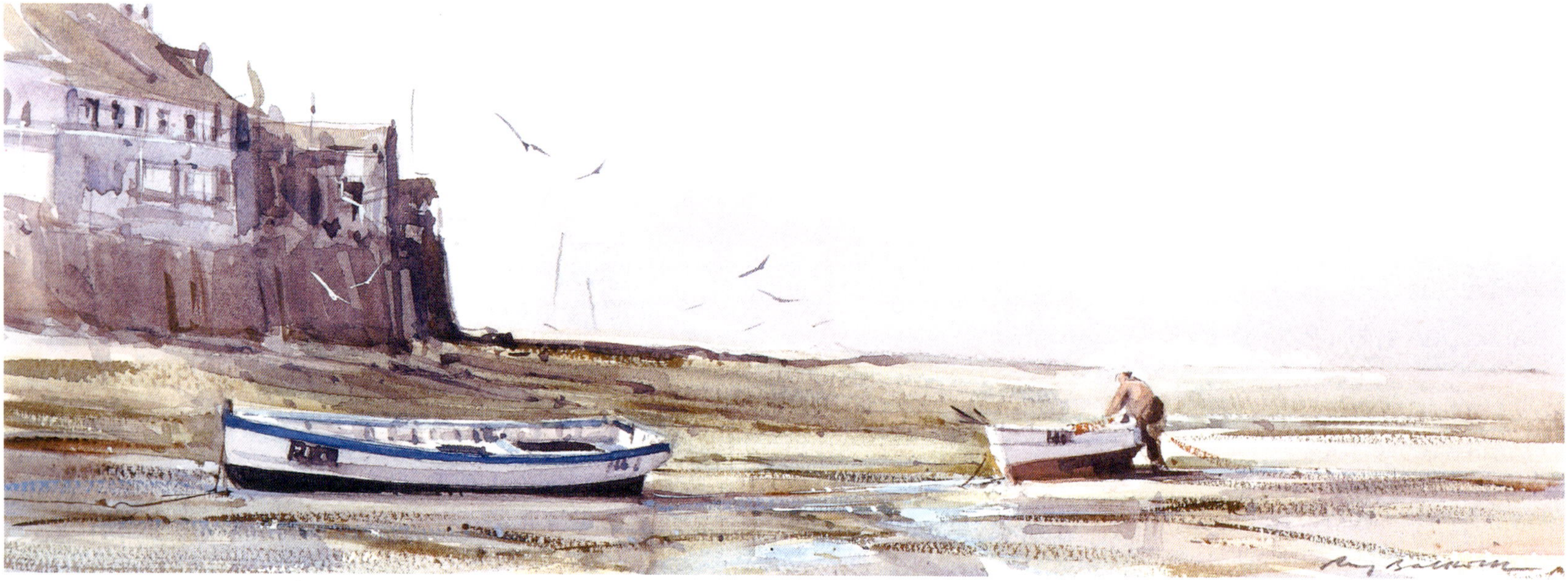

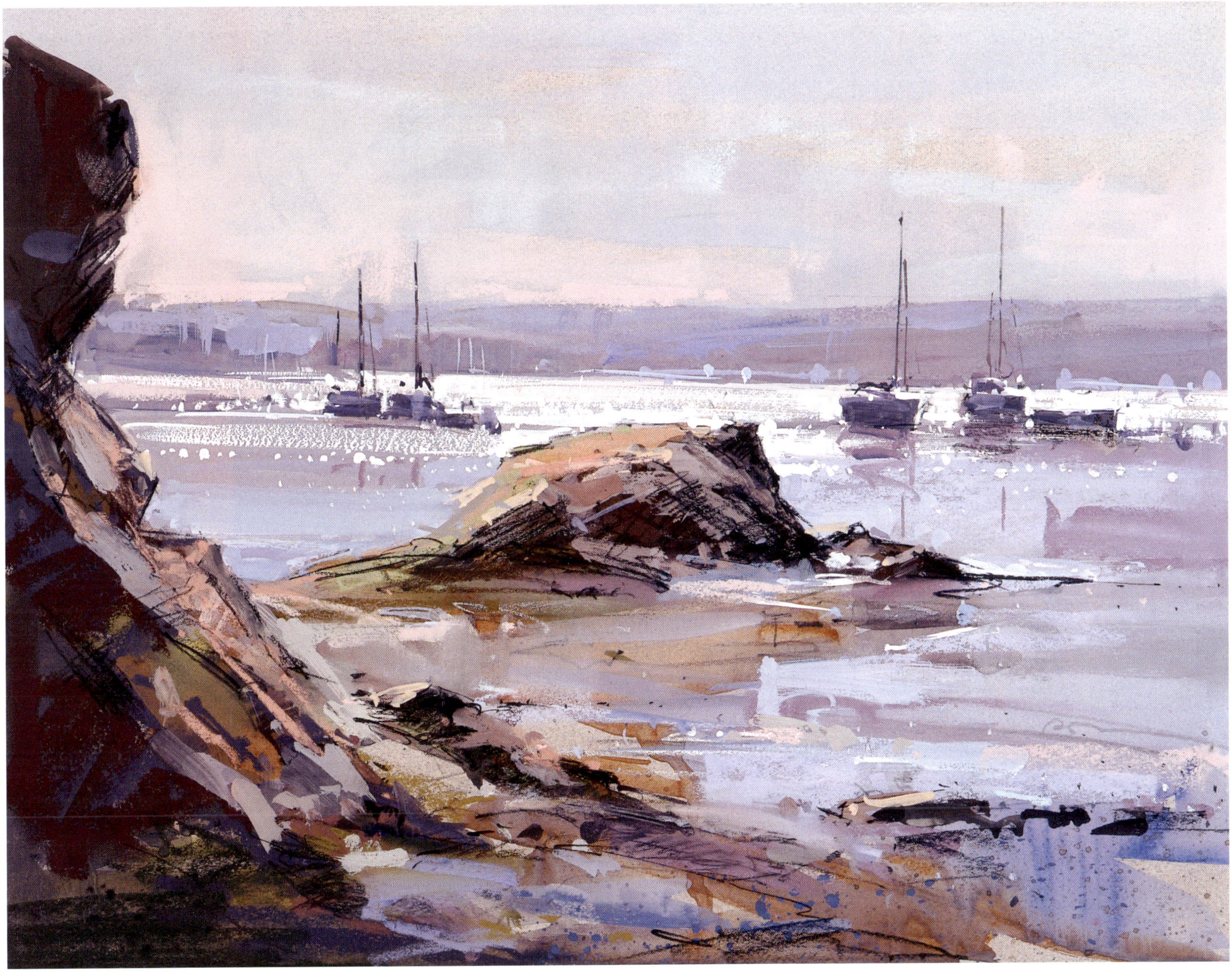

Ray Balkwill. *Darling Rock, Lympstone*
Mixed Media 13x17in (33x43cm)

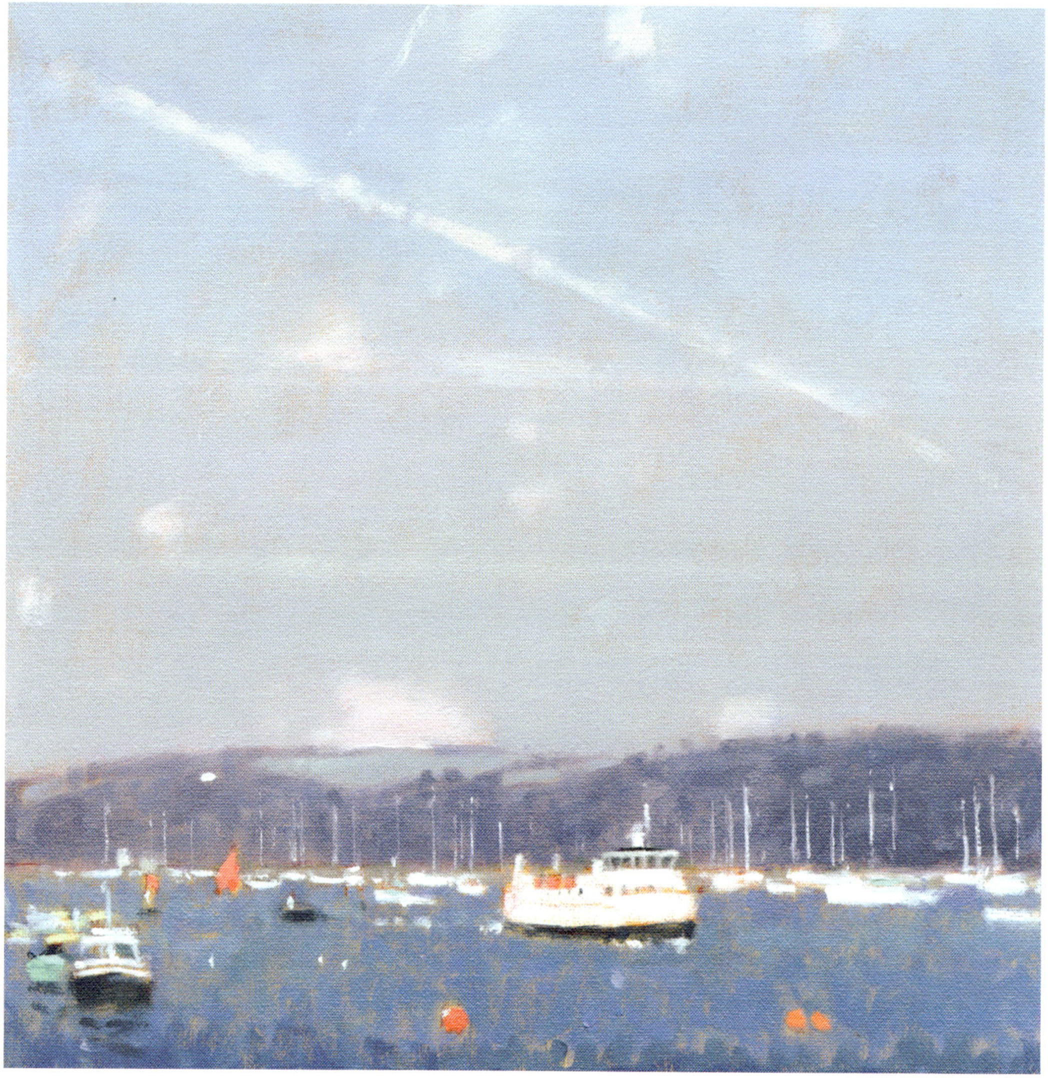

Stephen Brown. *Dartmouth*
Oil 12x12in (30x30cm)

A ferry arrives back in Dartmouth from its journey up the river to Totnes. This river trip is a quiet and relaxing way to see some of the finest of Devon's landscape, passing as it does, the village of Dittisham and the house at Greenway, once the home of Agatha Christie.

Lionel Aggett.
Grey Calm, Topsham
Pastel 20x20in
(500x500cm)

This vast open space beyond the Goat Walk, in airy contrast to the tightly-knit street pattern, is spellbinding. The light here, under all conditions, is very special.

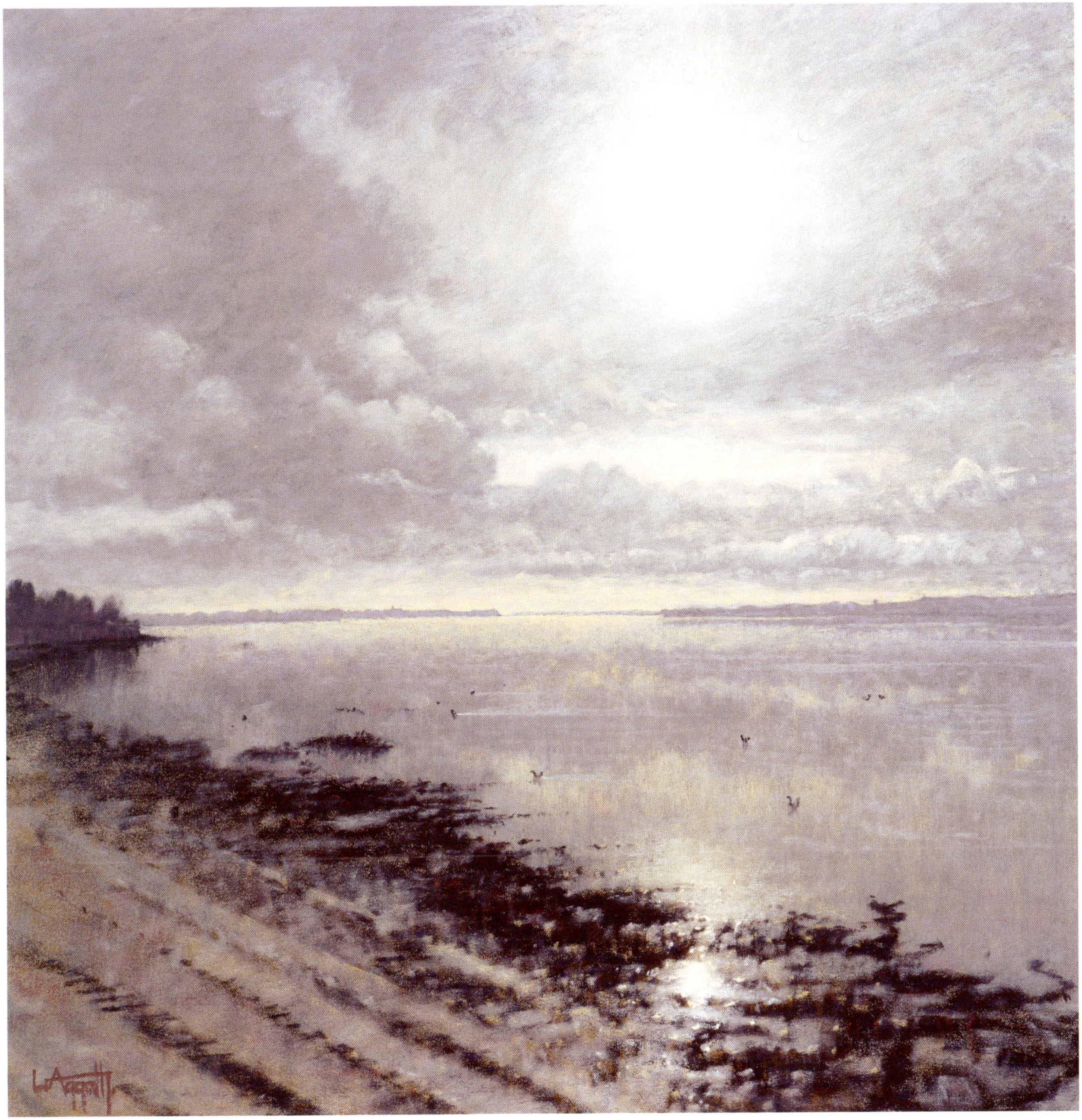

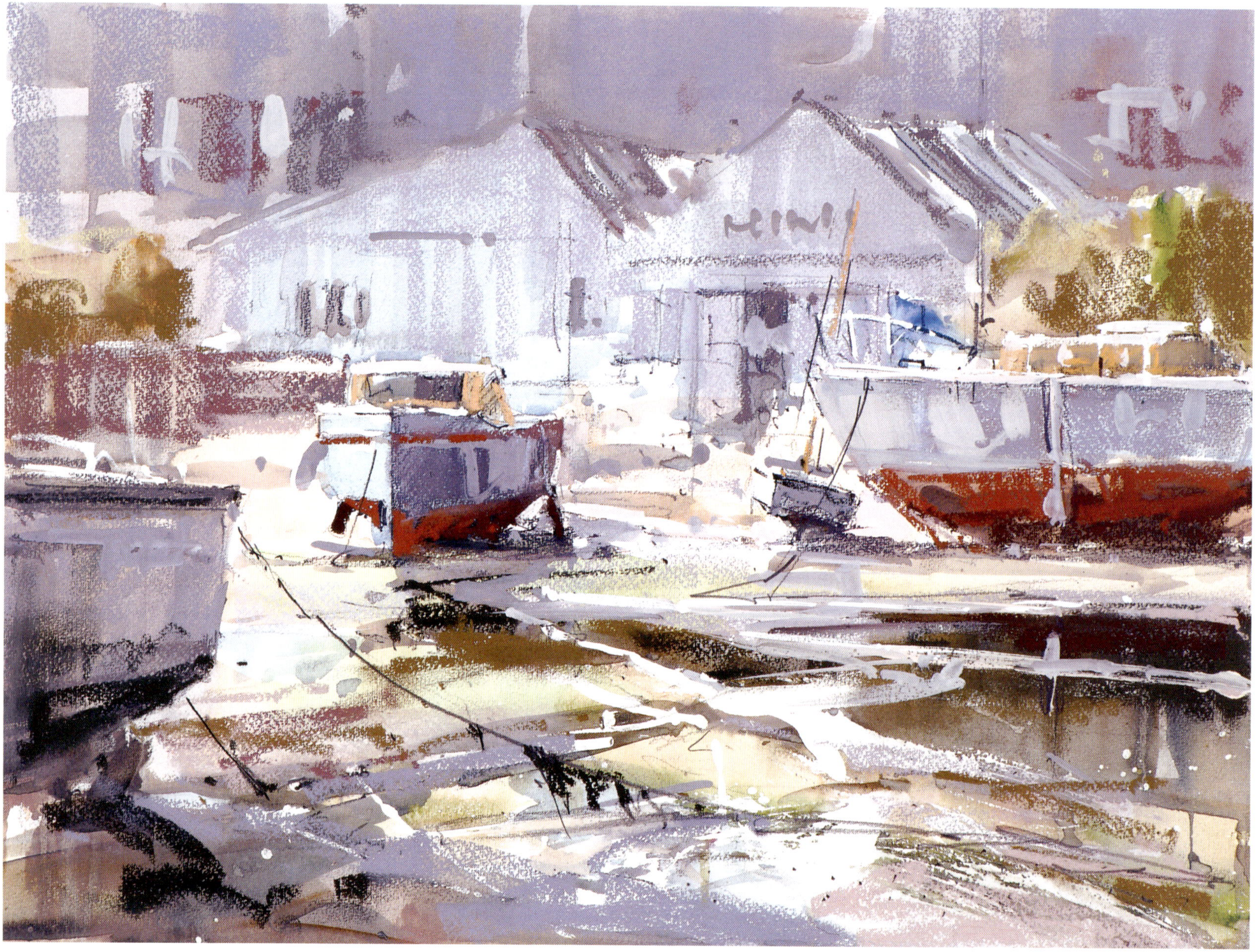

Ray Balkwill. *Low Water, Shelly Gut, Exmouth*
Mixed Media 13x18in (33x46cm)

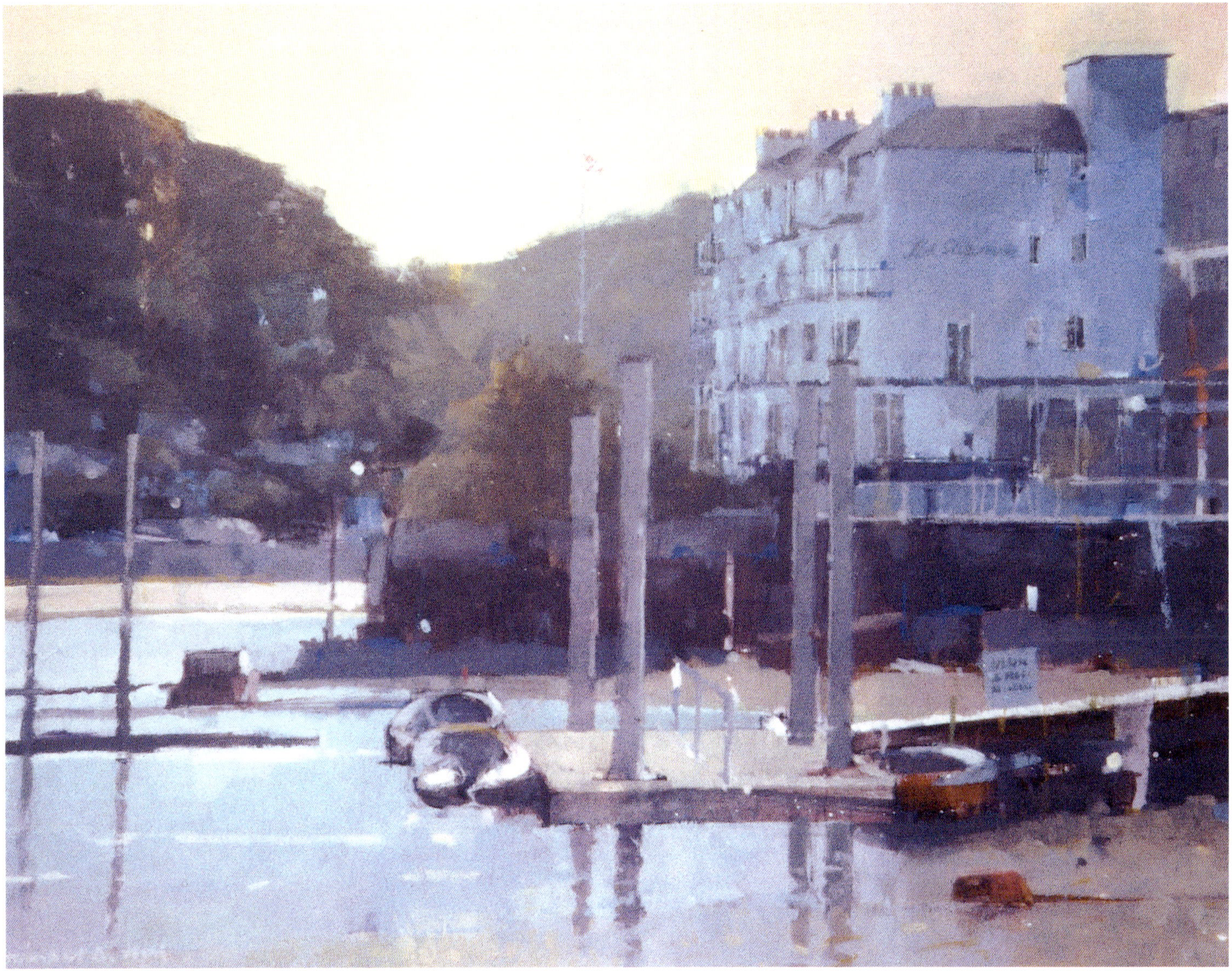

Michael Hill. *Old Salcombe Hotel, Low Tide*
Acrylic 16x12in (40x30cm)

Low tide at Salcombe during the Summer evening is a magical time. Gone are the hundreds of sailing boats, which parade continuously up and down the estuary. The place becomes still and reflective, and presiding over the scene is The Old Salcombe Hotel which seems to glow in the evening light.

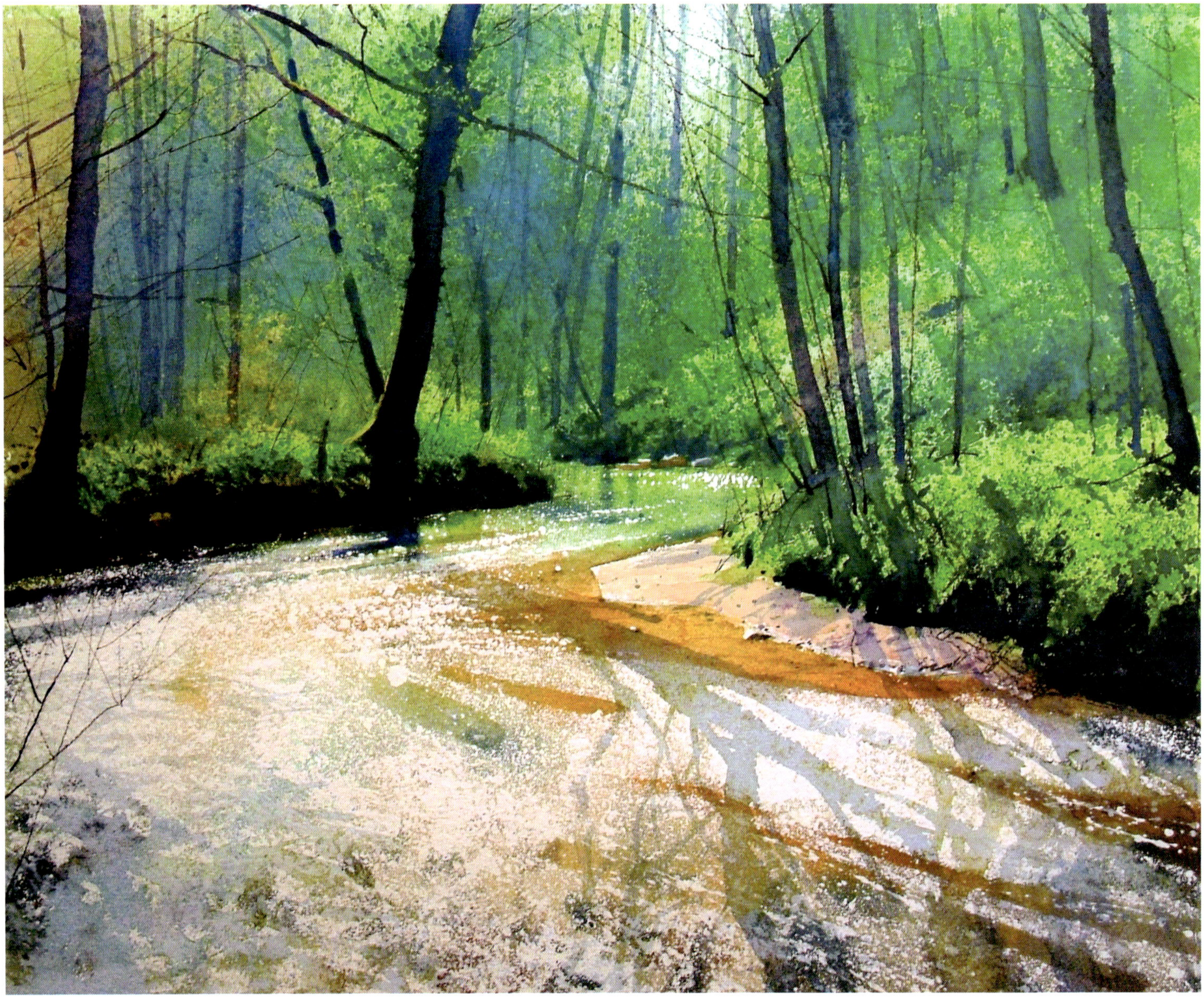

Richard Thorn. *Gently Downstream*
Watercolour 21x25in (53x64cm)

Tony Williams. *Tug at Bideford Quay*
Oil 16x22in (40x56cm)

Seen here at 6.15am on a summer morning, giving me the chance to describe the colours of a shivering cool early light that anticipates the heat of the coming day, with that first shaft of warm colour from the sun hitting the tug and the quayside ironwork.

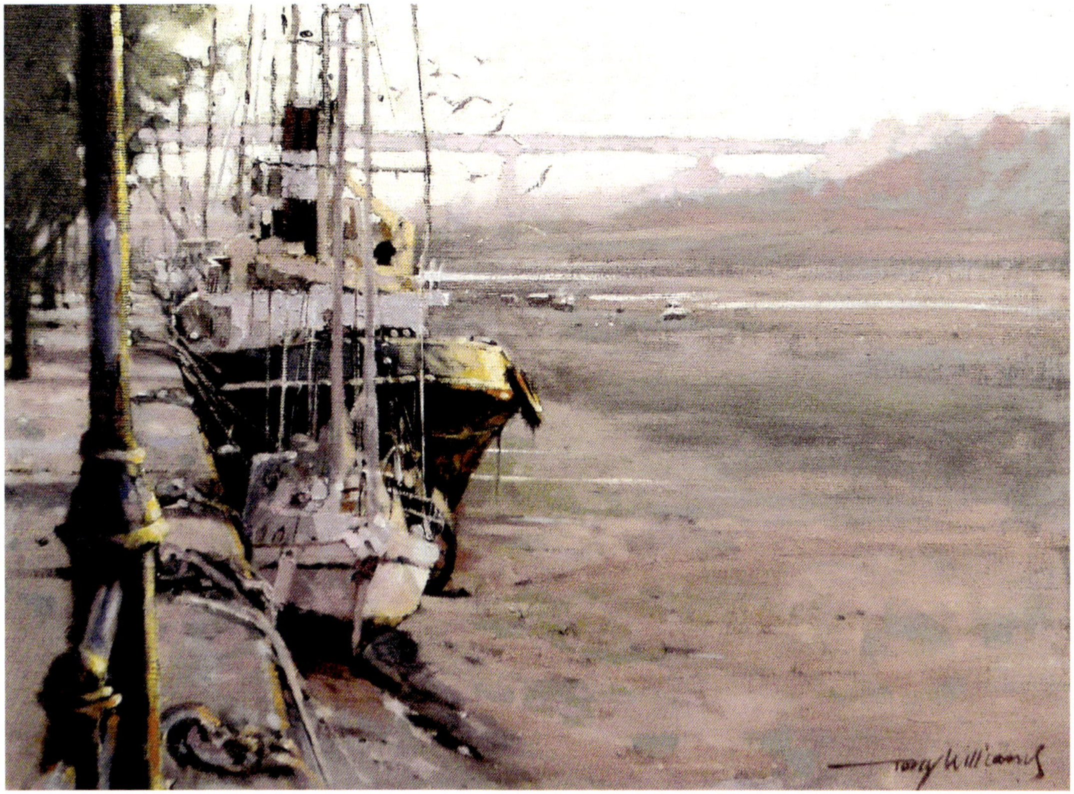

Judy Hempstead. *Veiled Estuary, Otter Head*
Mixed Media 9.5x28.5in (24x73cm)

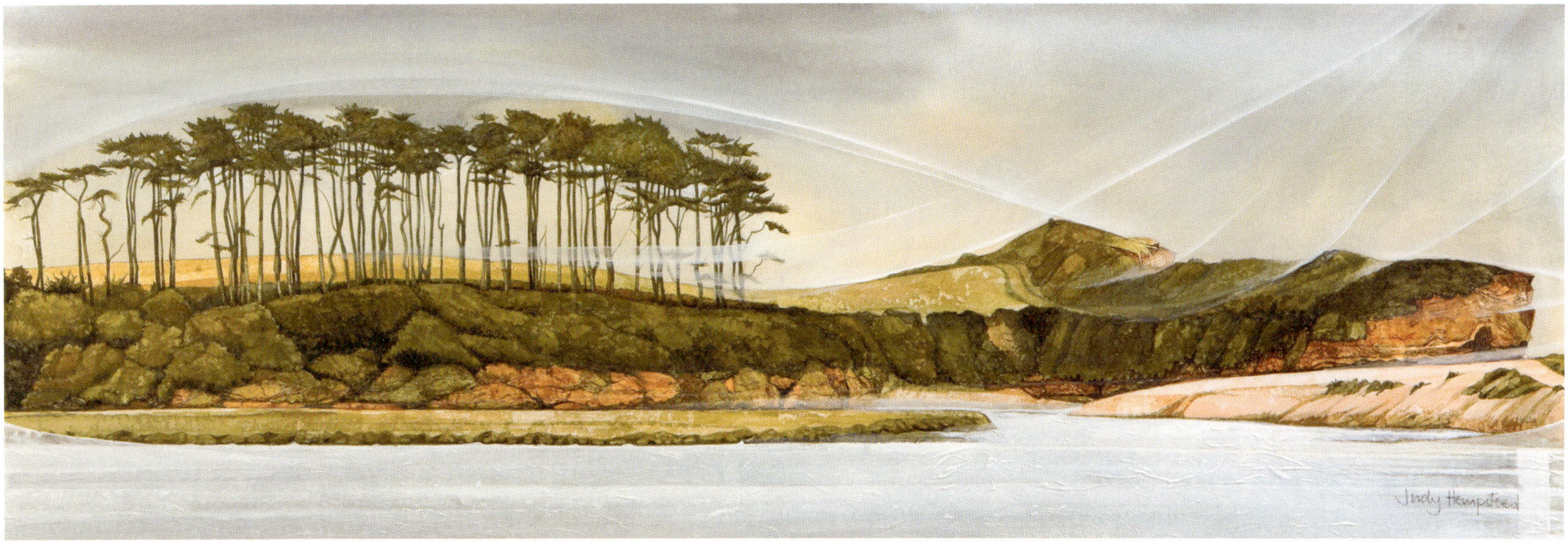

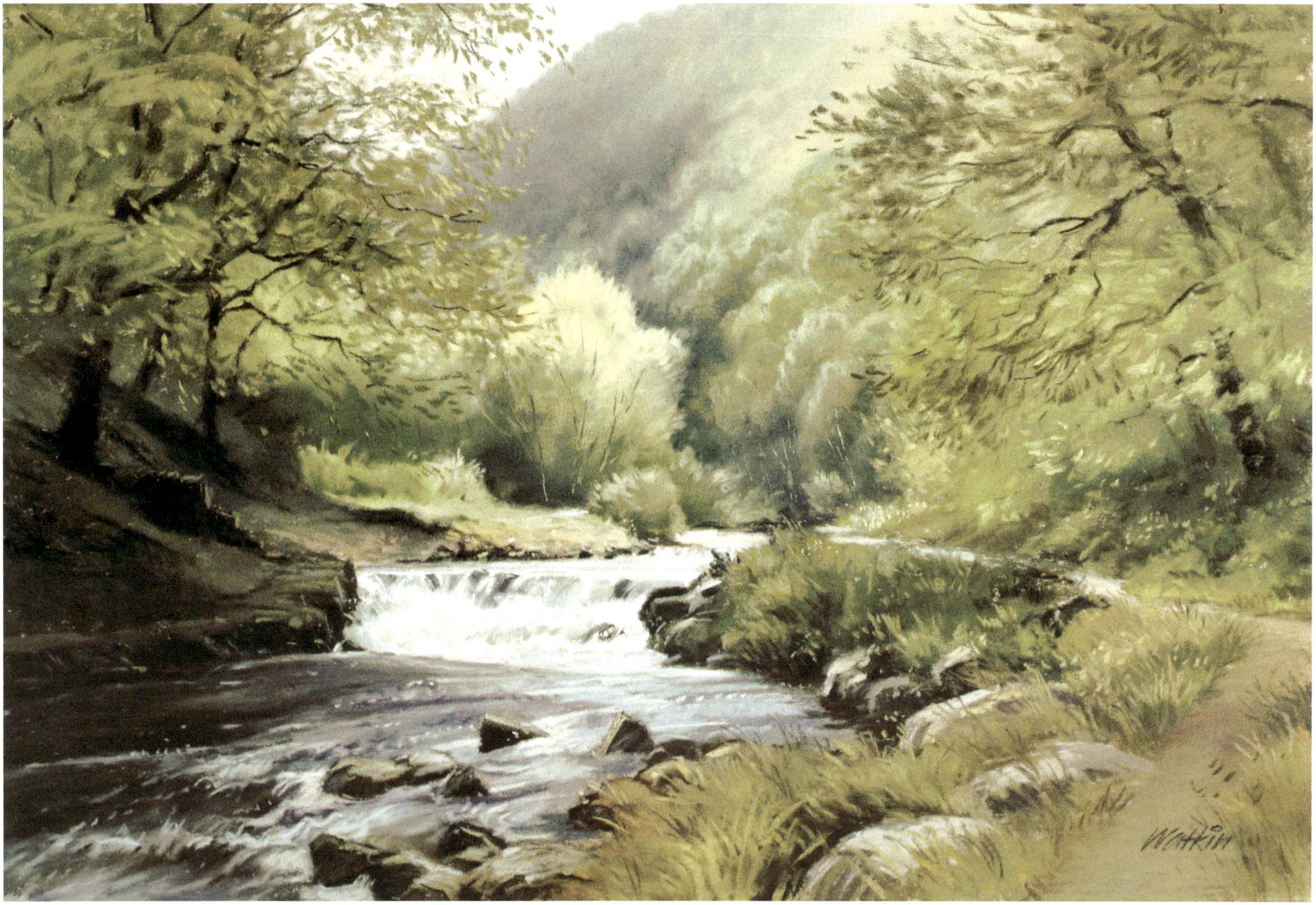

Barry Watkin. *Waterfall near Watersmeet*
Pastel 15x22in (38x56cm)

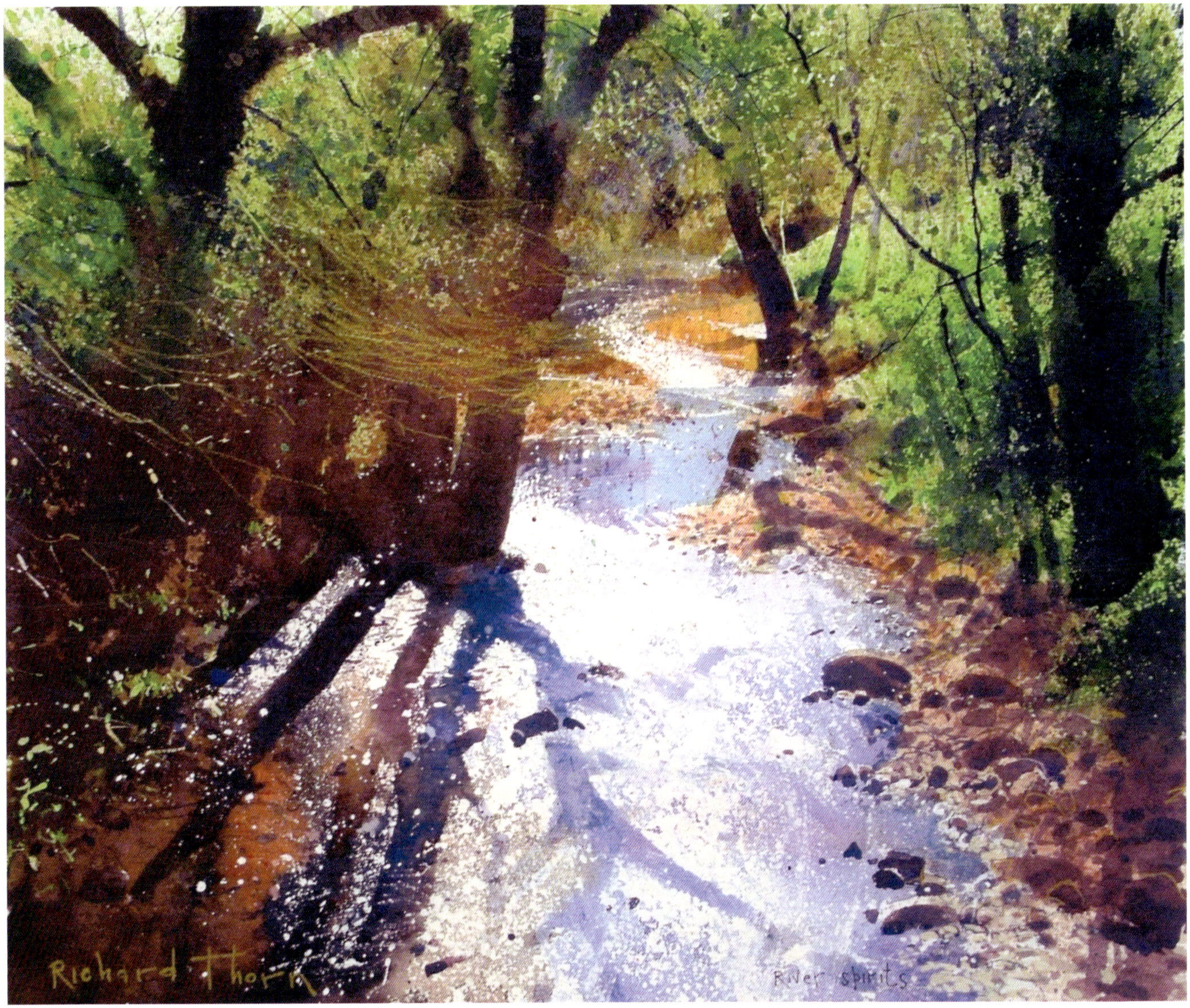

Richard Thorn. *River Spirits*
Watercolour 17x19in (43x48cm)

They say that 'Every picture tells a story' and this book certainly reaffirms this old adage. Therefore, I thought it appropriate to end on a favourite story of mine.

Nestling on the banks of the East Okement River and set deep below the road bridge and railway viaduct at Fatherford is a small unpretentious bungalow called 'Molcote'. On a recent painting trip back to this enchanting valley of my youth, I met by chance the present owners and they told me how it came to be there and why it was so called. In 1965 when the railway line finally closed under the Beeching cuts, a redundant steam train driver was given squatter's rights on a small piece of railway land. It was there that he built a small humble home and named it 'Molcote', this being an acronym for 'My Own Little Corner Of The Earth.' It may be an easy cliché, but each of us has a need for our own 'little corner of the earth' somewhere. It goes without saying of course, that mine is to be found in this beautiful county of Devon.

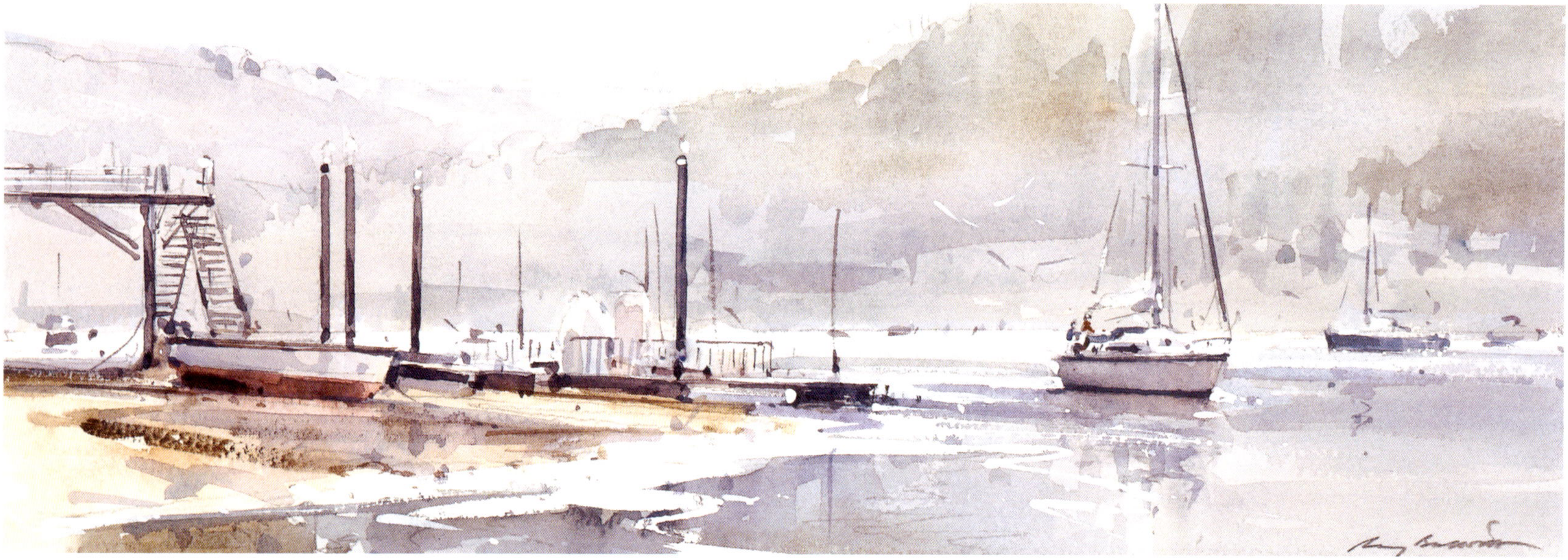

Ray Balkwill. *Summer Haze, River Dart*
Watercolour 5x14in (13xx36cm)

Ray Balkwill. *Waterfall, East Okement River*
Mixed Media 11x12in (28x30cm)

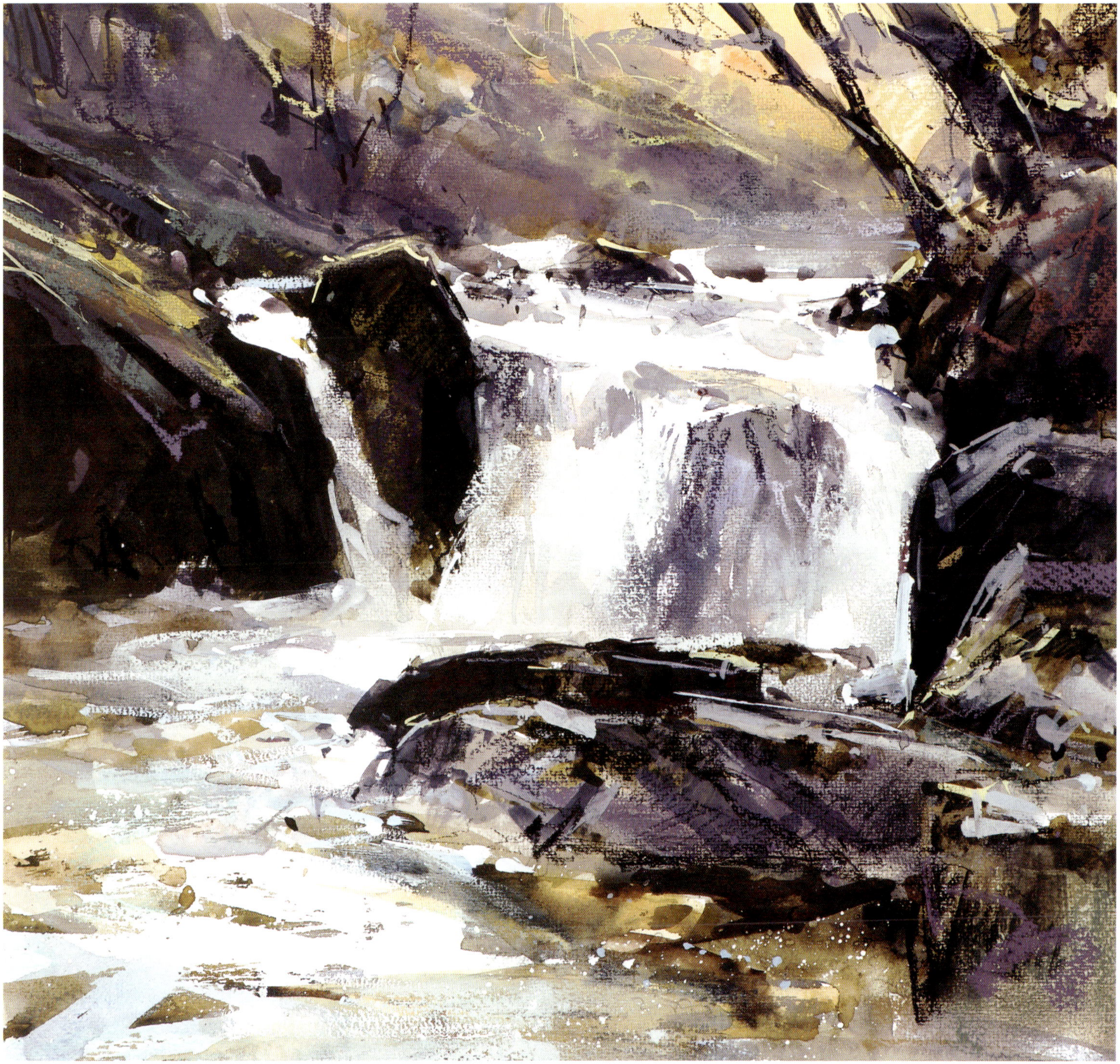

Bibliography and Further Reading

Aggett, Lionel. *Andalucia and Las Alpujarras*, Halsgrove, 2002

Aggett, Lionel. *The Heart of Devon*, Halsgrove, 2003

Aggett, Lionel. *France*, Halsgrove, 2005

Aggett, Lionel. *Italy*, Halsgrove, 2007

Allbrook, Colin. *Colin Allbrook's North Devon*, Halsgrove, 2002

Bailey, Anthony. *Standing in the Sun, A Life of J.M.W. Turner*, Sinclair-Stevenson, 1997

Baker, Jane C. *A Vision of Dartmoor, Paintings by F.J. Widgery 1861-1942*, Victor Gollancz Ltd, 1988

Balkwill, Ray. *Watercolour Plus...*, David & Charles, 2002

Balkwill, Ray. *Ray Balkwill's Exe Estuary*, Halsgrove, 2004

Balkwill, Ray. *Learn to Paint Coastal Landscapes*, Collins, 2006

Balkwill, Ray. *Painting Landscapes with Atmosphere*, David & Charles. 2006

Beacham, Peter. *Down the Deep Lanes*, Devon Books, 2000

Beer, Trevor. *Trevor Beer's Wildlife of North Devon*, Halsgrove, 2001

Crawshaw, Alwyn. *The Artist at Work*, Collins, 1984

Earle, John. *Dartmoor – Walks into History*, Halsgrove, 2003

Holmes, Richard. *Coleridge – Early Visions*, Hodder & Stoughton. 1989

Hoskins, W.G. *Devon and its People*, A. Wheaton & Co. Ltd, 1959

Howard, Peter. *Landscapes, The Artists' Vision*, Routledge, 1991

Hughes,Ted. *Poems Selected by Simon Armitage*, Faber & Faber. 2000

Lane, John. *In Praise of Devon*, Green Books Ltd, 1998

Le Messurier, Brian. *Dartmoor Artists*, Halsgrove, 2002

Leggett, Daverick and Stewart Edmondson. *Wild Land, Burning Hearts*, Poetry and Paintings, *Meridian Press*, 2005

Morgan, Michael. *Michael Morgan RI*, Halsgrove, 2004

Morgan, Michael. *80 @ 80 The Watercolour Paintings of Michael Morgan RI*, Halsgrove, 2008

Pery, Jenny. *Alan Cotton – On a Knife Edge*, Halsgrove, 2003

Ravilious, James. *A Corner of England*, Devon Books, 1995

Smiles, Sam & Pidgley, Michael. *The Perfection of England, Artist Visitors to Devon c. 1750-1870*, Royal Albert Memorial Museum, Exeter, 1995 Exhibition catalogue.

Smiles, Sam. *Light into Colour; Turner in the South West.* Tate St Ives, 2000 Exhibition Catalogue

Sheldon, Gilbert. *Transactions of the Devonshire Association, Vol. 63, 'Devonshire Scenery as depicted in English Prose Literature'* 1931

Trewin, J.C. *The West Country Book,* Webb & Bower, 1981

Williamson, Henry. *Tarka the Otter*, G.P. Putnam & Sons, 1927